Junior Worldmark Encyclopedia of Physical Geography

Junior Worldmark Encyclopedia of
Physical Geography

VOLUME 4

Morocco to Slovakia

Karen Ellicott and Susan B. Gall,
Editors

Detroit • New York • San Diego • San Francisco • Cleveland • New Haven, Conn. • Waterville, Maine • London • Munich

JUNIOR WORLDMARK ENCYCLOPEDIA OF PHYSICAL GEOGRAPHY

Editors
Karen Ellicott and Susan Bevan Gall

Associate Editors
Robert J. Groelsema, Ph.D.,
Jeneen Hobby, Ph.D., Maura Malone,
and Rosalie Wieder

Graphics and Layout
Steven Ollay

Project Editor
Allison McNeill

Imaging and Multimedia
Christine O'Bryan

Cover Design
Cynthia Baldwin

Composition
Evi Seoud

Manufacturing
Rita Wimberley

Cover photographs reproduced courtesy of Digital Stock (Matterhorn), Photodisc (Rice terraces, Luzon Island; Grand Canyon), and Corbis (Victoria Falls).

While every effort has been made to ensure the reliability of the information presented in this publication, The Gale Group, Inc. does not guarantee the accuracy of the data contained herein. The Gale Group, Inc. accepts no payment for listing; and inclusion in the publication of any organization, agency, institution, publication, service, or individual does not imply endorsement by the editors or publisher. Errors brought to the attention of the publisher and verified to the satisfaction of the publisher will be corrected in future editions.

Library of Congress Cataloging-in-Publication Data

Junior worldmark encyclopedia of physical geography / Karen Ellicott and Susan Bevan Gall, editors.
  v. cm.
Includes bibliographical references.
Contents: v. 1. Afghanistan to Comoros -- v. 2. Congo, Democratic Republic of the to India -- v. 3. Indonesia to Mongolia -- v. 4. Morocco to Slovakia -- v. 5. Slovenia to Zimbabwe.
  ISBN 0-7876-6265-8 (set : hardcover) -- ISBN 0-7876-6266-6 (v. 1) -- ISBN 0-7876-6267-4 (v. 2) -- ISBN 0-7876-6268-2 (v. 3) -- ISBN 0-7876-6269-0 (v. 4) -- ISBN 0-7876-6633-5 (v. 5)
  1. Physical geography--Encyclopedias, Juvenile. [1. Physical geography--Encyclopedias.] I. Ellicott, Karen. II. Gall, Susan B.
  GB58.J86 2003
  910'.02'03--dc21
                    2003009019

Printed in the United States of America
10 9 8 7 6 5 4 3 2 1

Contents
Volume 4

Cumulative Contents

CUMULATIVE CONTENTS

Countries of the World, by Continent

Africa

Algeria
Angola
Benin
Botswana
Burkina Faso
Burundi
Cameroon
Cape Verde
Chad
Comoros
Congo, Democratic Republic of the
Congo, Republic of
Côte d'Ivoire
Djibouti
Egypt
Equatorial Guinea
Eritrea
Ethiopia
Gabon
Gambia, The
Ghana
Guinea
Guinea-Bissau
Guyana
Kenya
Lesotho
Liberia
Libya
Madagascar
Malawi
Mali
Mauritania
Mauritius
Morocco
Mozambique
Namibia
Niger
Nigeria
Rwanda
São Tomé and Príncipe
Senegal
Seychelles
Sierra Leone
Somalia
South Africa
Sudan
Swaziland
Tanzania

Togo
Tunisia
Uganda
Zambia
Zimbabwe

Asia

Afghanistan
Armenia
Azerbaijan
Bahrain
Bangladesh
Bhutan
Brunei
Cambodia
China
Cyprus
East Timor
Georgia
India
Indonesia
Iran
Iraq
Israel
Japan
Jordan
Kazakhstan
Korea, North (Democratic People's Republic of)
Korea, South (Republic of)
Kuwait
Kyrgyzstan
Laos
Lebanon
Malaysia
Mongolia
Myanmar
Nepal
Oman
Pakistan
Philippines
Qatar
Russia
Saudi Arabia
Singapore
Sri Lanka
Syria
Taiwan
Tajikistan
Thailand

Turkey
Turkmenistan
United Arab Emirates
Uzbekistan
Vietnam
Yemen

Australia
Australia

Europe
Albania
Andorra
Austria
Belarus
Belgium
Bosnia and Herzegovina
Bulgaria
Croatia
Czech Republic
Denmark
Estonia
Finland
France
Germany
Greece
Hungary
Iceland
Ireland
Italy
Latvia
Liechtenstein
Lithuania
Luxembourg
Macedonia
Malta
Moldova
Monaco
Netherlands
Norway
Poland
Portugal
Romania
Russia
San Marino
Serbia and Montenegro
Slovakia
Slovenia
Spain
Sweden
Switzerland
Ukraine
United Kingdom
Vatican City

North America
Antigua and Barbuda
Bahamas
Barbados
Belize
Canada
Costa Rica
Cuba
Dominica
Dominican Republic
Ecuador
El Salvador
Guatemala
Haiti
Honduras
Jamaica
Mexico
Nicaragua
Panama
Puerto Rico
Saint Kitts and Nevis
Saint Lucia
Saint Vincent and the Grenadines
United States of America

Oceania
Note: The island nations lying in the Pacific Ocean are not part of any continent.

Fiji
Kiribati
Marshall Islands
Micronesia
Nauru
New Zealand
Palau
Papua New Guinea
Samoa
Solomon Islands
Tonga
Tuvalu
Vanuatu

South America
Argentina
Bolivia
Brazil
Chile
Colombia
Paraguay
Peru
Suriname
Trinidad and Tobago
Uruguay
Venezuela

Reader's Guide

Junior Worldmark Encyclopedia of Physical Geography presents a comprehensive survey of the physical geography of 192 countries of the world plus Taiwan, Antarctica, and Puerto Rico.

The entries are arranged alphabetically by country in five volumes. Following the format of other popular titles in the *Junior Worldmark* series, information in each entry is presented in a consistent format, allowing student researchers to find information and compare countries quickly and easily.

A topographic map—with notable mountain ranges and peaks, lakes, rivers, deserts, and coastal areas labeled—accompanies each entry. In addition, more than 200 photographs illustrate the varied landscapes found in the countries of the world. Adding further interest are the "Did You Know?" boxes appearing in the entries, noting interesting or unusual geographic features or facts or explaining regional geographic references.

Organization

Each volume begins with the contents listed for that volume, followed by a cumulative table of contents for all five volumes in the set. To help researchers who wish to identify a country within one of the world's continents, a finder table—Countries of the World by Continent—appears at the front of each volume. Words to Know, a glossary of terms related to geography, completes the front matter. Entries for individual countries follow. Although all numbered rubrics are included in every entry, entries vary in length depending primarily on the geographic complexity of the country's land area.

Each entry begins with a list of key facts about the physical characteristics of the country; measurements are provided in both metric and English units. Student researchers should be reminded that geography is an imprecise science, and measurements of geographical features may vary from source to source.

Key Facts

Official name
The countries of the world are referred to by a common name; the more formal official name is listed here.

Area
The country's area, usually including islands, is provided in square kilometers and square miles.

Highest point on mainland
The height, in meters and feet, is given for the highest point on the mainland portion of the country. For most countries, this is also the highest point anywhere in the country.

Highest point in territory
For some countries with islands and territories, the highest point not on the mainland is provided in meters and feet.

Lowest point on land
The elevation, in meters and feet, for the lowest point on the mainland portion of the country is provided.

Hemispheres

The country's hemispheres (Northern, Southern, Eastern, and Western) help the researcher locate the country on the globe.

Time zone

The time zone of the country's capital is provided, with the time related to Greenwich Mean Time (GMT). For some large countries, more than one time zone may be listed.

Longest distances

Measurements in kilometers and miles of the country's widest points from north to south and east to west are given. For some countries, longest distances may be measured on a slight diagonal (northwest to southeast, for example).

Land boundaries

The total distance making up the country's borders with other nations is provided in kilometers and miles, followed by the border distances with the individual neighboring countries.

Coastline

Coastline measurements, in kilometers and miles, are approximate. Coastline measurements are likely to vary from source to source.

Territorial sea limits

The territory extending into the ocean over which the country claims control or jurisdiction. Territorial sea limits are given in kilometers and nautical miles, and generally govern activities such as fishing and mineral rights.

The first four numbered rubrics offer a general overview of the country.

1 ⊕ LOCATION AND SIZE

This section gives the reader an overview of where the country lies and provides its relation to the bodies of water around it. Also included is information about whether the country is divided into states, provinces, or other internal administrative units.

2 ⊕ TERRITORIES AND DEPENDENCIES

Many countries exercise jurisdiction over territories—often islands—that are not part of the mainland. This section lists any such territories and dependencies.

3 ⊕ CLIMATE

The general climate of the country is described, with a table providing seasonal temperature ranges included for many countries. General information about rainfall and snow patterns is also included here.

4 ⊕ TOPOGRAPHIC REGIONS

An overview of the general topography (shape of the country's land surface) is provided, with key features (mountain ranges, plateaus, deserts, valleys, lakes, rivers) noted.

The next eight numbered rubrics—5 through 12—describe specific geographic features. All entries include all eight headings. Since all countries do not include every geographic feature, individual entries note the absence of specific features.

5 ⊕ OCEANS AND SEAS

The oceans and seas bounding the country are listed. Subheadings describe specific features of the country and its coastal areas. Subheads are used in entries as appropriate and may include:

Seacoast and Undersea Features

Includes discussion of nearby undersea features of note, such as deep ocean trenches or coral reefs.

Sea Inlets and Straits

Includes major bays, gulfs, sounds, channels, straits, and other sea inlets that characterize the coastal areas.

Islands and Archipelagos

Major islands and island chains are described here.

Other Coastal Features

Includes notable peninsulas, isthmuses, and describes the type and quality of the coastal areas.

6 ⊕ INLAND LAKES

Major and significant lakes are included. When a lake straddles a border between two countries, it is covered in both entries. Major man-made reservoirs are also included in this section in some entries.

7 ⊕ RIVERS AND WATERFALLS

Describes important rivers, giving length and general characteristics. Also includes major waterfalls.

8 ⊕ DESERTS

Arid and semi-arid flatland regions are described.

9 ⊕ FLAT AND ROLLING TERRAIN

Areas that range from flat and treeless to rounded terrain are described.

10 ⊕ MOUNTAINS AND VOLCANOES

Mountain peaks, including volcanoes, are described here, typically in the context of a mountain range.

11 ⊕ CANYONS AND CAVES

Notable canyons and cave systems are described.

12 ⊕ PLATEAUS AND MONOLITHS

Regions of high elevation but with relatively flat terrain and monoliths (huge stone outcroppings) are described here.

The final two numbered rubrics describe notable man-made features, and provide resources for further study. Supplementing the Further Reading suggestions provided in each entry is the Selected Sources for Further Study that appears in the back of each volume.

13 ⊕ MAN-MADE FEATURES

Notable man-made features—such as dams, canals, major bridges, tunnels, and other structures—that affect a country's geography are described.

14 ⊕ FURTHER READING

This section lists selected books and Web sites that provide more information on the country's geography.

Additional Features

Additional reference materials appear at the back of each volume. Researchers looking for comparative information on some of the world's key geographic features can refer to a series of Appendixes. These provide the following rankings: continents by area;

countries by area; countries by population; oceans and seas by area; oceans by depth; islands by area; deserts by area; mountain peaks by height; volcanoes by height; rivers by length; waterfalls by height; lakes by area; and lakes by depth. The seven wonders of the ancient world and seven wonders of the natural world are described in the final two appendixes. Lastly, a listing of selected references for the further study of physical geography completes the backmatter. Volume 5 contains a cumulative general index to all five volumes. Topographic world maps appear on each volume's endsheets.

Photographs

The photographs in *Junior Worldmark Encyclopedia of Physical Geography* were assembled with assistance from ARAMCO; Raoul Russo, UNESCO imaging; Marcia L. Schiff, AP/Wide World Photos; Maura Malone, EPD Photos; and Mimi Dornack, National Geographic Imaging.

Comments and Suggestions

We welcome your comments and suggestions for features to be included in future editions. Please write: Editors, *Junior Worldmark Encyclopedia of Physical Geography*, U•X•L, 27500 Drake Road, Farmington Hills, Michigan 48331-3535; call toll-free: 1-800-877-4253; fax to (248) 699-8097; or send e-mail via http://www.gale.com.

Words to Know

A

aboriginal ⊕ Something that is the first or earliest known of its type in a country or region, such as an aboriginal forest.

aborigines ⊕ The first known inhabitants of a country and their descendents.

acid rain ⊕ Rain (or snow) that has become slightly acidic by mixing with industrial air pollution.

alluvial plain ⊕ Flatlands containing deposits of alluvium.

alluvium ⊕ Clay, silt, sand, or gravel deposited by running water, such as a stream or river.

Antarctic Circle ⊕ (also called South **Frigid Zone**) The parallel of latitude approximately 66°33′ south and the region that lies between this latitude and the south pole; the region surrounding Antarctica.

aquatic ⊕ Of or relating to the water, particularly the animals and plants that live there.

aqueduct ⊕ A pipe or channel, usually man-made, that carries water from a remote source. Also, a bridge-like structure that carries water over obstacles.

aquifer ⊕ An underground layer of porous rock, sand, or gravel that holds water.

arable land ⊕ Land that is naturally suitable for cultivation by plowing and is used for growing crops.

archipelago ⊕ A group of islands or a body of water containing many islands.

Arctic ⊕ Relating to the northernmost part of the Earth that lies within and around the Arctic Circle. Also, **arctic**: anything that is frigidly and invariably cold.

Arctic Circle ⊕ (also called the North **Frigid Zone**) The parallel of latitude approximately 66°33′ north and the region that lies between this latitude and the north pole.

arid ⊕ Extremely dry, particularly applied to regions of low rainfall where there is little natural vegetation and agriculture is difficult.

artesian well ⊕ A type of well where underground pressure forces water to overflow up to the surface.

atmosphere ⊕ The air surrounding the Earth's surface.

atoll ⊕ An island consisting of a strip or ring of coral surrounding a central lagoon.

avalanche ⊕ A swift sliding of snow or ice down a mountain.

B

badlands ⊕ Eroded and barren land.

Balkan Peninsula ⊕ The southernmost peninsula of Europe, which is surrounded by the Adriatic, Ionian, Aegean, and Black seas

Balkan States ⊕ (also called The Balkans) Those countries that lie on or near the Balkan Peninsula; includes Albania, Bulgaria, continental Greece, southeast Romania, European Turkey, Serbia and Montenegro, Slovenia, Croatia, Bosnia and Herzegovina, and Macedonia.

Baltic States ⊕ The countries of Estonia, Latvia, and Lithuania. These independent countries were once provinces of Russia and all border on the Baltic Sea.

barren land ⊕ Unproductive land that is partly or entirely treeless.

barrier island ⊕ An island parallel to the shore that was formed by wave and tidal action and protects the shore from rough ocean waves.

barrier reef ⊕ A coral reef that lies parallel to the coast, often forming a lagoon along the shore.

basalt ⊕ Black or nearly black dense rock, usually formed by the solidification of magma or from some other high-temperature geological event.

basin ⊕ A depression on land or on the ocean floor. Usually relatively broad and gently sloped, as compared to a trench, canyon, or crater.

bay ⊕ A wide inlet of a sea or a lake.

bayou ⊕ A stagnant or slow-moving body of water.

beach ⊕ An area of sediment deposited along the shoreline of a large body of water through the action of waves and the process of erosion.

bedrock ⊕ Solid rock lying under loose earth.

bight ⊕ A bend in a coastline that forms an open bay.

bluff ⊕ Elevated area with a broad, steep cliff face.

bog ⊕ Wet, soft, and spongy ground where the soil is composed mainly of decayed or decaying vegetable matter.

bora ⊕ A very cold wind blowing from the north in the Adriatic Sea region.

broadleaf forest ⊕ A forest composed mainly of broadleaf (deciduous) trees, as opposed to a coniferous forest.

butte ⊕ An elevated, flat-topped area, similar to but smaller than a plateau or mesa.

C

caldera ⊕ A crater formed by the eruption of a volcano.

canal ⊕ An artificial waterway constructed to connect two bodies of water or for irrigation of farmland.

canyon ⊕ A deep gorge cut by a river, usually found in arid regions and often surrounded by plateaus.

cape ⊕ A part of the coast that protrudes into a body of water.

Caribbean ⊕ The region that includes the Caribbean Sea, its islands, and the Central or South American coastal areas of the sea.

catchment ⊕ Area that collects water.

cave ⊕ Hollow man-made or natural passages in the Earth with an opening to the surface.

cay (or key) ⊕ A small, low-lying island or reef formed by coral or sand.

Caucasus ⊕ Region between the Black and Caspian seas that forms the traditional boundary between Europe and Asia; includes the countries of Georgia, Azerbaijan, and Armenia, as well as parts of southwestern Russia.

Central America ⊕ A region of southern North America that extends from the southern border of Mexico to the northern border of Colombia; includes the countries of Belize, Guatemala, Honduras, El Salvador, Nicaragua, Costa Rica, and Panama

channel ⊕ A narrow body of water that connects two larger areas of water; an area where water flows through a narrow restricted path.

cliff ⊕ A high, vertical face of rock.

climate ⊕ Weather conditions pertaining to a specific area.

cloud forest ⊕ A tropical forest that is covered in clouds throughout most of the year, usually located on mountain peaks.

coast ⊕ Typically, the land that borders an ocean or sea.

coastal ⊕ Relating to the area along the coast.

coastal plain ⊕ A fairly level area of land along the coast of a land mass.

coniferous forest ⊕ A forest consisting mainly of evergreen trees such as pine, fir, and cypress trees.

conifers ⊕ Trees and plants that have needle-like, or scale-like, leaves and also produce cones; evergreens.

contiguous ⊕ Sharing an edge or boundary or connected without any breaks, as in *the 48 contiguous states*.

continent ⊕ One of the seven major land masses of Earth.

continental climate ⊕ A climate typical of the interior of a continent. Particulars can vary widely depending on the region, but in general, areas with a continental climate have greater variations in daily and seasonal temperatures than areas with a maritime climate.

continental divide ⊕ An extensive elevated region of land that separates the drainage basins of a continent so that the rivers on either side of the divide flow in opposite directions.

continental shelf ⊕ A shallow submarine plain extending from the coast of a continent into the sea and varying in width; typically the shelf ends in a steep slope to the ocean floor.

coral reef ⊕ A ridge in warm water areas of the ocean made up of the limestone and calcium deposits of coral animals.

cordillera ⊕ A continuous ridge, range, or chain of mountains; part of the principal mountain system of a continent or country.

crater ⊕ A bowl-shaped depression on the surface of the Earth, generally with relatively deep, steep, sides. The most common type of crater is a caldera, formed by volcanic eruption. Other craters are created by explosions or by impact, such as from a meteoroid.

cyclone ⊕ A violent rotating wind storm, particularly one that originates in the southwestern Pacific or the Indian Ocean. Cyclones rotate counterclockwise in the northern hemisphere and clockwise in the southern hemisphere.

D

dam ⊕ A structure built across a river that restricts its flow, causing a reservoir to form behind it. Dams are often used to generate hydropower.

deciduous ⊕ Relates to trees or shrubs that shed their leaves on a regular basis, as opposed to those that retain them (coniferous).

deforestation ⊕ The removal or clearing of a forest, usually to enable the land to be used for another purpose, such as agriculture or settlements.

delta ⊕ Triangular-shaped deposits of soil formed at the mouths of large rivers. They are formed out of the silt carried by the river and have the effect of forcing the river to split into distributary channels, sometimes over a very wide area.

depression ⊕ Any place where the Earth's surface is lower than the surrounding terrain.

desert ⊕ Any dry land area with little precipitation and sparse vegetation; often a sandy region but also includes areas of permanent cold that are generally lacking plant life.

desertification ⊕ The process where land that supports vegetation gradually becomes desert as a result of climatic changes, land mismanagement, or both.

dike ⊕ An artificial riverbank built up to control the flow of water.

discontiguous ⊕ Not connected to or sharing a boundary with.

distributary ⊕ A stream that branches off from a river and never rejoins it, flowing independently into another body of water.

doldrums ⊕ An area near the equator characterized by variable winds and periods of calm.

dormant volcano ⊕ A volcano that has not exhibited any signs of activity for an extended period of time.

dune ⊕ A mound or ridge of loose, wind-blown sand.

E

Earth ⊕ Fifth-largest planet in the solar system; its orbit is third from the sun, its circumference is 40,064 kilometers (24,900 miles) at the equator and 40,000 kilometers (24,860 miles) when measured around the poles. The diameter at the equator is 12,753 kilometers (7,926 miles) and, from pole to pole, 12,711 kilometers (7,900 miles).

earthquake ⊕ Shaking or other movement of the earth that is caused by tectonic shifts or volcanic activity.

East Asia ⊕ A subregion of Asia that includes the countries of China, Mongolia, Korea, and the islands of Taiwan and Japan.

easterlies ⊕ Winds or air currents blowing more or less consistently from east to west.

Eastern Europe ⊕ A geopolitical term that usually refers to those countries in the east of Europe that were once allied with the Soviet Union under the Warsaw Pact (1955-1991). Today, the independent countries of the region include: Albania, Bulgaria, Czech Republic, Slovakia, Hungary, Croatia, Slovenia, Bosnia and Herzegovina, Poland, Romania, Serbia and Montenegro, and Macedonia.

Eastern Hemisphere ⊕ The half of the Earth's surface that extends east of the Prime Meridian to the 180th meridian.

eddy ⊕ An air or water current that follows a course different from that of the main flow and usually has a swirling circular motion.

El Niño ⊕ The warming of the ocean off the west coast of South America that causes a change in climate elsewhere in the world, especially in North America. El Niño conditions have occurred about every four to twelve years.

enclave ⊕ A country or portion of a country that lies entirely within the boundaries of one other country. Also, a culturally distinct community within a country.

endangered species ⊕ A plant or animal species that is at risk of becoming extinct.

endemic ⊕ Anything that is native to, unique to, or characteristic of a specific place or region.

equator ⊕ An imaginary line running around the middle of the Earth halfway between the North and South Poles. Identified as 0° latitude, it divides the Northern and Southern Hemispheres.

erosion ⊕ Changes in the shape of the Earth's surface as a result of damage from wind, water, or ice.

escarpment ⊕ (also called scarp land) A steep slope that separates areas of different elevations.

estuary ⊕ The region where a river and a large lake or sea meet so that their waters gradually blend into each other.

Eurasia ⊕ The land mass that contains the continents of Europe and Asia.

exclave ⊕ Part of a country that is separated from the larger, main portion of the country by foreign territory.

F

Far East ⊕ Traditionally, those countries that are a part of East Asia and the easternmost portion of Siberia. Often, the term includes the countries of Southeast Asia as well.

fault ⊕ (also called a fault line) A fracture in the Earth's crust where the rock formation splits, allowing the opposing sides to shift. Most commonly found along the boundaries between tectonic plates, the shifting sometimes causes earthquakes.

fen ⊕ Wet, soft, and spongy ground where the soil is composed mainly of decayed or decaying vegetable matter and is fed by surrounding soils and groundwater. Fens are similar to bogs but have higher nutrient levels.

fjord ⊕ A relatively narrow arm of the sea that indents deeply into the land, with generally steep slopes or cliffs on each side.

flood ⊕ The flow of excessive quantities of water over land that is generally above water.

flood plain ⊕ An area of low-lying land bordering a stream of water where floods, and the resulting deposits of alluvium, occur frequently.

Frigid Zone ⊕ Either of the extreme north and south latitude zones of the Earth. The North Frigid Zone lies between the North Pole and the Arctic Circle. The South Frigid Zone lies between the South Pole and the Antarctic Circle. The climate of these regions is characterized by extreme cold throughout the year.

G

game reserve ⊕ An area of land reserved for wild animals that are hunted for sport or for food.

geopolitical ⊕ Refers to the relationship between geographic, political (or governmental), and cultural aspects of a nation or region.

geothermal energy ⊕ Energy derived from the heat that constantly and naturally radiates out from the center of the Earth. Also used to describe the radiation itself.

geyser ⊕ A hot spring that periodically erupts through an opening in the surface of the Earth, spewing boiling water and steam.

glacier ⊕ A large body of ice that moves along the Earth's surface.

gorge ⊕ A deep, narrow passage with steep, rocky walls.

grassland ⊕ An area where the vegetation is mostly grasses and other grass-like plants, often providing a transition between forests and deserts.

Greenwich Mean Time ⊕ The time at Greenwich, England, in the United Kingdom. This time is used as a basis for calculating time throughout most of the world. It is also called universal time, and is abbreviated GMT.

groundwater ⊕ Water located below the earth's surface, providing a source for wells and springs.

gulf ⊕ A large inlet of a sea or ocean that is partially enclosed by land, such as by capes or peninsulas.

Gulf Stream ⊕ Warm ocean current flowing from roughly the Gulf of Mexico northeast along the coast of North America, then east toward Europe.

H

harbor ⊕ A protected inlet along the shore of a sea or lake that is deep enough for ships to anchor.

hardpan ⊕ A layer of hardened clay soil, usually underlying a thin layer of topsoil.

hardwoods ⊕ Deciduous trees, such as cherry, oak, maple, and mahogany, that produce very hard, durable, and valuable lumber.

harmattan ⊕ An intensely dry, dusty wind felt along the coast of Africa between Cape Verde and Cape Lopez. It prevails at intervals during the months of December, January, and February.

headland ⊕ Slightly elevated land lying along or jutting into a body of water.

headstream ⊕ Stream that forms the source of a river.

headwater ⊕ Source of a stream or river.

heath ⊕ Uncultivated land with low shrubs.

hemisphere ⊕ Any half of the globe. The Northern and Southern Hemispheres are divided by the equator while the Eastern and Western Hemispheres are divided by the Prime Meridian and 180° longitude.

hill ⊕ A rounded area of elevation rising more or less prominently above the surrounding, flatter landscape. Hills are generally no more than 300 meters (1,000 feet) high.

Humboldt Current ⊕ A cold ocean current that runs north from Antarctica along the west coast of South America, primarily from June to November.

hurricane ⊕ A tropical storm originating in the Atlantic or Pacific Oceans, generally with winds over 74 miles per hour.

hydropower ⊕ (also called hydroelectric power) Electricity generated by the flow of water through the turbines of river dams.

I

iceberg ⊕ A massive block of floating ice that has broken off of a glacier or an ice shelf through a process known as calving.

ice caps ⊕ Ice sheets covering less than 50,000 square kilometers (19,000 square miles). They form primarily in polar and sub-polar regions, generally occupying high and relatively flat regions.

ice shelves ⊕ Sheets of ice that extend from the edge of a continent over the surface of the ocean, with ocean water flowing beneath them. They typically range from approximately 200–1000 meters (500–3,500 feet) thick. The Arctic Ocean is partly covered by ice shelves and the continent of Antarctica is almost completely surrounded by them.

indigenous ⊕ A native species; vegetation that originates from or occurs naturally within a particular region.

Indochina ⊕ A subregion that includes the peninsular countries of southeast Asia that lie between India and China, including: Vietnam, Laos, Cambodia, Thailand, Myanmar (Burma), and the mainland territory of Malaysia. The term indicates that the culture in these countries has been influenced by both Indian and Chinese traditions.

inlet ⊕ Any water filled indentation along a coast or shore, such as a bay or gulf; a narrow passage through which water from an ocean or other large body of water passes, usually into a bay or lagoon.

International Date Line ⊕ An arbitrary, imaginary line at about 180° longitude that designates where one day begins and another ends.

island ⊕ A land mass entirely surrounded by water.

isthmus ⊕ A narrow strip of land that connects two larger bodies of land such as two continents, a continent and a peninsula, or two parts of an island. An isthmus is bordered by water on two sides.

K

karst ⊕ An area of limestone characterized by caverns and rock formations that are caused by erosion and underground streams.

key. *See* **cay.**

L

Labrador Current ⊕ A North Atlantic current that flows southward from polar waters along the east coast of Canada.

lagoon ⊕ A shallow body of water, often connected with or barely separated from a nearby ocean or sea by coral reefs or sandbars.

lake ⊕ A large inland body of standing water.

landlocked country ⊕ A country that does not have direct access to an ocean; a country that is completely surrounded by other countries.

landslide ⊕ A flow of muddy soil or loose rock that is usually triggered by heavy rainfall in areas where the terrain is steep.

Latin America ⊕ A geopolitical term that relates to the countries that are south of the United States in the Western Hemisphere, particularly countries where the Latin-based languages (or Romance languages) of Spanish, Portuguese, and French are spoken.

latitude ⊕ (also called parallel) An imaginary line running around the Earth parallel to the equator. The equator is at 0° latitude and divides the Earth into two sets of lines of latitude, north and south. Each set covers 90°.

lava ⊕ Molten rock (magma) that has been poured out on the Earth's surface, usually through a volcano.

leeward ⊕ The direction identical to that of the prevailing wind.

littoral ⊕ A coastal region or shore; or, the area between the high water and low water marks of a shore or coastal region.

loam ⊕ Light soil consisting of clay, silt, and sand.

loess ⊕ A windblown accumulation of fine yellow clay or silt.

longitude ⊕ (also called meridian) An imaginary line that extends along the surface of the Earth directly from one pole to another. The Earth is divided into 360 degrees of longitude, with 0° being designated as the Prime Meridian.

M

Maghreb ⊕ Region in northwest Africa made up of Algeria, Morocco, and Tunisia.

magma ⊕ Molten rock beneath the Earth's surface that has been melted by the heat of the Earth's interior. When magma breaches the Earth's surface it is known as lava.

mangrove ⊕ A tree that abounds on tropical shores in both hemispheres. It is characterized by its numerous roots that arch out from its trunk and descend from its branches. Mangroves form thick, dense growths along the tidal mud, covering areas that are hundreds of miles long.

marine life ⊕ The life that exists in or is formed by the seas and oceans.

maritime climate ⊕ The climate and weather conditions typical of areas bordering large bodies of water. Generally, areas close to water have more even temperatures than areas with a continental climate.

marsh ⊕ An area of soggy land, usually covered wholly or in part by shallow water and containing aquatic vegetation.

massif ⊕ The central part of a mountain or the dominant part of a range of mountains.

mean temperature ⊕ The air temperature unit measured by adding the maximum and minimum daily temperatures together and diving the sum by two; an average temperature.

Mediterranean ⊕ The region surrounding the Mediterranean Sea.

Mediterranean climate ⊕ A wet-winter, dry-summer climate with a moderate annual temperature range, as is typically experienced by countries along the Mediterranean Sea.

meridian. *See* **longitude.**

mesa ⊕ An isolated, elevated, flat-topped area of land, typically larger than a butte but smaller than a plateau.

Mesopotamia ⊕ The name means, "between rivers," and refers to the territory between and around the Tigris and Euphrates rivers (currently a part of Iraq). This area has been nicknamed "The Cradle of Civilization" because it was home to the ancient empires of Babylon, Sumer, and Assyria, among others. The Tigris and Euphrates are also two of the four rivers mentioned in the Biblical story of Eden.

Middle East ⊕ A geopolitical term that designates those countries of southwest Asia and northeast Africa that stretch from the Mediterranean Sea to the borders of Pakistan and Afghanistan, including the Arabian Peninsula. This area was considered to be the midpoint between Europe and East Asia, usually called the Far East. The term is sometimes used to include all the countries of that general region that are primarily Islamic.

mistral ⊕ In southern France, a cold, dry, northerly wind.

moist tropical climate ⊕ A weather pattern typical to the tropics, known for year-round high temperatures and large amounts of rainfall.

monolith ⊕ A large, natural rock formation, usually one that is isolated from other areas of high elevations; a large, stone block, column, or figure.

monsoon ⊕ Seasonal change in the wind direction of Southeastern Asia, leading to wet and dry seasons. A monsoon develops when there is a significant difference in air temperatures over the ocean and the land.

moor ⊕ A poorly drained open area containing peat and heath.

moraine ⊕ A deposit of rocky earth deposited by a glacier.

mountain ⊕ A lofty elevation of land, generally higher than 300 meters (1,000 feet), but varying greatly depending on the surrounding terrain, with little surface area at its peak; commonly formed in a series of ridges or in a single ridge known as a mountain range.

N

nature preserve ⊕ An area (often a park) where one or more specific species of plants and/or animals are protected from harm, injury, or destruction.

Northern Hemisphere ⊕ The northern half of the Earth's surface, as measured from the equator to the North Pole.

O

oasis ⊕ Originally, a fertile spot in the Libyan Desert where there is a natural spring or well and vegetation; now refers to any fertile tract in the midst of a wasteland.

ocean ⊕ The entire body of saltwater that covers almost three-fourths of the Earth's surface; any of the five principal divisions of the ocean.

Oceania ⊕ Oceania is a term that refers to the islands in the region that covers the central and south Pacific and its adjacent seas; sometimes includes Australia, New Zealand, and the Malay Archipelago (an large group of islands off the southeast coast of Asia).

P

pampas ⊕ Grass-covered plain of South America.

panhandle ⊕ A long narrow strip of land projecting like the handle of a frying pan.

parallel. *See* **latitude.**

peneplain ⊕ A flat land surface that has been subjected to severe erosion.

peninsula ⊕ A body of land surrounded by water on three sides.

permafrost ⊕ A frozen layer of soil that never thaws.

petroglyph ⊕ Ancient carvings or line drawings created on the surface of rocks by prehistoric peoples; often found in caves.

plain ⊕ An expansive area free of major elevations and depressions.

plateau ⊕ A relatively flat area of an elevated area of land.

plate tectonics ⊕ A set of theories about the Earth's structure used by many geologists to explain why land masses and oceans are arranged as they are and why seismic activity occurs. According to plate tectonics the Earth's surface, including the bottom of the oceans, rests on a number of large tectonic plates. These plates are slowly moving over the interior layers of the Earth. Where they grind against each other, earthquakes and other seismic activity occurs, and the shape of the land gradually changes.

polar circle ⊕ (also called the polar region) A circular region around the North and South Poles that separates the frigid polar zones from the temperate zones. The Earth has two polar circles, the Arctic Circle in the north and the Antarctic Circle in the south.

polar climate ⊕ A humid, severely cold climate controlled by arctic-like air masses, with no warm or summer season.

polder ⊕ A low land area reclaimed from a body of water and protected by dikes or embankments.

pole (geographic pole) ⊕ The extreme northern and southern points of the Earth's axis, where the axis intersects the spherical surface. The geographic North Pole is located at 90°N latitude/ 0° longitude. The geographic South Pole is located at 90°S latitude/0° longitude.

pole (magnetic pole) ⊕ Either of two points on the Earth's surface, close to the geographic North Pole and South Pole, where the magnetic field is most intense. The North Magnetic Pole is located at 78°N latitude/104°W longitude in the Queen Elizabeth Islands of northern Canada. The South Magnetic Pole is located at 66°S latitude/139°E longitude on the Adélie Coast of Antarctica.

pond ⊕ A small body of still, shallow water.

prairie ⊕ An area of level grassland that occurs in temperate climate zones.

Prime Meridian ⊕ The meridian designated as 0° longitude that runs through Greenwich, England, site of the Royal Observatory. All other longitudes are measured from this point.

R

rainforest ⊕ A dense forest of tall trees with a high, leafy canopy where the annual rainfall is at least 254 centimeters (100 inches) per year.

rain shadow ⊕ An area that receives very little precipitation due to natural barriers, such as mountains, which keep rain clouds from covering the region.

Ramsar ⊕ The Ramsar Convention on Wetlands of International Importance is an international organization concerned with the preservation and protection of major wetland environments throughout the world.

ravine ⊕ A steep, narrow valley or gorge, usually containing the channel for a stream.

reef ⊕ String of rocks or coral formations, usually on a sandy bottom, that are barely submerged.

reforestation ⊕ Systematically replacing forest trees that were lost due to fire or logging.

reservoir ⊕ A lake that was formed artificially by a dam.

Ring of Fire ⊕ The region of seismic activity roughly outlined by a string of volcanoes that encircles the Pacific Ocean.

river ⊕ A substantial stream of water following a clear channel as it flows over the land.

riverine ⊕ Related to a river or the banks of a river.

S

Sahel ⊕ Sahel is an Arabic word meaning "shore." It refers to the 5,000 kilometer (3,125 mile) stretch of savanna that is the shore or edge of the Sahara desert. The Sahel spreads west to east from Mauritania and Senegal to Somalia.

salinization ⊕ An accumulation of soluble salts in soil. This condition is common in irrigated areas with desert climates, where water evaporates quickly in poorly drained soil due to high temperatures. Severe salinization renders soil poisonous to most plants.

salt pan ⊕ (also salt flat) An area of land in a sunny region that is periodically submerged in shallow water, usually due to tides or seasonal floods. The sun causes the shallow water to evaporate and leave the salt it contained behind on the ground.

sand bar ⊕ A deposit of sedimentary material that lies in the shallow water of a river, lake, or sea.

savanna ⊕ (also spelled savannah) A treeless or near treeless plain of a tropical or subtropical region dominated by drought-resistant grasses.

Scandinavia ⊕ The region of northwestern Europe that lies on the peninsula bordered by the Atlantic Ocean, the Baltic Sea, and the Gulf of Bothnia. Even though Norway and Sweden are the only two countries that lie directly on this peninsula, the countries of Denmark, Iceland and Finland are usually considered to be Scandinavian countries in a cultural context.

sea ⊕ A body of salt water that is connected to (and therefore a part of) the ocean; sometimes, a name given to a large lake.

sea level ⊕ The level of the ocean's surface, specifically the average between the levels at high tide and low tide. Sea level is often designated as 0 meters (0 feet) and is used as the baseline for measuring elevations and depressions on land and on the ocean floor.

seasonal ⊕ Dependant on the season. The flow of rivers and volume of lakes often varies greatly between seasons, as can vegetation.

seasons ⊕ Regular variations in weather patterns that occur at the same times every year.

sedimentary rock ⊕ Rock, such as sandstone, shale, and limestone, formed from the hardening of material deposits.

seismic activity ⊕ Relating to or connected with an earthquake or earthquakes in general.

semiarid ⊕ A climate where water and rainfall is relatively scarce but not so rare as to prohibit the growth of modest vegetation. Semiarid areas are often found around arid deserts and semiarid land is sometimes called a desert itself.

shoal ⊕ A shallow area in a stream, lake, or sea, especially a sand bank that lies above water at low tide or during dry periods.

shore ⊕ Typically, the land that borders a lake or river; may also be used to designate the land bordering an ocean or sea.

sierra ⊕ A rugged, jagged, irregular chain of hills or mountain.

silt ⊕ Fine, gravel-like, inorganic material, usually sand and coarse clay particles, that is carried by the flow of a river and deposited along its banks. Silt is generally very fertile soil.

skerry ⊕ A rocky island.

slough ⊕ A marshy pond that occurs in a river inlet.

softwoods ⊕ Coniferous trees with a wood density that is relatively softer than the wood of those trees referred to as hardwoods.

sound ⊕ A wide expanse of water, usually separating a mainland from islands or connecting two large bodies of water; often lies parallel to the coastline.

South Asia ⊕ A subregion of Asia that includes the countries of Afghanistan, Pakistan, India, Bangladesh, and Nepal.

Southeast Asia ⊕ A subregion of Asia that lies between India on the west, China to the north, and the Pacific Ocean to the east. The region includes the Indochina Peninsula of the South China Sea, the Malay Peninsula, and the Indonesian and Philippine Archipelagos The countries of Southeast Asia are: Brunei, Cambodia, Indonesia, Laos, Malaysia, Myanmar, the Philippines, Singapore, Thailand, and Vietnam.

Southern Hemisphere ⊕ The southern half of the Earth's surface between the equator and the South Pole.

Southwest Asia ⊕ A subregion of Asia that includes Turkey and extends southward through the Arabian Peninsula. Iran can also be included in the region.

spring ⊕ Water flowing from the ground through a natural opening.

stalactites ⊕ Deposits of calcium carbonate formed in a cavern or cave that hang down from the ceiling like icicles.

stalagmites ⊕ Deposits of calcium carbonate formed in a cavern or cave that rise up from the floor like cones or columns.

steppe ⊕ A flat, mostly treeless, semiarid grassland, marked by extreme seasonal and daily temperature variations. Although sometimes used to describe other areas, the term applies primarily to the plains of southeastern Europe and Central Asia.

strait ⊕ Narrow body of water connecting two larger bodies of water.

stream ⊕ Any flowing water that moves generally downhill from elevated areas towards sea level.

subarctic climate ⊕ A high latitude climate. The continental subarctic climate has very cold winters; short, cool summers; light precipitation; and moist air. The marine subarctic climate is a coastal and island climate with polar air masses causing high levels of precipitation and extreme cold.

subcontinent ⊕ A land mass of great size, but smaller than any of the continents; a large subdivision of a continent.

subtropical climate ⊕ A middle latitude climate dominated by humid, warm temperatures and heavy rainfall in summer, with cool winters and frequent cyclonic storms.

T

taiga ⊕ An area of open forest made up of coniferous trees.

tectonic ⊕ Relating to the structure of the Earth's crust.

tectonic plate ⊕ According to the theory of plate tectonics, the outer layer of the Earth consists of a series of large plates of rock called tectonic plates. The largest plates have entire oceans or continents on their surface.

Temperate Zone ⊕ The parts of the Earth lying between the Tropics and the polar circles. The North Temperate Zone is the area between the Tropic of Cancer and the Arctic Circle. The South Temperate Zone is the area between the Tropic of Capricorn and the Antarctic Circle. Temperate zones are marked by the greatest seasonal variations in temperature; however, temperatures and rainfall tend to stay within a moderate range, without extremes.

terraces ⊕ Successive areas of flat lands.

terrain ⊕ General characteristics of the Earth's surface in a region, including its characteristic vegetation.

tidal bore ⊕ A distinctive type of wave that travels up a shallow river or estuary on the incoming tide. It is a dramatic phenomenon that occurs in few places in the world; the incoming tidal waters flow against the river's current.

tidal wave. *See* **tsunami**.

tide ⊕ The rise and fall of the surface of a body of water caused by the gravitational attraction of the sun and moon.

timber line ⊕ The point of high elevation on a mountain above which the climate is too severe to support trees.

topography ⊕ The surface features of a region; also, the study of such features.

tornado ⊕ A violent, whirling wind storm that forms a funnel-shaped cloud and moves in a path over the surface of the Earth.

Torrid Zone ⊕ The part of the Earth's surface that lies between the Tropic lines, so named for the warm, humid, character of its climate.

trade winds ⊕ Winds that consistently blow from the northeast and southeast toward the equator.

trench ⊕ A steep-sided depression in the ocean floor where the water is very deep.

tributary ⊕ Any stream that flows into another larger stream.

tropical monsoon climate ⊕ One of the tropical rainy climates; it is sufficiently warm and rainy to produce tropical rainforest vegetation, but also has a winter dry season.

Tropic of Cancer ⊕ A latitudinal line located 23°27′ north of the equator, the highest point on the globe at which the sun can shine directly overhead.

Tropic of Capricorn ⊕ A latitudinal line located 23°27′ south of the equator, the lowest point on the globe at which the sun can shine directly overhead.

tsunami ⊕ A powerful, massive, and destructive ocean wave caused by an undersea earthquake or volcanic eruption.

tundra ⊕ A nearly level, treeless area whose climate and vegetation are characteristically arctic due to its position near one of the poles; the subsoil is permanently frozen.

typhoon ⊕ Violent hurricane occurring in the region of the South China Sea, usually in the period from July through October.

U

UNESCO ⊕ The United Nations Educational, Scientific, and Cultural Organization. An international organization promoting peace and security around the world through education, science, culture, and communication.

V

valley ⊕ An elongated depression through which a stream of water usually flows, typically an area that lies between mountains, hills, and/or other uplands.

vegetation ⊕ Plants, including trees, shrubs, grasses, and other plants.

volcano ⊕ A hole or opening through which molten rock and superheated steam erupt from the interior of the Earth. Also, a mountain created by the accumulation of these ejected materials.

W

wadi ⊕ Dry stream bed, usually in a desert region in southwest Asia or north Africa.

waterfall ⊕ A steep, natural descent of water flowing over a cliff or precipice to a lower level.

watershed ⊕ An area of shared water drainage, where all the rainfall drains into a common river or lake system.

waves ⊕ The alternate rise and fall of ridges of water, generally produced by the action between the wind and the surface of a body of water.

weather ⊕ Atmospheric conditions at a given place and time.

Western Europe ⊕ A geopolitical term that usually refers to those countries of Europe that are allies of the United States and Canada under the North Atlantic Treaty Organization (NATO, established 1949). The original European countries in NATO were Belgium, France, Great Britain, Italy, Luxembourg, the Netherlands, and Portugal. Today, Western European countries also include Germany, Spain, Ireland, amd Austria. Though Denmark is geographically part of Europe, it is culturally considered as part of Scandinavia.

Western Hemisphere ⊕ The half of the Earth's surface that lies west of the Prime Meridian to 180° longitude.

West Indies ⊕ The islands lying between North America and South America made up of the Greater Antilles (Cuba, Haiti, Dominican Republic, Jamaica, and Puerto Rico), the Lesser Antilles (Virgin Islands, Trinidad and Tobago, Barbados), and the Bahamas.

wildlife sanctuary ⊕ An area of land set aside for the protection and preservation of animals and plants.

windward ⊕ Facing into the prevailing wind, or lying closest to the direction from which the wind is blowing.

Junior
Worldmark
Encyclopedia of
Physical
Geography

Morocco

- **Official name:** Kingdom of Morocco
- **Area:** 446,550 square kilometers (172,414 square miles)
- **Highest point on mainland:** Mount Toubkal (4,165 meters/13,665 feet)
- **Lowest point on land:** Sebkha Tah (55 meters/180 feet below sea level)
- **Hemispheres:** Northern and Western
- **Time zone:** Noon = noon GMT
- **Longest distances:** 1,809 kilometers (1,124 miles) from northeast to southwest; 525 kilometers (326 miles) from southeast to northwest

- **Land boundaries:** 2,081 kilometers (1,254 miles) total boundary length; Algeria 1,559 kilometers (969 miles); Spain (Ceuta) 6.3 kilometers (3.9 miles); Spain (Melilla) 9.6 kilometers (6.0 miles); Western Sahara 443 kilometers (275 miles)
- **Coastline:** 1,140 miles (1,835 kilometers)
- **Territorial sea limits:** 22 kilometers (12 nautical miles)

1 ⊕ LOCATION AND SIZE

Morocco is located at the northwest corner of the African continent, bordering the North Atlantic Ocean and the Mediterranean Sea. It shares land borders with the two Spanish enclaves of Ceuta and Melilla, Algeria, and the Western Sahara. The Moroccan-controlled Western Sahara also borders on Mauritania. With an area of about 446,550 square kilometers (172,414 square miles), the country is slightly larger than the state of California. Morocco is divided into thirty-seven provinces and two wilayas (special districts).

2 ⊕ TERRITORIES AND DEPENDENCIES

The Western Sahara is claimed and administered by the government of Morocco; surrounding countries challenge Morocco's claim, however. The Western Sahara covers an area of about 252,120 square kilometers (97,344 square miles).

3 ⊕ CLIMATE

Morocco has two climatic zones: coastal and interior. Temperature variations are relatively small along the Atlantic coast, while the interior is characterized by extreme variations. The north and central areas have a Mediterranean climate, moderate and subtropical, cooled by the Mediterranean Sea and Atlantic Ocean. These areas characteristically have warm, wet winters and hot, dry summers. The average temperature hovers around 20°C (68°F). In the northern part of the interior, the climate is predominantly semiarid. Winters can be quite cold, and summers can be very hot. In the mountain ranges temperatures can drop as low as -18°C (0°F). Mountain peaks in both the Atlas and Er Rif mountain ranges are snow-capped throughout most of the year.

The western slopes of the Atlas Mountains receive a great deal of rain, but at the expense

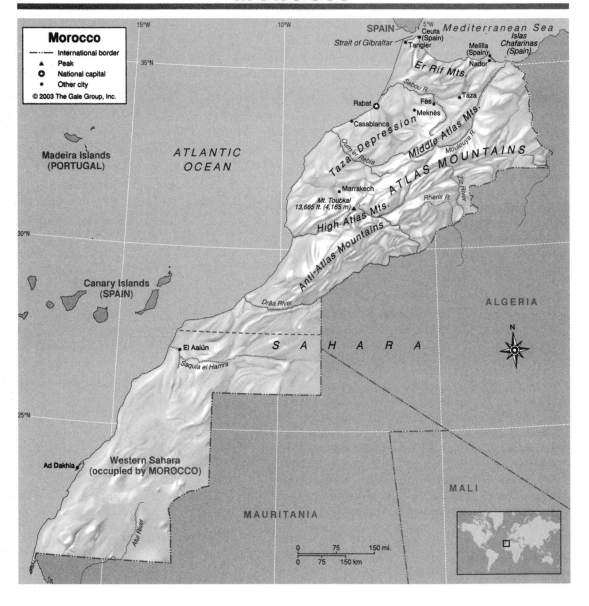

of the interior, since the mountains block the central areas from the Atlantic or Mediterranean. The two rainy seasons are in April and May and in October and November. A maximum annual rainfall of 75 to 100 centimeters (30 to 40 inches) occurs in the northwest. Other parts of the country receive much less precipitation. Half of all of the arable land

receives no more than 35 centimeters (14 inches) of rain per year.

4 ⊕ TOPOGRAPHIC REGIONS

Morocco has four distinct geographic regions. In the north, there is a fertile coastal plain along the Mediterranean. The Atlas Mountains, extending across the country from southwest to northeast and into Algeria,

ARAMCO/Brynn Bruijn

Desert sands of Morocco.

comprise another region. A third area is a wide arc of coastal plains lining the country's western seaboard, bounded by the Er Rif and Atlas mountain ranges. Finally, south of the Atlas Mountains are semiarid grasslands that merge with the Sahara Desert along the southeastern borders of the country.

Morocco provides habitats for dozens of bird species, from large raptors to woodpeckers, waterfowl, and songbirds.

5 ⊕ OCEANS AND SEAS

Seacoast and Undersea Features

The Mediterranean Sea is north of Morocco. It is an almost completely landlocked body of water that lies between southern Europe, north Africa and southwest Asia. Morocco's western coast faces the Atlantic Ocean.

Sea Inlets and Straits

The Strait of Gibraltar connects the Mediterranean Sea with the Atlantic Ocean and separates Morocco from Spain.

Coastal Features

The Mediterranean coast between Tangier and Nador has a string of creeks, bays, sheltered beaches, and cliffs, all of which are ideal for recreational use. The Atlantic coast is often rocky, but it also has some long stretches of fine sand and calm bays, including the harbors at Rabat and Casablanca.

6 ⊕ INLAND LAKES

Lake Semara is in the Western Sahara. Lake Chiker, near Taza, is usually dry during the summer months. The Middle and High Atlas Mountains contain mountain lakes that reach impressive depths, including Tigalmamine

EPD/Saxifraga

The Todra Gorge is in the Atlas Mountains of Morocco.

(16 meters/53 feet); Sidi Ali (65 meters/213 feet); and Isti (95 meters/311 feet).

7 ⊕ RIVERS AND WATERFALLS

Morocco has the most extensive river system in North Africa. The principal rivers flowing south or westward into the Atlantic Ocean are the Rebia (555 kilometers/344 miles long), Sebou (Sebu; 500 kilometers/310 miles long), Bouregreg (250 kilometers/155 miles long), Tensift (270 kilometers/167 miles long), and Drâa (1,200 kilometers/744 miles long). The Drâa is Morocco's longest river, but it is seasonal. It marks part of the border with Algeria and is sometimes dry, since it runs through the desert.

The Ziz and Rheris both flow south out of the Atlas Mountains into the heart of the Sahara. The Moulouya (Muluya) flows 560 kilometers (347 miles) northeast from the Atlas to the Mediterranean, making it the longest river in the country that consistently reaches the sea.

8 ⊕ DESERTS

Morocco lies within the border of the Sahara Desert. The Sahara Desert, which covers an area of 9,065,000 square kilometers (3,500,000 square miles) is the largest desert in the world. It covers the entire region of North Africa, from the Atlantic coast in the west to the Red Sea in the east. It borders the Mediterranean Sea and the Atlas Mountains in the north and extends into a southern region known as the Sahel and the Sudan. Scientists believe that during the Ice Age (about fifty thousand to one hundred thousand years ago), the Sahara was covered with shallow lakes that provided water for large areas of lush vegetation.

The Western Sahara, as part of the greater Sahara Desert, has a terrain that is composed mostly of sand, gravel, or small stones. It is relatively flat except for a region of rocky highlands in the east.

9 ⊕ FLAT AND ROLLING TERRAIN

With the exception of the Er Rif, all of Morocco north of the Atlas Mountains is a fertile plain. This area is also known as the Taza Depression. There are also some semiarid grasslands in the south beyond the Atlas Mountains. These eventually give way to the Sahara Desert. Semiarid plains can also be found in northern Western Sahara.

10 ⊕ MOUNTAINS AND VOLCANOES

The Atlas Mountains are the largest and most important mountain range in North Africa, extending from Morocco to Tunisia for about 2,400 kilometers (1,488 miles) in a series of creased mountain chains. Morocco's portion of the Atlas Mountains includes the Middle Atlas, High Atlas, and Anti-Atlas.

The High Atlas (also called Western Atlas or Great Atlas) is the highest of the three, stretching for more than 644 kilometers (400 miles), with ten peaks of over 3,965 meters (13,000 feet). Mount Toubkal, south of Marrakech, reaches to 4,165 meters (13,665 feet)—the highest point in the country. The Middle Atlas stretches for 251 kilometers (156 miles) east of the High Atlas, extending into Algeria. Mount Bounaceur is the highest point in the Middle Atlas, at 3,326 meters (10,909 feet). West and south of the High Atlas is the Anti-Atlas range. Although not as tall as the High Atlas, the terrain in the Anti-Atlas is very rugged. It is about 403 kilometers (250 miles) long. South of the Atlas is the Sirwa, a volcanic outcropping and a ridge of black lava that connects the High Atlas and Anti-Atlas. The Sirwa reaches a maximum height of 2,822 meters (9,254 feet).

The Er Rif Mountains near the northern coast are not part of the Atlas ranges. They are made up of steep cliffs. The highest peak in the Er Rif is Tidghine (2,465 meters/8,085 feet), south of Ketama.

11 ⊕ CANYONS AND CAVES

Toghobeit Cave is located in the Er Rif cliffs. At 722 meters (3,918 feet) deep it is one of the most fantastic open caverns in the world.

The Ziz River cuts through the Atlas Mountains to form the Ziz Gorge. At the southern end of the gorge, there are artificial lakes created by the Hassan Addakhil Dam. At the northern end is the Tunnel de Légionnaire, which creates a passageway from the Ziz Mountains to the Ziz Valley.

The Todra Gorge is also in the Atlas Mountains, near the town of Tinerhir. The gorge has steep rock faces that rise as much as 300 meters (984 feet) and has become a popular site for rock climbers.

12 ⊕ PLATEAUS AND MONOLITHS

There are no plateau regions in Morocco.

DID YOU KN⊕W?

Kasbah, or Casbah, is a term often heard in association with Morocco. Rather than being a specific place or region, it is a term that usually refers to the oldest section of a city. Often, this is the marketplace of the city. Sometimes the term refers to an ancient castle or palace.

---

13 ⊕ MAN-MADE FEATURES

Morocco relies very heavily on its system of river dams and reservoirs for drinking water, irrigation, and electricity. Some of the main dams in the country are the Bin El Ouidane, Moulay Youssef, and Moulay Hassan I. The Al Wahda Dam, at 90 meters (295 feet) high, is the second-largest dam in Africa.

14 ⊕ FURTHER READING

Books

Demeude, Hugues. *Morocco*. Köln, Germany: Evergreen, 1998.

Italia, Bob. *Morocco*. Minneapolis, MN: Abdo Publications, 2000.

Solyst, Annette. *Morocco*. New York: Friedman/ Fairfax, 2000.

Jacobshagen, H. Volker, ed. *The Atlas System of Morocco: Studies on Its Geodynamic Evolution*. New York: Springer-Verlag, 1988.

Wilkins, Frances. *Morocco*. Philadelphia: Chelsea House, 2001.

Web Sites

Association for Freedom & Regulation of the Western Sahara (ARSO): Western Sahara Geography. http://www.arso.org/05-2.htm (accessed April 4, 2003).

Mozambique

- **Official name:** Republic of Mozambique
- **Area:** 801,590 square kilometers (309,496 square miles)
- **Highest point on mainland:** Mount Binga (2,436 meters/7,992 feet)
- **Lowest point on land:** Sea level
- **Hemispheres:** Southern and Eastern
- **Time zone:** 2 P.M. = noon GMT
- **Longest distances:** Not available

- **Land boundaries:** 4,571 kilometers (2,840 miles) total boundary length; Malawi 1,569 kilometers (975 miles); South Africa 491 kilometers (305 miles); Swaziland 105 kilometers (65 miles); Tanzania 756 kilometers (470 miles); Zambia 419 kilometers (260 miles); Zimbabwe 1,231 kilometers (765 miles)
- **Coastline:** 2,470 kilometers (1,535 miles)
- **Territorial sea limits:** 22 kilometers (12 nautical miles)

1 ⊕ LOCATION AND SIZE

Mozambique is located on the southeast coast of Africa between the countries of Tanzania and South Africa, with an eastern coastline on the Mozambique Channel. The country shares land borders with six nations. With a total area of about 801,590 square kilometers (309,496 square miles), the country is slightly less than twice the size of California. Mozambique is administratively divided into ten provinces.

2 ⊕ TERRITORIES AND DEPENDENCIES

Mozambique has no outside territories or dependencies.

3 ⊕ CLIMATE

Between the months of November and March, temperatures are usually between 27°C and 29°C (81°F and 84°F) throughout most of the country, though temperatures are lower in the interior uplands. Between April and October, temperatures are cooler, averaging between 18°C and 20°C (64°F and 68°F).

The wet season runs from November through March, when 80 percent of all rainfall occurs. Rainfall is lowest in the southwest portion of the country, which receives an annual average of 30 centimeters (12 inches). It is highest near the western hills and the central areas near the Zambezi River, as well as along the central coast, where annual averages are between 135 and 150 centimeters (53 and 59 inches).

4 ⊕ TOPOGRAPHIC REGIONS

Mozambique is a topographically diverse nation. The Zambezi River divides the country into distinct northern and southern halves. The north is known for its mountainous regions and plateaus, notably the Livingstone-Nyasa Highlands, the Shire (or Namuli) Highlands, and the Angonia Highlands in the northeast. The westernmost regions are particularly mountainous, giving way to plateaus and uplands as one travels eastward. South of the Zambezi are the more fertile plains, most notably in the area surrounding the river. In the center of the country are uplands,

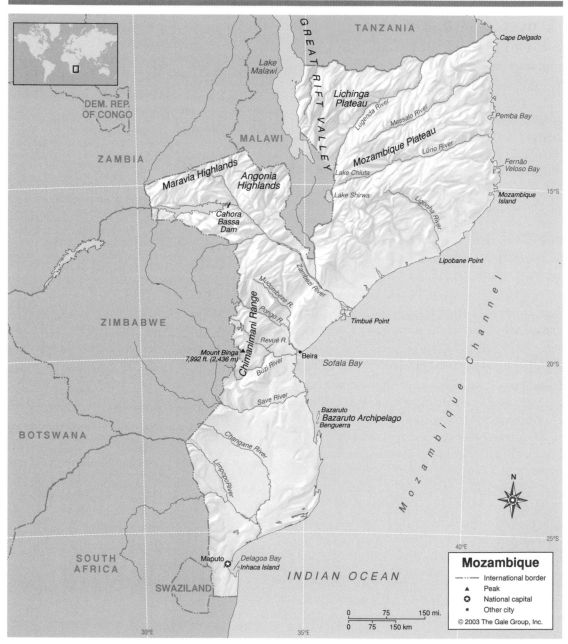

marshes, and coastal lowlands. Inland areas are dry and thus do not support much vegetation. By area, the country is approximately 44 percent coastal lowlands, 26 percent higher hills and plateaus, 17 percent lower plateaus and hills, and 13 percent mountains. Mozambique is located on the African Tectonic Plate and experiences little or no tectonic activity.

5 ⊕ OCEANS AND SEAS

Seacoast and Undersea Features

Bordering Mozambique to the east is the Mozambique Channel, which is a strait in the Indian Ocean that separates Africa from the island of Madagascar. The channel is approximately 1,600 kilometers (1,000 miles) long, and at its widest point, it stretches more than 950 kilometers (600 miles). This area is particularly susceptible to cyclones. Many coral reefs line the channel, attracting large numbers of divers from around the world. Coral islands also exist in the channel.

Sea Inlets and Straits

Several bays dot the coastline, including (from south to north) Delagoa Bay, Sofala Bay, Fernão Veloso Bay, and Pemba Bay.

Islands and Archipelagos

Mozambique has many small offshore islands along its coastline. Mozambique Island (Ilha de Moçambique), located 3 kilometers (2 miles) off the coast of the Nampula province, is a small but culturally significant island. Formerly a Portuguese colonial capital, this 2.5-kilometer- (1.5-mile-) long and 0.6-kilometer- (0.4-mile-) wide island is accessible via a mainland bridge. The United Nations Educational, Scientific, and Cultural Organization (UNESCO) has designated the island a World Heritage Site.

Inhaca Island, located 30 kilometers (18.6 miles) from Maputo, is a 12.5-kilometer– (7.8-mile–) long and 7.5-kilometer– (4.7-mile–) wide island known for its sandy beaches and ideal diving and fishing locations.

The Bazaruto Archipelago, also known as the Paradise Islands, is located 10 kilometers (6 miles) off the country's coast and was formed from sands deposited by the Limpopo River thousands of years ago. Santa Carolina, Bazaruto, Ibo, Benguerra, and Magaruque are the most popular islands in the archipelago, boasting clear blue waters, sandy beaches, palm trees, coral reefs, crocodiles, many species of tropical fish, and other tropical wildlife such as the samango monkey. The region was declared a national park in 1970.

Coastal Features

The expansive coastlines of Mozambique are jagged, with numerous bays and beaches. The coastal areas are ideal for the cultivation of rice, maize, sugar cane, and cashews. The coastal waters are rich in prawns, one of the country's leading exports. Fishermen often frequent the coastlines, as small and large fish are abundant.

Located in the southeast of Mozambique, Tofo (sometimes Tofu) and Barra Beaches are known for their sand dunes, mangroves, and palm groves, as well as for their tropical wildlife, including parrots and monkeys. Wimbi Beach is particularly notable for its coral reefs, a favorite among snorkelers. Its white coral beaches, lined by palm trees, provide an ideal tropical setting. The beaches of Mozambique are well preserved, and wildlife thrives, including humpback whales, turtles, flamingoes, dolphins, and manta rays.

Some notable points along the coast are Timbué Point and Lipobane Point. Cape Delgado is located near the northernmost point of the coast.

6 ⊕ INLAND LAKES

Three lakes in northern Mozambique form part of the border with Malawi: Lake Malawi, Lake Chiuta, and Lake Shirwa.

Navigable Lake Malawi (also known as Lake Nyasa) borders Mozambique and Tanzania. The lake has an incredible 29,600 kilometers (11,400 square miles) of surface

AP Photo/Cobus Bodenstein

A woman works her field on the outskirts of Maputo, Mozambique.

area, about one-third of which is situated within Mozambique's territory. Its deepest waters, which reach a maximum depth of 706 meters (2,316 feet), are found in this part of the lake.

7 ⊕ RIVERS AND WATERFALLS

Mozambique is rich in rivers, with twenty-five of them throughout the country. Many of these rivers flow out from the western highlands to the Indian Ocean or to the Mozambique Channel in the east. Water flow tends to fluctuate, owing to the rainy and dry seasons. The rivers overflow between January and March, while they slow to a trickle between June and August.

The longest and most important river is the Zambezi River, with a total length of 2,650 kilometers (1,650 miles). It flows southeast across the heart of Mozambique into the Indian Ocean; historically, this river has been the principal means of transport between inland central Africa and the coast. Its waters make the soil in the land surrounding it some of the most fertile land in the country. From the Maravia Highlands downstream, the valley is low-lying and has a very gentle slope, with an elevation of less than 152 meters (500 feet). Upstream, the river enters a narrow gorge; this constriction prompted the construction of the Cahora Bassa Dam.

The Limpopo River in the south flows through Botswana, Zimbabwe, Mozambique, and South Africa. It is fed mainly by the Changane River and drains the Limpopo Basin. It is susceptible to serious flooding, the effects of which are compounded when cyclones occur in the wet months. Also particularly notable is the Save (or Sabi) River in the center of the country, which, along with the Búzi and Revué Rivers, drains the southern Mozambique Plain. In the northeast draining the Mozambique Plateau are the Lugenda River, the Messalo River, the Lúrio River, and the Ligonha River.

Much of the area around the mouth of the Zambezi and south to the lower reaches of the Pongo River and its tributary, the Mucombeze, is marshy, hindering north-south communications and promoting the spread of disease. Mangrove swamps are common near the coast of the Sophala and Zambezia provinces. These wetlands provide excellent conditions for many marine species, most notably prawns.

8 ⊕ DESERTS

There are no desert regions in Mozambique.

9 ⊕ FLAT AND ROLLING TERRAIN

Low-lying areas close to the major rivers in Mozambique are particularly fertile and support a variety of plants and trees, including lemon, orange, lychee, and mango.

Much of southern and central Mozambique that is inland from the coastline suffers from poor, sandy, infertile soil. Little vegetation other than dry scrubs can be supported on this land.

Approximately two-thirds of the land supports woodland vegetation. Most of Mozambique's forested areas are located along plateaus and contain the *miombo* forest type: dry, deciduous trees of varying heights. The northernmost regions, as well as those surrounding the mouth of the Zambezi River, are the richest in woodland. Tropical forests are also prevalent, with lush vegetation and African game species such as zebras, wildebeests, and even elephants; mangroves, however, are relatively rare and are found near coastal regions.

The area in northeastern Mozambique between the Lúrio and Ligonha Rivers contains some of the most magnificent vertical granite rock faces in all of Africa; consequently, it is a favorite rock-climbing destination. Rolling hills are commonly found east of areas with particularly mountainous terrain. Vegetation is sparse in these savannahs and this land does not support many crops.

10 ⊕ MOUNTAINS AND VOLCANOES

Mountainous regions in Mozambique are found throughout the western end of the country. Most mountain peaks rise from plateau regions, although many mountains are isolated in the landscape. The Great Rift Valley, which starts in Jordan near Syria, terminates in Mozambique near Beira at Sofala Bay. A wide variety of animal species, including lions, reside in this area.

The country shares with Zimbabwe the Chimanimani Mountain Range, which contains Mozambique's highest peak, Mount Binga (2,436 meters/7,992 feet). Alluvial gold has been extracted from these mountains.

DID YOU KN⊕W?

Mozambique lies at the southern end of the Great Rift Valley, which is a massive fault system that stretches over 6,400 kilometers (4,000 miles) from the Jordan Valley in Israel to the middle of Mozambique at about Sofala Bay. In general, the Great Rift Valley ranges in elevation from 395 meters (1,300 feet) below sea level at the Dead Sea to 1,830 meters (6,000 feet) above sea level in south Kenya. The western branch contains the troughs and rivers that have become part of the African Great Lakes system. A large number of volcanoes lie along this rift, which was created by the violent underground collisions between the African Plate (Nubian) to the west and the Eurasian, Arabian, Indian, and Somalian Plates to the east. There are no active volcanoes located in Mozambique, however.

11 ⊕ CANYONS AND CAVES

There are no major canyons or caves in Mozambique.

12 ⊕ PLATEAUS AND MONOLITHS

There are many plateaus of varying elevations throughout the northwestern portion of Mozambique, which generally increase in elevation as one travels westward. These plateaus help support many farmers, providing land on which to grow cash crops as well as feed for livestock.

The province of Niassa, bordering Lake Malawi in northern Mozambique, is the largest and highest in the country. The Lichinga Plateau, which reaches elevations of up to 1,500 meters (4,920 feet), covers 25 percent of Niassa. The entire province has an average elevation of 700 meters (2,296 feet). The plateau is a heavily wooded savannah, with dry and open woodland areas covered with acacia trees. On the other side of the Lugenda River is the Mozambique Plateau. This plateau is similar to the Lichinga, though lower in elevation. It reaches from the center of the country all the way to the Indian Ocean.

The Angonia and Maravia Highlands, in northwest Mozambique on the Zambia border, are some of the most fertile lands in all of Mozambique. Crops such as peaches, apples, and potatoes are grown in this area.

13 ⊕ MAN-MADE FEATURES

The Cahora Bassa Dam, the largest hydroelectric power dam in Africa, powers the capital city of Maputo and provides electricity for parts of South Africa and Zimbabwe as well. The dam is built along the upper part of the Zambezi River and has formed a very large reservoir. During the wet seasons, heavy rains from Zambia and Zimbabwe cause significant water flow along the Zambezi River, so that often the reservoir of the Cahora Bassa begins to swell, threatening the structure of the dam. When this occurs, one or more of the gates of the dam are opened, releasing water downstream that then tends to flood areas along the river. During some particularly dry seasons, however, the water level in the Zambezi River drops so low that parts of the river become impassable.

14 ⊕ FURTHER READING

Books

Darch, Colin. *Mozambique*. Santa Barbara, CA: Clio Press, 1987.

James, R. S. *Mozambique*. New York: Chelsea House, 1988.

Lauré, Jason. *Mozambique*. Chicago: Children's Press, 1995.

Slater, Mike. *Mozambique*. London: New Holland, 1997.

Waterhouse, Rachel. *Mozambique: Rising from the Ashes*. Oxford: Oxfam, 1996.

Web Site

Mozambique: Welcome to Our Beautiful Country. http://www.mozambique.mz/eindex.htm (accessed June 18, 2003).

Myanmar

- **Official name:** Union of Myanmar
- **Area:** 678,500 square kilometers (261,969 square miles)
- **Highest point on mainland:** Hkakabo Razi (5,881 meters/19,295 feet)
- **Lowest point on land:** Sea level
- **Hemispheres:** Northern and Eastern
- **Time zone:** 6:30 P.M. = noon GMT
- **Longest distances:** 1,931 kilometers (1,200 miles) from north to south; 925 kilometers (575 miles) from east to west

- **Land boundaries:** 5,876 kilometers (3,643 miles) total boundary length; Bangladesh 193 kilometers (120 miles); China 2,185 kilometers (1,355 miles); India 1,463 kilometers (907 miles); Laos 235 kilometers (146 miles); Thailand 1,800 kilometers (1,116 miles)
- **Coastline:** 1,930 kilometers (1,197 miles)
- **Territorial sea limits:** 22 kilometers (12 nautical miles)

1 ⊕ LOCATION AND SIZE

Myanmar is located in Southeast Asia, bordered by India and Bangladesh in the northwest, China in the northeast, Laos in the east, Thailand in the east and southeast, and the Indian Ocean to the south and the west. It is slightly smaller than the state of Texas.

2 ⊕ TERRITORIES AND DEPENDENCIES

Myanmar has no territories or dependencies.

3 ⊕ CLIMATE

Myanmar has a tropical climate with three seasons: a cool winter from November to February, a hot season in March and April, and a rainy season from May through October, when the southwest monsoon arrives. The average annual temperature is 28°C (82°F). Temperatures can dip below 0°C (32°F) in mountainous areas, and soar as high as 45°C (113°F) on the central plains. Humidity ranges from 66 percent to 83 percent. Most of the country's rainfall occurs during the monsoon. Annual average rainfall is 508 centimeters (200 inches) along the coast and 76 centimeters (30 inches) for central regions. Frost and snow occur in the high mountains of the north.

4 ⊕ TOPOGRAPHIC REGIONS

Myanmar, the largest nation of mainland Southeast Asia, has an extraordinary variety of terrain, from glaciers in the north to coral reefs in the south. There are four major topographic areas: mountains in the north and west, the Shan Highlands in the east, the plains of central Myanmar, and the delta and valley regions in the south near the Irrawaddy and Sittang Rivers.

In the late 1980s, the military government changed the name of the country from Burma to Myanmar; the government also changed the names or spellings of many geographic features.

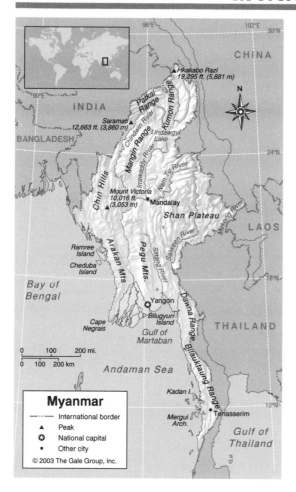

Myanmar

— — — International border
▲ Peak
✪ National capital
● Other city

© 2003 The Gale Group, Inc.

Islands and Archipelagos

Offshore, there are many large islands and hundreds of smaller ones. The islands of Myanmar's western coast and delta have been formed by erosion of the shoreline. Just off the northwest coast, the large islands of Ramree (1,350 square kilometers/520 square miles) and Cheduba (523 square kilometers/202 square miles) are part of the Ramri Group. Bilugyun is a large island on the southwest coast. Also in the southwest is an undersea ridgeline that forms the Mergui Archipelago— some nine hundred islands ranging in size from Kadan Island (440 square kilometers/170 square miles) to small rocks.

Coastal Features

In the northwest of Myanmar, the coast has rocky ridges with deep channels. After Cape Negrais, Myanmar's southern delta coast is formed by silt from the Irrawaddy and other rivers. From the mouth of the Sittang River, the coast stretches to the south, studded with inlets, rocky cliffs, and coral reefs.

6 ⊕ INLAND LAKES

An earthquake likely formed Myanmar's largest lake: Indawgyi, with an area of 116 square kilometers (45 square miles). The second-largest inland lake is the shallow Inle Lake, which covers about 67 square kilometers (26 square miles) on the Shan Plateau. It is the residue of an inland sea that is still shrinking. The lower Chindwin River basin has several crater lakes. Most other lakes and ponds are situated in the courses of former rivers.

7 ⊕ RIVERS AND WATERFALLS

The Irrawaddy (Ayeyarwady) River, which is 2,170 kilometers (1,350 miles) long, is Myanmar's primary drainage system. Rising in the far north of Myanmar, the Irrawaddy flows south across the entire country before entering the sea through a nine-channel delta. It is the

5 ⊕ OCEANS AND SEAS

Seacoast and Undersea Features

Myanmar's western shores curve along the Bay of Bengal, coming to a point at Cape Negrais. The Irrawaddy delta and the southeastern region's coasts together frame the upper corner of the Andaman Sea, joining at the Gulf of Martaban. All of these bodies of water are parts of the Indian Ocean.

Sea Inlets and Straits

There are no notable sea inlets or straits off Myanmar.

An Irrawaddy River gorge.

longest river found entirely within Myanmar. The Irrawaddy's most important tributary is the Chindwin River (960 kilometers/600 miles), which drains the northwest. The Sittang (Sittoung) River (483 kilometers/300 miles) rises just south of Mandalay and parallels the Irrawaddy on its eastern flank. The lower valleys of the Irrawaddy and Sittang Rivers form a vast, low-lying delta area of about 25,900 square kilometers (10,000 square miles) that continually expands into the sea due to silting.

Myanmar's other large river, the Salween (Thanlwin), rises in China and flows south across the Shan Plateau in eastern Myanmar. The Salween covers 1,325 kilometers (823 miles) within Myanmar, in a series of rapids and waterfalls that run through steep, narrow valleys.

In the eastern Shan State the mighty Mekong River (4,200 kilometers/2,600 miles) forms Myanmar's 235-kilometer (146-mile) border with Laos. In the southeast, many short streams run westward to the Andaman Sea, most notably the Tenasserim. There are also a number of small rivers in the southwest, flowing south out of the mountains into the Bay of Bengal.

8 ⊕ DESERTS

The "dry zone" of north-central Myanmar has seven rainless months each year, during which its rivers go dry and windstorms are frequent.

9 ⊕ FLAT AND ROLLING TERRAIN

The vast deltas and flood plains of the Irrawaddy and Sittang Rivers form the heart of Myanmar and provide its most productive

EPD/Cynthia Bassett

Mount Popa is the site of the annual Festival of the Spirits each spring.

farmland. Bamboo grows extensively in many parts of the country.

Myanmar used to be rich in rainforests, monsoon forests, and mangrove forests. Now, most of these woodlands are gone due to deforestation. The country's remaining forest cover, now less than 30 percent, is found mostly in the relatively inaccessible mountain areas of the north and northeast. The loss of forest cover in Myanmar not only has threatened animal and plant populations, but also has caused landslides, flooding, and drought.

Steep, craggy limestone hills with many caves are found in the Shan Plateau and in the southeastern part of the country. Elsewhere in Myanmar there are foothill areas leading up to the mountain chains.

10 ⊕ MOUNTAINS AND VOLCANOES

There are many mountain ranges throughout the country. Myanmar's northern mountains, including the Patkai and Kumon ranges, are among the southernmost extensions of the Himalayas. These mountains are very high and rugged; they include Hkakabo Razi at the northernmost tip of the country. At 5,881 meters (19,295 feet), it is the highest peak in the nation.

The mountains run south along the western border with India and Bangladesh. This belt is composed of many ranges, including the Patkai, the Mangin, and the Chin Hills, which continue southward to the extreme southwestern corner of the country. The Arakan (Rakhine) Mountains extend southeastward along the coast. Notable peaks in the west include Saramati (3,860 meters/12,663 feet) and Mount Victoria (3,053 meters/10,016 feet). To the southeast of Mount Victoria, almost 2500 kilometers (160 miles) south of Mandalay, lies Mount Popa, a spectacular extinct volcano that rises 1,518 meters (5,009 feet) from the surrounding plains.

The Pegu Yoma (Bago) Mountains are in central Myanmar. In the southeast, the Dawna and Bilauktaung ranges mark the border with Thailand on the Malay Peninsula.

11 ⊕ CANYONS AND CAVES

The Shan Plateau features deep limestone river gorges. The most notable are the gorge of the Salween (Thanlwin) River and Gokteik Gorge, which is cut by the Namtu River.

12 ⊕ PLATEAUS AND MONOLITHS

In northeast Myanmar, the Shan Plateau—149,743 square kilometers (57,816 square miles) in area—rises to an average elevation of about 914 meters (3,000 feet). Its western edge is clearly marked by a north-south cliff that often rises 610 meters (2,000 feet) in a single step.

13 ⊕ MAN-MADE FEATURES

Several artificial lakes and dams can be found throughout the river regions. The largest of the dams is the Thaphanseik Dam in Kyunhla Township, which was completed in 2001.

14 ⊕ FURTHER READING

Books

Steinberg, David J. *The Future of Burma: Crisis and Choice in Myanmar*. New York: Asia Society, 1990.

Yin, Saw Myat. *Myanmar*. New York: Marshall Cavendish, 2002.

Yip, Dora. *Welcome to Myanmar*. Milwaukee, WI: Gareth Stevens, 2001.

Web Sites

AsianInfo.Org: Myanmar. http://www.asianinfo.org/asianinfo/myanmar/myanmar.htm (accessed April 11, 2003).

Myanmar's Informative Resources on Culture, Travel, and Business. http://www.myanmars.net/ (accessed April 11, 2003).

Namibia

- **Official name:** Republic of Namibia
- **Area:** 825,418 square kilometers (318,696 square miles)
- **Highest point on mainland:** Konigstein (2,606 meters/8,550 feet)
- **Lowest point on land:** Sea level
- **Hemispheres:** Southern and Eastern
- **Time zone:** 2 P.M. = noon GMT
- **Longest distances:** 1,498 kilometers (931 miles) from south-southeast to north-northwest; 880 kilometers (547 miles) from east-northeast to west-southwest (excluding the Caprivi Strip)

- **Land boundaries:** 3,824 kilometers (2,376 miles) total boundary length; Angola 1,376 kilometers (855 miles); Botswana 1,360 kilometers (845 miles); South Africa 855 kilometers (531 miles); Zambia 233 kilometers (145 miles)
- **Coastline:** 1,572 kilometers (977 miles)
- **Territorial sea limits:** 22 kilometers (12 nautical miles)

1 ⊕ LOCATION AND SIZE

Namibia is located on the southwest Atlantic coast of Africa, bordering Angola and Zambia to the north, Botswana to the east, and South Africa to the southeast. With a total area of about 825,418 square kilometers (318,696 square miles), the country is slightly more than half the size of Alaska. Namibia is administratively divided into thirteen regions.

2 ⊕ TERRITORIES AND DEPENDENCIES

Namibia has no outside territories or dependencies.

3 ⊕ CLIMATE

Along the coast, the average temperature ranges from 23°C (73°F) in summer to 13°C (55°F) in winter. Inland, the temperatures may be somewhat higher, except at the higher elevations, where temperatures are lower.

There is little rainfall in Namibia. The rainy season is from November to March, with most of the rainfall occurring from January to March. Rain typically occurs during widely scattered, brief thunderstorms. Average annual rainfall along the Atlantic Coast is less than 5 centimeters (2 inches). About 35 centimeters (14 inches) of rain fall in the central highlands, while 70 centimeters (28 inches) of rain is the yearly average in the northeast. Because of the erratic rainfall, droughts are frequent; some areas of the country may go years without receiving any rain. The country's highest rainfall occurs in the northeast, where there is woodland savannah featuring dense vegetation covering the plains.

4 ⊕ TOPOGRAPHIC REGIONS

Namibia is primarily a large desert and semi-desert plateau with an average elevation of 1,080 meters (3,543 feet). There are four distinct topographical regions in Namibia: the

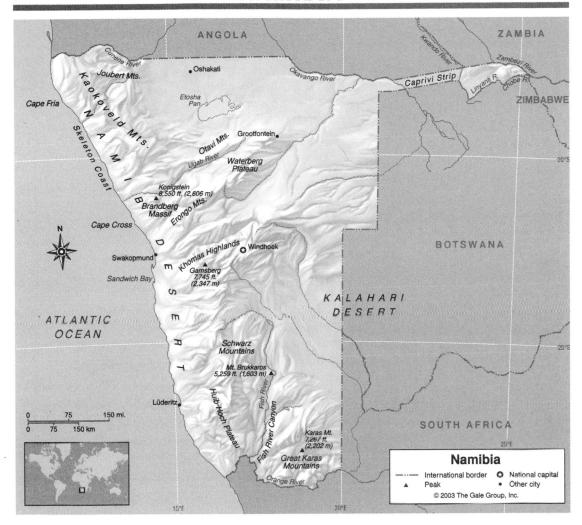

coastal Namib Desert, the central plateau, the southeastern Kalahari Desert, and the northeastern woodland savannah. Extending from the northeast corner of the country is the Caprivi Strip, a narrow panhandle extending between Angola and Zambia on the north and Botswana on the south. Namibia lies on the African Tectonic Plate.

5 ⊕ OCEANS AND SEAS

Seacoast and Undersea Features

Namibia has a western coastline on the Atlantic Ocean. The cold Benguela ocean current, which flows from Antarctica north along the west coast of Africa, contributes to the overall climate of Namibia and causes the dense fog that almost always hangs over much of the coast, especially in the north.

Sea Inlets and Straits

Sandwich Harbor, the coastal area around Sandwich Bay, is a wetland fed both by salt water flowing with the tides and by fresh water seeping up from aquifers. It attracts a wide variety of wading birds and serves as a breeding ground for marine life.

EPD/Cynthia Bassett

Namibia's Namib Desert has some of the highest sand dunes in the world.

Islands and Archipelagos

Namibia has only twelve small, rocky islands off of its coast. The islands are uninhabited except for colonies of penguins and the scientists who are researching them.

Coastal Features

The 500-kilometer (300-mile) stretch of Atlantic Coast, from roughly the Cunene River on the Angola border to the Ugab River, is known as the Skeleton Coast. Dramatic sand dunes, deep canyons, and mountains line this remote, foggy shore. It marks the extreme western edge of the Namib Desert. The Skeleton Coast got its name from the many shipwrecks that occurred there. A park covering about 16,000 square kilometers (6,200 square miles) is maintained in the area south of Cape Fria.

Just north of the city of Swakopmund is Cape Cross, home to Africa's largest colony of cape fur seals, numbering between one hun-dred thousand and two hundred thousand. In 1486, the Portuguese explorer Diogo Cao became the first European to visit Namibia; he erected a cross to honor the Portuguese king, and that is how the cape got its name.

Access to the coast south of Lüderitz to the South African border is restricted, since it is an area rich in diamonds.

6 ⊕ INLAND LAKES

The Etosha Pan in northwestern Namibia is known both as the "Great White Place," because of the appearance of its dry, saline, clay soil, and also as the "Land of Dry Water," because it is a dry lake for much of the year. It has been protected as a nature preserve since 1907. The intermittent Ekuma and Oshigambo Rivers feed the Etosha Pan, periodically creating a large, shallow lake where flamingoes congregate. There are no other major lakes in Namibia.

DID YOU KN🌐W?

The elephant herds that roam northwest Namibia dwell in the desert. They seem to have adapted to the dry, sandy conditions by having larger feet and smaller bodies than other elephants. There are only two countries in the world where elephants live in desert conditions: Namibia and Mali. Most elephants inhabit savannah (grassland) or forest regions.

7 🌐 RIVERS AND WATERFALLS

The only permanent rivers lie on or near the country's borders. The Cunene River forms the northwestern border with Angola, and the Okavango River forms the northeastern border. The Zambezi River, though one of the longest rivers in Africa with a total length of 2,650 kilometers (1,650 miles), touches Namibia only where it forms the far eastern border of the Caprivi Strip with Zambia. The system of the Kwando, Linyanti, and Chobe Rivers forms the easternmost border between the Caprivi Strip and Botswana. The Orange River forms the southern border with South Africa.

Along the northern border with Angola, the Cunene River courses to the Atlantic Ocean. Two dramatic waterfalls lie on the Cunene. Epupa Falls is actually a series of cascades created by the river dropping almost 60 meters (200 feet) over the short distance of just 1.5 kilometers (1 mile). At full flood stage, the Ruacana Falls swell to 120 meters (400 feet) high and 700 meters (2,300 feet) wide.

During the rainy season (generally from November to March), the intermittent rivers may be filled with water and may even pose flash-flood hazards, while at other times they are dry riverbeds, sometimes dotted with pools filled with fish. Intermittent rivers that flow west to the Atlantic Ocean include the Kuiseb, Swakop, Omaruru, Hoarusib, Hoanib, Ugab, and Khumib. The Nossob, a tributary of the Orange River, flows along the Kalahari Desert into Botswana. Another Orange River tributary, the Fish, flows throughout south-central Namibia. Intermittent rivers that flow north include the Marienfluss, the Omatako, and the Cuvelai, which flows from its source in Angola to the Etosha Pan.

8 🌐 DESERTS

The Namib Desert follows the full length of the Atlantic coastline and varies in width from 50 to 140 kilometers (30 to 88 miles). The terrain features dramatic stretches of dunes, dry riverbeds, and deep canyons, sometimes lined with majestic rock formations. From Swakopmund to Lüderitz, some of the highest sand dunes found anywhere in the world extend inland about 70 kilometers (44 miles). Remains of shipwrecks also dot the beach.

The Kalahari Desert lies in the east-central portion of the country and straddles the border with Botswana. The Kalahari features relatively flat expanses of red sand covered in some areas with sparse vegetation.

9 🌐 FLAT AND ROLLING TERRAIN

African savannah (grassland) dotted by solitary shrubs and trees are common in vast areas of the country, except for the desert on the western coast.

10 🌐 MOUNTAINS AND VOLCANOES

Konigstein, the highest mountain in Namibia, reaches 2,606 meters (8,550 feet). It belongs to a range known as the Brandberg Massif.

In 1917, the White Lady rock painting was discovered in a ravine called Maack's Shelter, which is at the base of the Konigstein. West of the Brandberg rise the Gobobose Mountains, which contain an extinct volcano, the Messum Crater. Just south of the Brandberg Massif, in the region northeast of Swakopmund, are the sharp peaks of Groot Spitzkoppe (1,728 meters/5,702 feet) and Klein Spitzkoppe (1,584 meters/5,227 feet). The Kaokoveld Mountains are located about 60 kilometers (40 miles) north of the Brandberg. They run along the Namib Desert parallel to the coast. At their northern extent they run into the Joubert Mountains. Twyfelfontein is a west-facing mountain slope located in the Kaokoveld Mountains that is covered with more than two thousand rock engravings (where the designs have been chipped into the rock). Some of the carvings date from about 3,300 B.C.

The Khomas Highlands run east to west from Windhoek toward the sea and include the flat-topped Gamsberg (2,347 meters/7,745 feet). In the north-central region there are two mountain ranges: the Erongo Mountains, which are about 150 kilometers (94 miles) from the Brandberg with maximum elevations of about 2,319 meters (7,653 feet), and the Otavi Mountains, which are even further north. Northeast of Windhoek are the Eros Mountains, which reach a maximum elevation of 1,900 meters (6,270 feet).

In the south, there are two main mountain ranges. The Schwarz Mountains run north to south along the western bank of the Fish River. The highest peak of the Schwarz is Mount Brukkaros at 1,603 meters (5,259 feet). The Great Karas Mountains run southwest to northeast across the southeastern corner of the country, beginning to the east of Fish River Canyon. The highest point in this range is Karas Mountain, which reaches an altitude of 2,202 meters (7,267 feet). The country's

DID YOU KN🌐W?

Namibia is the first country in the world to include protection of the environment and sustainable utilization of wildlife in its government's constitution. About 15.5 percent of the country's land has been set aside as national parks.

second-highest peak, Von Moltkeblick (2,480 meters/8,184 feet), rises among the Auas Mountains in southeastern Namibia.

11 🌐 CANYONS AND CAVES

Fish River Canyon lies in the dry, stone-covered plain in south-central Namibia. With an estimated length of 160 kilometers (100 miles), a maximum width of 27 kilometers (17 miles), and a depth of 550 meters (1,815 feet), it is the second-largest natural gorge in Africa.

12 🌐 PLATEAUS AND MONOLITHS

The central plateau has elevations between 1,000 and 2,000 meters (3,300 and 6,600 feet). The terrain features mountain peaks, rock formations, and broad sweeping plains or savannah. In the northwest, the plateau runs into the Kaokoveld, a remote and desolate area of high elevation, home to many rare species of African animals. Further east toward the center of the country, just south of Grootfontein in an area known as the Kaukauveld, the red sandstone Waterberg Plateau rises about 200 meters (660 feet) above the savannah and extends for more than 50 kilometers (30 miles). It is the centerpiece of a large area that was designated as parkland in 1972 to protect the habitat of rare and endangered species. The southwestern corner of the country sits on the Huib-Hoch Plateau.

North of the Ugab River are two interesting geological features: Burnt Mountain, a hill displaying outcroppings of purple, black, and gray rock; and a dramatic mass of perpendicular volcanic rock called the Organ Pipes.

13 ⊕ MAN-MADE FEATURES

There are at least ten dams built along Namibia's rivers for the sole purpose of containing river and rainwater for drinking and irrigation. These include the Von Boch and Swakopport Dams on the Swakop River, the Hardop Dam on the Fish River, and the Frienenau Dam on the Kuiseb River. Unfortunately, these catchment areas do not always provide an adequate amount of water for the surrounding areas, since the rivers are occasionally dry and much of the rainfall waters can evaporate soon after a rain. Boreholes (a type of well) have been dug in many areas to access underground water sources. Water is then distributed to villages and settlements by pumps. Nearly 73 percent of the country's water supply comes from these boreholes. This water is not always filtered or completely suitable for drinking, however, and lack of rainfall can make even these sources run dry. During drought seasons, village water supplies may be damaged or destroyed by elephants and other animals in search of fresh water.

14 ⊕ FURTHER READING

Books

Allen, Benedict. *The Skeleton Coast: A Journey through the Namib Desert.* London: BBC Books, 1997.

Ballard, Sebastian. *Namibia Handbook.* Lincolnwood, IL: Passport Books, 1999.

DID YOU KN⊕W?

Namibia is one of the world's leading producers of gem-quality diamonds. The most significant diamond mine areas are in the southwest and belong jointly to the De Beers Consolidated Diamond Mines and the Namibian government. Under the name Namdeb, they mine about half of the world's diamonds. In the Oranjemund Mine, located on the southern coast of the country, diamond deposits are found under the beachfront soils and under the coastal sea floor.

Bannister, Anthony. *Namibia: Africa's Harsh Paradise.* London: New Holland, 1990.

Grotpeter, John J. *Historical Dictionary of Namibia.* Meutchen, NJ: Scarecrow Press, 1994.

Lauré, J. *Namibia.* Chicago: Children's Press, 1993.

Web Sites

Cardboard Box Travel Shop: Namibian Geography. http://www.namibian.org/travel/namibia/ geography.htm (accessed April 11, 2003).

E-Tourism: Namibia. http://www.e-tourism.com.na (accessed April 11, 2003).

Nauru

- **Official name:** Republic of Nauru
- **Area:** 21 square kilometers (8.1 square miles)
- **Highest point on mainland:** Unnamed central plateau (61 meters/202 feet)
- **Lowest point on land:** Sea level
- **Hemispheres:** Southern and Eastern
- **Time zone:** 11:30 P.M. = noon GMT
- **Longest distances:** 5.6 kilometers (3.5 miles) from north-northeast to south-southwest; 4 kilometers (2.5 miles) from west-northwest to east-southeast
- **Land boundaries:** None
- **Coastline:** 30 kilometers (18.6 miles)
- **Territorial sea limits:** 22 kilometers (12 nautical miles)

1 ⊕ LOCATION AND SIZE

Nauru is an oval-shaped island in the western Pacific Ocean, 42 kilometers (26 miles) south of the equator. The closest neighboring land is the island of Banaba, which is part of the country of Kiribati. With a total area of 21 square kilometers (8.1 square miles), Nauru is the smallest nation in Asia, roughly one-tenth the size of Washington, D.C.

2 ⊕ TERRITORIES AND DEPENDENCIES

Nauru has no territories or dependencies.

3 ⊕ CLIMATE

Nauru has a tropical climate that is tempered by sea breezes. The westerly monsoon season occurs from November to February. Temperatures range from 23°C to 32°C (75°F to 91°F). Nauru experiences widely variable rainfall, ranging from 31 centimeters (12 inches) to as much as 457 centimeters (180 inches). Rainfall provides most of the nation's water supply.

4 ⊕ TOPOGRAPHIC REGIONS

A coastal plain at the perimeter of the island gradually rises to a fertile section no wider than 275 meters (902 feet). A coral cliff rises from this belt to a central plateau.

5 ⊕ OCEANS AND SEAS

Nauru is located in the west-central Pacific Ocean.

Seacoast and Undersea Features

The island is surrounded by a coral reef, which is exposed at low tide and dotted with pinnacles. The reef is bounded seaward by deep water.

Sea Inlets and Straits

Nauru has a smooth coastline without significant indentations.

Coastal Features

Beaches line the coral reef that encircles Nauru.

6 ⊕ INLAND LAKES

The permanent, often brackish Buada Lagoon (Lake Buada) is the only lake of significance on the island.

7 ⊕ RIVERS AND WATERFALLS

Nauru has no rivers.

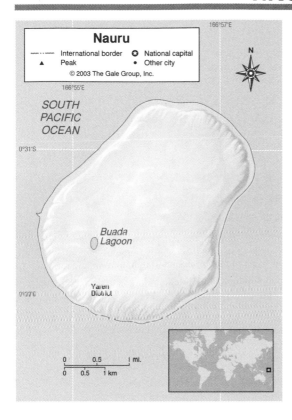

Nauru

— — — International border ✛ National capital
▲ Peak • Other city

© 2003 The Gale Group, Inc.

SOUTH PACIFIC OCEAN

166°57'E
166°55'E
0°31'S

Buada Lagoon

Yaren District

0 0.5 1 mi.
0 0.5 1 km

DID YOU KN☉W?

Nauru and the other fifteen low-lying countries of the Pacific Islands Forum face the environmental crisis of rising sea levels due to global warming. The consequences of climate change include destruction of freshwater sources, more intense storms, loss of crops to seawater, and coastal erosion.

making the nation one of the largest phosphate-rock islands in the Pacific.

13 ⊕ MAN-MADE FEATURES

The landscape does not include any prominent man-made features.

14 ⊕ FURTHER READING

Books

McDaniel, Carl N. *Paradise for Sale: Back to Sustainability.* Berkeley: University of California Press, 2000.

U.S. Department of State. "Background Notes, Nauru." Washington, DC: Bureau of Public Affairs, Office of Public Communication, Editorial Division, U.S. Department of State, 1988.

Web Sites

Lonely Planet World Guide, Destination Nauru. http://www.lonelyplanet.com/destinations/ pacific/nauru/ (accessed April 9, 2003).

Ocean 98: Welcome to Nauru. http://www. ocean98.org/seahnaur.htm (accessed April 9, 2003).

Pacific Island Travel. Nauru. http://www.pacifi cislandtravel.com/nauru/introduction.html (accessed April 9, 2003).

8 ⊕ DESERTS

There are no deserts on Nauru.

9 ⊕ FLAT AND ROLLING TERRAIN

Nauru's coastal strip consists of sandy beaches fringed by palm trees.

10 ⊕ MOUNTAINS AND VOLCANOES

There are no mountains on Nauru.

11 ⊕ CANYONS AND CAVES

Nauru's coral reefs include a large underwater grotto known as the Cave. A popular spot for divers, the Cave is some 30 meters (98 feet) below sea level.

12 ⊕ PLATEAUS AND MONOLITHS

A central plateau of phosphate-bearing rock comprises four-fifths of Nauru's landmass,

Nepal

- **Official name:** Kingdom of Nepal
- **Area:** 140,800 square kilometers (54,363 square miles)
- **Highest point on mainland:** Mount Everest (8,850 meters/29,035 feet)
- **Lowest point on land:** Kanchan Kalan (70 meters/230 feet)
- **Hemispheres:** Northern and Eastern
- **Time zone:** 5:45 P.M. = noon GMT

- **Longest distances:** 885 kilometers (550 miles) from southeast to northwest; 201 kilometers (125 miles) from northeast to southwest
- **Land boundaries:** 2,926 kilometers (1,818 miles) total boundary length; China 1,236 kilometers (768 miles); India 1,690 kilometers (1,050 miles)
- **Coastline:** None
- **Territorial sea limits:** None

1 ⊕ LOCATION AND SIZE

Nepal is a mountainous, landlocked South Asian country situated on the southern slopes of the Himalayas between China's Tibet region to the north and India to the south. Nepal has a total area of 140,800 square kilometers (54,363 square miles), or slightly more than the state of Arkansas.

2 ⊕ TERRITORIES AND DEPENDENCIES

Nepal has no territories or dependencies.

3 ⊕ CLIMATE

Nepal has four seasons: Winter from December through February is cold and clear, with some snow; spring from March through May is warm, with some rain showers; summer from June through August is the season of the monsoon rains; and autumn from September through November is cool and clear. Nepal's climate also varies by elevation. Above 4,877 meters (16,000 feet), the temperature stays below freezing, and there is permanent snow and ice. The average January temperature in the Kathmandu Valley ranges from 2°C to 18°C (36° to 64°F); in July, it warms to 20°C to 29°C (68°F to 84°F). In the Tarai the annual temperatures range from 7°C to 40°C (44°F to 104°F). Roughly 80 percent of Nepal's precipitation happens during the summer monsoon season. Annual rainfall in the Kathmandu Valley averages 130 centimeters (51 inches), from as little as 25 centimeters (10 inches) to as much as 600 centimeters (236 inches).

4 ⊕ TOPOGRAPHIC REGIONS

Nepal can be divided into three distinct geographic regions, each of which forms an east-west horizontal band across the rectangle-shaped country: the Mountain Region, which constitutes almost three-fourths of the total area; the central hill area, which includes the Kathmandu Valley; and the Tarai, a narrow, flat belt that extends along the boundary with India in the northern part of the Gangetic Plain.

5 ⊕ OCEANS AND SEAS

Nepal is a landlocked country. The nearest sea access is 644 kilometers (400 miles) to the southeast on the Indian Ocean's Bay of Bengal.

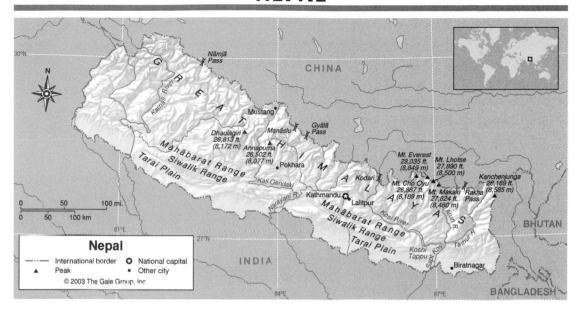

6 ⊕ INLAND LAKES

Rara Lake is Nepal's largest body of water, with an area of approximately 11 square kilometers (4 square miles). It is located at an elevation of 2,990 meters (9,600 feet) in the remote northwest of the country. The world's highest lake, Tilicho, is located in eastern Nepal, at an elevation of 4,919 meters (16,140 feet). A 1999 survey found 2,323 glacial lakes in Nepal.

7 ⊕ RIVERS AND WATERFALLS

Numerous streams and rivers flow generally southward out of Nepal's northern mountains, then meander across the Tarai Plain and finally join the Ganges in northern India. Three separate river systems, each having its headwaters on the Tibetan plateau, drain almost all of Nepal. The Kosi River drains the Eastern Mountains; the Narayani, the Western Mountains; and the Karnali, the Far Western Mountains. The Narayani's Kali Gandak tributary flows between the region's highest peaks, Dhaulagiri and Annapurna. The Kosi River has seven major tributaries; the principal one, the Arun, rises almost 160

kilometers (100 miles) inside the Tibetan plateau. The Karnali River is noted for its deep gorges and rapid current.

8 ⊕ DESERTS

There are no deserts in Nepal.

9 ⊕ FLAT AND ROLLING TERRAIN

The Tarai region, with a total area of 23,220 square kilometers (8,969 square miles), consists mainly of an alluvial plain along the boundary with India. A northern extension of the Gangetic Plain, the Tarai varies between 46 and 183 meters (150 and 600 feet) in altitude and between 8 and 88 kilometers (5 and 55 miles) in width.

Nepal's central hill region is north of the Tarai, and south of the Great Himalayas; its hills are called the Pahar complex. At 600 to 4,000 meters (1,968 to 13,123 feet), these two ranges of hills, the Siwalik and the Mahabharat, exceed the heights of mountains in many other countries. Siwalik range (sometimes called the Churia Hills or Churia range), on the northern edge of the Tarai, rises

EPD/Cynthia Bassett

The world's highest mountain peak, Mount Everest, lies on the border between Nepal and China.

to nearly 1,524 meters (5,000 feet). The narrow Mahabharat range parallels the Siwalik some 32 kilometers (20 miles) to the north; summits in the Mahabharat reach elevations above 3,048 meters (10,000 feet). The hill region also includes the populous Kathmandu Valley, just south of the junction between the Eastern and Western Mountains. This circular basin of only 565 square kilometers (218 square miles) contains some of Nepal's largest cities, including the nation's capital, Kathmandu.

Wetlands are estimated to cover about 5 percent of Nepal. Nepal has four wetlands of particular importance. Koshi Tappu, covering 175 square kilometers (68 square miles) of the Tarai, is a nature reserve on the flood plain of the Sapta Kosi River. A mixture of marshes, mud flats, and reed beds, it provides a habitat for water birds as well as the last wild herds of water buffalo in Nepal. Three other wetlands designated as significant by Nepal's government are Ghodaghodi Tal, Beeshazar Tal, and the Jagdishpur Reservoir. All three are biodiverse habitats for birds, fish, and reptiles.

10 ⊕ MOUNTAINS AND VOLCANOES

The complex mountain mass within Nepal's borders contains seven of the world's ten highest peaks. Six of them are more than 7,924 meters (26,000 feet) above sea level. Nepal's Mountain Region is part of the Himalayas, formed by the collision of the Indian subcontinent with the Asian landmass around twenty-five million years ago. The Great Himalayas are in the north. In northeastern Nepal, the Great Himalayas generally define the country's boundary with Tibet; in the northwest, they lie just to the south of the boundary. South of

The wild yak, still found in the mountains of Nepal, can survive at higher altitudes than any other mammal. Thanks to their large lung capacity, they can exist at altitudes of up to 6,096 meters (20,000 feet); however, this endangered species has difficulty surviving below 3,048 meters (10,000 feet).

the Great Himalayas are the Lesser Himalayas, which in Nepal form the Mahabharat range. South of this system is the Siwalik range, part of the Outer Himalayas. Much lower than the Great Himalayas, the Mahabharat and the Siwalik belong to Nepal's Hill Region, although in most other countries they would be considered mountains.

Nepal's Mountain Region may be subdivided into three areas by two lines, one running generally northward from Kathmandu and the other about 241 kilometers (150 miles) to the west, extending northward from the foothills near the boundary with India. From east to west, these subdivisions are designated the Eastern Mountains, the Western Mountains and the Far Western Mountains. The whole Mountain Region is marked by a series of parallel north-south ridges flanking deep, narrow, southward-sloping valleys.

The Eastern Mountains contain five of the seven highest peaks in the world. The most famous of these is the world's highest summit, Mount Everest (Sagarmatha in Nepalese), at 8,850 meters (29,035 feet). It is located on the border with China. The world's third-tallest mountain, Kanchenjunga (8,585 meters/28,169 feet), towers along Nepal's eastern border with India. Among the tallest remaining peaks are Mount Lhotse (8,500 meters/27,890 feet); Mount Makalu (8,480 meters/27,824 feet); and Mount Cho Oyu (8,189 meters/26,867 feet).

The Western Mountains hold a jumble of ridges and deep valleys projecting at various angles from the main Himalayan range. Two mountains dominate the area: Dhaulagiri (8,172 meters/26,813 feet) and Annapurna at (8,077 meters/26,502 feet). The Far Western Mountain area is the driest and most sparsely inhabited section of the Mountain Region. Its scattered settlements are generally confined to its river valleys. Three passes in this area lead into Tibet.

11 🌐 CANYONS AND CAVES

Nepal has numerous deep canyons and river gorges. The world's deepest river gorge is said to be Kali Gandak (6,967 meters/22,860 feet deep), situated between the peaks of Dhaulagiri and Annapurna in north-central Nepal. The high-altitude valley of Mustang, north of the Himalayas, contains many dry, eroded canyons. Nepal's rivers carve mazes of canyons into the terrain, especially along the courses of the Bhote Koshi and the Karnali.

12 🌐 PLATEAUS AND MONOLITHS

Dolpo is a 5,439-square-kilometer (2,100-square-mile) plateau bordering Tibet in Nepal's northwest. It includes Shey-Phoksumdo National Park, which is a habitat for the rare snow leopard. In the far west, the Khaptad Plateau, which rises to 3,000 meters (9,842 feet), is a national park with grasslands and forests.

13 🌐 MAN-MADE FEATURES

Several large hydropower dams, intended to provide energy to India as well as to Nepal, have been built on Nepal's rivers and even more have been proposed, causing environmental controversies. The Karnali-Chisapani Bridge, which links western Nepal with a major east-west highway, is considered one of the most sophisticated engineering projects completed on the Asian continent.

14 ⊕ FURTHER READING

Books

Kelly, Thomas, and V. Carroll Dunham. *The Hidden Himalayas*. New York: Abbeville Press, 2001.

Krakauer, Jon. *Into Thin Air: A Personal Account of the Everest Disaster*. New York: Anchor Books, 1998.

Matthiessen, Peter. *The Snow Leopard*. New York: Penguin USA, 1996.

Web Sites

Nepal Internet Users Group: Nepal Net. http://www.panasia.org.sg/nepalnet (accessed March 20, 2003).

WelcomeNepal. http://www.welcomenepal.com/CountryInfo (accessed March 20, 2003).

The Netherlands

- **Official name:** Kingdom of the Netherlands

- **Area:** 41,526 square kilometers (16,033 square miles)

- **Highest point on mainland:** Vaalserberg (321 meters/1,053 feet)

- **Lowest point on land:** Prins Alexanderpolder (7 meters/23 feet below sea level)

- **Hemispheres:** Northern and Eastern

- **Time zone:** 1 P.M. = noon GMT

- **Longest distances:** 312 kilometers (194 miles) from north to south; 264 kilometers (164 miles) from east to west

- **Land boundaries:** 1,027 kilometers (638 miles) total boundary length; Germany 577 kilometers (359 miles); Belgium 450 kilometers (280 miles)

- **Coastline:** 451 kilometers (280 miles)

- **Territorial sea limits:** 22 kilometers (12 nautical miles)

---

1 ⊕ LOCATION AND SIZE

The Netherlands (formerly also known as Holland) is located in Western Europe between Belgium and Germany, bordering the North Sea. With an area of about 41,526 square kilometers (16,033 square miles), the country is slightly less than twice the size of the state of New Jersey. The Netherlands is divided into twelve provinces.

2 ⊕ TERRITORIES AND DEPENDENCIES

The two island groups of the Netherlands Antilles and the island of Aruba are dependencies of the Netherlands. All of these islands are located in the Caribbean Sea. Aruba and the Antilles islands of Curaçao and Bonaire are located just north of Venezuela. The other group of Antilles islands—Saba, Stint, Eustatius, and Sint Maarten (the Dutch portion of Saint Martin)—are located farther north, east of the Virgin Islands.

3 ⊕ CLIMATE

The Netherlands shares the temperate maritime climate common in much of northern and western Europe. The average temperature ranges from 1°C to 5°C (34°F to 41°F) in January and from 13°C to 22°C (55°F to 72°F) in July. Because the Netherlands has few natural barriers, such as high mountains, the climate varies little from region to region. Annual precipitation averages 76 centimeters (30 inches).

4 ⊕ TOPOGRAPHIC REGIONS

The Netherlands may be divided into two main regions, one comprising areas below sea level, called the Low Netherlands, and the other including land above sea level, called the High Netherlands. These classifications are based not only on differences in elevation, but also on differences in geological formation. The High Netherlands was formed mainly in the Pleistocene Age (which began about two million years ago and ended about ten thousand years ago) and is composed chiefly of sand and gravel. The Low Netherlands is relatively younger, having been formed in the Holocene Age (fewer than ten thousand years ago), and consists mainly of clay and peat. There are other differences as well. The High Netherlands is

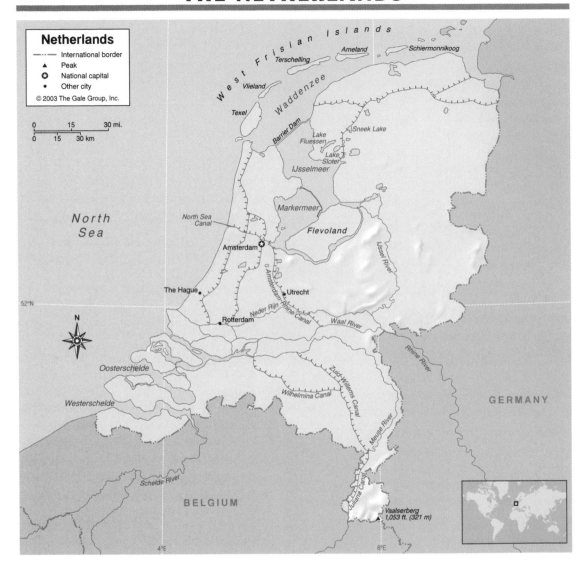

Netherlands
- – – – International border
- ▲ Peak
- ✪ National capital
- • Other city

© 2003 The Gale Group, Inc.

West Frisian Islands

Terschelling Ameland Schiermonnikoog

Vlieland Waddenzee

Texel

Barrier Dam

Lake Fluessen Sneek Lake

Lake Sloter

IJsselmeer

Markermeer

North Sea Canal

Flevoland

Amsterdam ✪

IJssel River

North Sea

The Hague •

52°N

Utrecht •

Amsterdam-Rhine Canal

Neder Rijn

Rotterdam •

Waal River

Rhine River

Oosterschelde

Zuid-Willems Canal

GERMANY

Westerschelde

Wilhelmina Canal

Meuse River

Schelde River

BELGIUM

Juliana Canal

Vaalserberg
▲ 1,053 ft. (321 m)

4°E   6°E

undulating and even hilly in places, with farms alternating with woodland and heath. The Low Netherlands is predominantly flat, and is intersected by natural and artificial waterways. Dunes and dikes protect the Low Netherlands against flooding. The western and northern regions of the country consist of about five thousand *polders* (plots of land reclaimed from the sea), which cover over 2,500 square kilometers (950 square miles).

5 ⊕ OCEANS AND SEAS

Seacoast and Undersea Features

The Netherlands has a western border on the North Sea, which is an arm of the Atlantic Ocean that separates Great Britain from northwest Europe.

Sea Inlets and Straits

The Waddenzee is a shallow body of water that stretches along the northern coast of the

Susan D. Rock

The Zaans Museum, a recreated traditional Netherlands village, features windmills.

country. It is separated from the North Sea by the West Frisian Islands and is protected as a popular nesting area for birds.

In the delta region at the southern coast, there are two major inlets: the Westerschelde and Oosterschelde.

Islands and Archipelagos

The West Frisian Islands were formed when the North Sea broke through a series of dunes along the Netherlands' ancient northern coastline. The area behind the dunes became the Waddenzee, while the tallest of the dunes remained intact, becoming the islands. From west to east, the largest of these islands are Texel, Vlieland, Terschelling, Ameland, and Schiermonnikoog. Vlieland Island is the site of a national park.

Coastal Features

The North Sea coastline of the Netherlands consists mostly of dunes. The low-lying sandy dunes of the northwestern coastline were created by the action of wind and water. In some areas, they are nearly 30 meters (100 feet) high.

Further south, the major rivers flow into the North Sea and form the delta region. This area is characterized by islands connected by dikes or dams, and waterways connected by canals.

6 ⊕ INLAND LAKES

There are many small lakes located in the northern and western portions of the Netherlands. In the northeast, more than thirty lakes are interconnected by canals. Some of the largest of these are Lake Fluessen, Lake Sloter, and Sneek Lake. Southwest

DID YOU KN⊕W?

The Netherlands was once famous for its windmills. Though these structures once covered the countryside, now there are many fewer operational windmills than before the invention of steam engines and other, more powerful, sources of energy.

of these is the nation's largest lake, IJsselmeer, a freshwater lake that was formed by the construction of the Afsluitdijk Barrier (completed in 1932). Prior to construction of the dam, this body of water was a shallow, salty arm of the North Sea known as the Zuider Zee. It now covers an area of about 1,210 square kilometers (467 square miles). South of the IJsselmeer is Marker Lake (Markermeer), another freshwater lake enclosed by a dam.

7 ⊕ RIVERS AND WATERFALLS

The Rhine (Rheine) River and the Meuse (Maas) River dominate the western and central part of the country. The Rhine is considered to be the nation's longest river. With a total length of 1,319 kilometers (820 miles), the river is formed by the confluence of two tributaries in eastern Switzerland; it then flows north and northwest through Germany before reaching the Netherlands. Inside the Netherlands, it branches out into two major arms: the Neder Rijn (called Lek in its lower course) and the Waal. They flow west, roughly parallel to each other and never farther apart than about 30 kilometers (19 miles). Both branches have many tributaries entering and leaving them before they reach the North Sea.

The Meuse River is the largest tributary of the Rhine in the Netherlands. It enters the country in the far southeast and flows north to the middle of the country before curving to the west. In this part of its course it is only a few miles south of the Waal; eventually, the two rivers meet and flow into the North Sea.

The IJssel River is a major branch of the Neder Rijn. It branches off from the Neder Rijn shortly after that river's beginning. The IJssel flows north, receives a number of small tributaries, and then empties into Lake IJsselmeer.

The Schelde (Scheldt or Escaut) River enters the Netherlands from Belgium in the southwest. It almost immediately widens into a broad estuary and flows into the North Sea.

8 ⊕ DESERTS

There are no desert regions in the Netherlands.

9 ⊕ FLAT AND ROLLING TERRAIN

The western and northern regions of the country consist of polders (land reclaimed from the sea), where the water level is mechanically controlled to stay about 1 meter (3 feet) below ground level, thus permitting cultivation. There are also polders that were reclaimed by earthen dikes in the late nineteenth century. The soil of these polders is marshy and too wet to be used for cultivation, but it may be used for grazing livestock. Polders do not necessarily lie below sea level, although most of them do. For example, the IJsselmeer polders are 3.5 meters (11.5 feet) below sea level, polders created by draining lakes can lie as much as 6.7 meters (22 feet) below sea level. In areas of young marine clay and along the rivers, many polders lie above the average sea level; consequently, it is not always necessary to pump the water out. Almost half of the land area of the Netherlands is made up of polders.

The highest point is Vaalserberg (321 meters/1,053 feet) in the hills of the South Limburg Plateau on the German border. Low hills created as the result of ancient glacial activity can be found in the eastern part of the country. These reach elevations of only about 100 meters (328 feet).

10 ⊕ MOUNTAINS AND VOLCANOES

There are no significant mountain ranges in the Netherlands.

11 ⊕ CANYONS AND CAVES

Near the city of Maastricht, the Caves of Mount St. Pieter were created by the excavation of marl, a stone used for building. The caves are connected through a labyrinth of over twenty thousand passageways. During World War I (1914–18) and World War II (1939–45), military personnel and civilians used the caves as emergency shelters and escape routes.

There are nearly 180 inactive limestone quarry mines scattered throughout the southern Limburg province. In the past, the fine-grained limestone has been used as a main ingredient in mortar, white paint, and chalk.

12 ⊕ PLATEAUS AND MONOLITHS

The South Limburg Plateau is the only part of the country not classified as lowland. The hills, some of which rise to over 300 meters (1,000 feet), comprise the foothills of the Central European Plateau. This is also virtually the only area of the country where rocks can be found at or near surface levels.

13 ⊕ MAN-MADE FEATURES

The Netherlands is famous for its vast system of dams and dikes, some of which date back many centuries. They were constructed to reclaim large swaths of land from the sea and stabilize the coastlines. Two of the most impressive are the Afsluitdijk and the Oosterschelde.

The Afsluitdijk is the largest and most famous dike in the Netherlands. It is a closure dike that connects the province of North Holland with Friesland. Construction of the 32-kilometer-long (20-mile-long) system

separated the Waddenzee from the newly created lake of Ijsselmeer.

The Oosterschelde Dam serves as a barrier that crosses the Oosterschelde inlet on the southern coast. The dam is 3 kilometers (2 miles) long and contains sixty-five pillars supporting sixty-two iron floodgates.

The Netherlands has an extensive system of canals that run throughout almost the entire country. The North Sea Canal connects Amsterdam and Marker Lake to the North Sea. The Amsterdam-Rhine River Canal is just one of several waterways that connect the city and that river. A network of canals—including the Wilhelmina, Zuid-Willems, and Juliana Canals—connects the southern part of the country to the Rhine River and to other canals in Belgium. In addition, many of the Netherlands's natural rivers, including all of its largest rivers, have had their shores reinforced (canalized) to prevent them from flooding or from shifting their courses.

14 ⊕ FURTHER READING

Books

Blom, J. C. H., and E. Lambert. *History of the Low Countries*. Translated by James C. Kennedy. Providence, RI: Berghahn Books, 1999.

Dash, Mike. *Tulipomania: The Story of the World's Most Coveted Flower and the Extraordinary Passions It Aroused*. New York: Crown, 2000.

Hintz, Martin. *The Netherlands*. New York: Children's Press, 1999.

Stergen, Theo van. *The Land and People of the Netherlands*. New York: HarperCollins, 1991.

Web Sites

The Royal Dutch Geographical Society (KNAG). http://www.knag.nl/english (accessed April 11, 2003).

Royal Netherlands Embassy in Washington, DC. http://www.netherlands-embassy.org (accessed April 11, 2003).

New Zealand

- **Official name:** New Zealand
- **Area:** 268,680 square kilometers (103,737 square miles)
- **Highest point on mainland:** Mount Cook (3,764 meters/12,349 feet)
- **Lowest point on land:** Sea level
- **Hemispheres:** Southern and Eastern
- **Time zone:** 12 midnight = noon GMT

- **Longest distances:** 1,600 kilometers (994 miles) from north-northeast to south-southwest; 450 kilometers (280 miles) from east-southeast to west-northwest
- **Land boundaries:** None
- **Coastline:** 15,134 kilometers (9,404 miles)
- **Territorial sea limits:** 22 kilometers (12 nautical miles)

1 ⊕ LOCATION AND SIZE

New Zealand lies in the southwestern Pacific Ocean and consists of two main islands and a number of smaller ones. The main North and South Islands, separated by the Cook Strait, lie on an axis running from northeast to southwest, except for the low-lying Northland Peninsula on the North Island. With a total area of 268,680 square kilometers (103,737 square miles), New Zealand is roughly the size of the state of Colorado.

2 ⊕ TERRITORIES AND DEPENDENCIES

New Zealand has three island dependencies in the Pacific Ocean.

The Cook Islands are located roughly halfway between New Zealand and Hawaii, in the middle of the South Pacific. The islands have local self-government but voluntarily rely on New Zealand to represent their interests in foreign affairs and defense. The Cook Islands consist of two island chains: seven low-lying coral atolls in the north, and eight larger and more elevated volcanic islands in the south.

Niue Island, which extends over more than 263 square kilometers (102 square miles), is one of the world's largest coral islands. Located east of the Cook Islands, Niue also governs itself in local affairs but depends on New Zealand in international matters.

Tokelau, another territory of New Zealand, is an island chain in the middle of the South Pacific northwest of the Cook Islands. It consists of three small coral atolls and surrounding islets.

Besides these three Pacific island groups, New Zealand also claims land in Antarctica in and near the Ross Sea.

3 ⊕ CLIMATE

New Zealand has a mild oceanic climate with little seasonal variation. Mean annual temperatures range from about 11°C (52°F) in the southern part of South Island to 15°C (59°F) in Northland, the northernmost part of the North Island. Daytime high temperatures in summer generally vary from 21°C to 27°C (70° to 81°F); winter highs are usually at least 10°C (50°F). Temperatures rarely extend beyond the extremes of -10°C (14°F) and 35°C

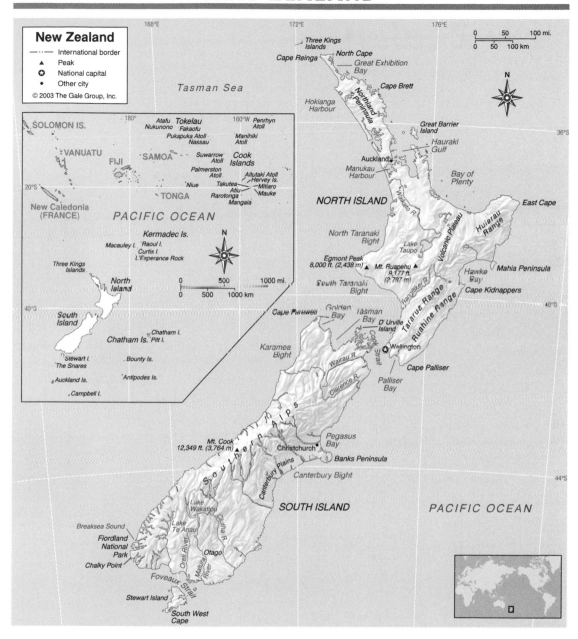

(95°F). Due to prevailing westerly and north-westerly winds, the western mountain slopes of both islands receive the heaviest rainfall. Average annual rainfall for the country as a whole ranges from 64 to 152 centimeters (25 to 60 inches). Precipitation amounts vary widely, however; on South Island, for example, central Otago Harbour receives as little as 30 centimeters (12 inches) per year, while southwestern Fiordland can get as much as 800 centimeters (315 inches).

EPD/Wilko Gijsbertsen

New Zealand's Volcanic Plateau has hot springs and bubbling mud pools.

4 ⊕ TOPOGRAPHIC REGIONS

New Zealand is very mountainous; more than 75 percent of its land exceeds an altitude of 200 meters (656 feet). The South Island covers an area of 149,883 square kilometers (57,870 square miles). Its major regions are the Canterbury Plains to the east; the central mountain highlands, which cover much of the island; and a narrow western coast. The North Island, which spans an area of 114,669 square kilometers (44,274 square miles), is characterized by hill country. The mountain highland here is narrow and lies to the east. North and west of the Kaimanawa Mountains is a volcanic plateau. There is little coastal lowland; even in Taranaki, where it is widest, Mount Egmont (also called Mount Taranaki) rises well over 2,438 meters (8,000 feet). The narrow northern peninsular section of the North Island is mostly low-lying, though its surface is broken and irregular in many places.

5 ⊕ OCEANS AND SEAS

New Zealand lies in the South Pacific Ocean to the southeast of Australia, across the Tasman Sea. At the Tamaki Isthmus on the North Island, these two bodies of water are separated by only 2 to 3 kilometers (1 to 2 miles) of land.

Sea Inlets and Straits

The North and South Islands are separated by the Cook Strait, which is 26 to 145 kilometers (16 to 90 miles) wide. The Foveaux Strait lies between the South Island and Stewart Island to the southeast. The North Island's bays include North and South Taranaki Bights to the west, Palliser Bay to the south, the wide Hawke Bay to the east, and the even wider Bay of Plenty to the northeast. The

New Zealand has several species of flightless birds, of which the most famous is the kiwi, the national emblem. These birds were able to evolve and survive on the islands because the environment lacked predators.

South Island's major bays include Golden Bay and Tasman Bay in the north, Karamea Bight at the northern end of the west coast, and Canterbury Bight and Pegasus Bay to the east.

Islands and Archipelagos

New Zealand's largest island, aside from its two primary landmasses, is Stewart Island to the southeast, which covers an area of 1,746 square kilometers (674 square miles). Other islands include the Chatham Islands (963 square kilometers/372 square miles) to the east and several other mostly uninhabited outlying islands, including the Auckland Islands (567 square kilometers/219 square miles).

Coastal Features

North Island has a more heavily indented coastline than South Island. The long arm of land that juts out to the northwest has so deep an indentation at its midsection that the land mass narrows to a width of only 2 or 3 kilometers (1 or 2 miles) at Auckland. The east coast and northern tip of Northland have multiple bays and harbors, while the west coast is almost completely smooth. The northern and southern ends of the South Island have numerous indentations, while the long eastern and western coastlines are smoother. In the east, the Banks Peninsula juts out somewhat less than halfway

down the coast. The coast of Fiordland to the southeast is broken up into numerous sounds and inlets. The northernmost part of North Island has many sand dunes.

6 ⊕ INLAND LAKES

New Zealand has many lakes. Those in the South Island are particularly noted for their magnificent scenery. The country's largest natural lake is Lake Taupo on the North Island, followed by Lakes Te Anau and Wakatipu on the South Island.

7 ⊕ RIVERS AND WATERFALLS

The rivers are shallow and swift, and only a few are navigable. The longest river is the Waikato (425 kilometers/264 miles), which flows northwestward across the North Island and empties into the Tasman Sea, as do the Wanganui and Rangitikei. Rivers that flow into the Pacific from the South Island include the Clutha, the Taieri, and the Clarence; the Mataura, Wairau, and Oreti flow from the South Island into the Foveaux Strait. The Clutha is the South Island's longest river, and its volume is the greatest of any river in the country.

8 ⊕ DESERTS

There are no deserts in New Zealand.

9 ⊕ FLAT AND ROLLING TERRAIN

Much of the land surrounding the mountain ranges and the Volcanic Plateau on North Island is hilly. North of Hawke Bay in the east, deeply corrugated embankments flank the mountain ranges. On the South Island, broken mounds dot the central section of the narrow coastal strip.

The Canterbury Plains on the east coast of South Island are New Zealand's largest plains area, stretching 320 kilometers (200 miles) in length and reaching widths of 64 kilometers (40 miles). The North Island has coastal plains bordering the Bay of Plenty and Hawke

EPD/Wilko Gijsbertsen

Fox Glacier is one of several glaciers covering parts of New Zealand's South Island.

Bay in the Taranaki region to the west, the Manawatu-Wanganui area south of the Volcanic Plateau, and the Waikato, Auckland, and Northland regions to the north.

The terrain of Northland, the northernmost part of the North Island, includes peat bogs and swamplands.

10 ⊕ MOUNTAINS AND VOLCANOES

Three-fourths of New Zealand is mountainous. Of the two main islands, South Island is by far the most rugged. A massive mountain chain called the Southern Alps runs the entire length of the island—some 483 kilometers (300 miles)—and outlying ranges extend to the north and the southwest. This range includes New Zealand's highest peak, Mount Cook (3,764 meters/12,349 feet), as well as about 350 glaciers, the largest of which is the Tasman Glacier (29 kilometers/18

miles long). There are at least 223 named peaks that are higher than 2,300 meters (7,546 feet) on the South Island. In contrast, the highest peak on the North Island, Ruapehu, reaches an elevation of only 2,797 meters (9,177 feet). The southernmost section of the South Island mountain system is Fiordland, at the island's southwestern edge. It is named for its deep, canyon-like valleys that are watered at the coast by saltwater fjords and inland by freshwater lakes.

The mountains of the North Island are a continuation of the South Island system. The Tararua, Ruahine, Kaimanawa, and Huiarau ranges extend across the island on the same southwest-to-northeast axis as the higher mountains to the south. The landscape to the west is dominated by the extinct volcano of Mount Taranaki (Mount Egmont), at an elevation of 2,518 meters (8,260 feet).

11 ⊕ CANYONS AND CAVES

At 40,600 meters (133,209 feet) long, the Bulmer Caverns in Mount Owen on South Island are among the longest in the world. Their average depth is 749 meters (2,457 feet).

12 ⊕ PLATEAUS AND MONOLITHS

The wide Volcanic Plateau, with its terrain of lava, pumice stone, and volcanic ash, lies north and west of the Kaimanawa range on the North Island. Hill country with short but steep slopes occupies most of its rim. The elevation of the plateau decreases and its slopes become gentler toward the western coast.

13 ⊕ MAN-MADE FEATURES

Lake Benmore is New Zealand's largest artificial lake. The 8,879-meter (29,132-foot) Kaimai Tunnel at Apata is New Zealand's longest railroad tunnel, as well as the longest in the Southern Hemisphere.

14 ⊕ FURTHER READING

Books

Hanbury-Tenison, Robin. *Fragile Eden: A Ride Through New Zealand.* Topsfield, MA: Salem House, 1989.

New Zealand. Eyewitness Travel Guides. New York: Dorling Kindersley, 2001.

Sinclair, Keith, ed. *The Oxford Illustrated History of New Zealand.* New York: Oxford University Press, 1997.

Web Sites

New Zealand Official Tourism Site. http://www.purenz.com/ (accessed April 17, 2003).

Lonely Planet World Guide. http://www.lonelyplanet.com/destinations/australasia/new_zealand/ (accessed April 17, 2003).

Nicaragua

- **Official name:** Republic of Nicaragua
- **Area:** 129,494 square kilometers (49,998 square miles)
- **Highest point on mainland:** Mogotón Peak (2,438 meters/7,999 feet)
- **Lowest point on land:** Sea level
- **Hemispheres:** Northern and Western
- **Time zone:** 6 A.M. = noon GMT
- **Longest distances:** 472 kilometers (293 miles) from north to south; 478 kilometers (297 miles) from east to west

- **Land boundaries:** 1,231 kilometers (765 miles) total boundary length; Costa Rica 309 kilometers (192 miles); Honduras 922 kilometers (573 miles)
- **Coastline:** 910 kilometers (565 miles)
- **Territorial sea limits:** 370 kilometers (200 nautical miles)

1 ⊕ LOCATION AND SIZE

Nicaragua is the largest country in Central America. It is located north of Costa Rica and south of Honduras, between the Pacific Ocean and the Caribbean Sea. With a total area of about 129,494 square kilometers (49,998 square miles), the country is slightly smaller than the state of New York. Nicaragua is administratively divided into fifteen departments and two autonomous regions.

2 ⊕ TERRITORIES AND DEPENDENCIES

Nicaragua has no outside territories or dependencies.

3 ⊕ CLIMATE

In Nicaragua, temperature is affected more by elevation than by season. On the flat lands (in the east and west), daytime temperatures average 29°C (85°F) and night temperatures drop below 21°C (70°F). In the central highlands temperatures are lower, about 21°C (70°F) in the daytime and about 15°C (60°F) at night. In the very high mountains, temperatures can approach freezing after dark.

The rainy season (winter, or *invierno*) is from May through November and the dry season (summer, or *verano*) is from June through October. The Mosquito Coast gets the greatest amount of yearly rainfall, from 230 to 508 centimeters (90 to 200 inches). Less rain, about 76 to 229 centimeters (30 to 90 inches) per year, falls on the Central Highlands; precipitation here occurs over a longer period of the year. On the Pacific Coast, annual rainfall ranges from 102 to 152 centimeters (40 to 60 inches).

Periodically, hurricanes have caused severe damage on Nicaragua. The most devastating storms in recent years were Hurricane Mitch (October 1998) and Hurricane Joan (November 1988).

4 ⊕ TOPOGRAPHIC REGIONS

The country is shaped like an equilateral triangle with its southwest/northeast side along the Honduran border, the north/south side along

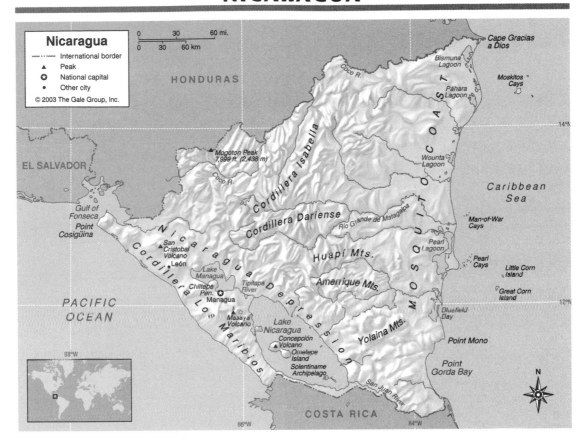

Nicaragua

- – – – – International border
- ▲ Peak
- ✪ National capital
- • Other city

© 2003 The Gale Group, Inc.

0   30   60 mi.
0   30   60 km

HONDURAS

EL SALVADOR

Gulf of
Fonseca
Point
Cosigüina

▲ Mogoton Peak
7,999 ft. (2,438 m)

Coco R.

Cordillera Isabella

Cordillera Dariense

Río Grande de Matagalpa

Nicaragua Depression

Cordillera Los Maribios

▲ San
Cristobal
Volcano
León

Chiltepe
Pen.
✪ Managua

Lake
Managua

Tipitapa
River

Masaya
Volcano

Lake
Nicaragua

Concepción
Volcano ▲
Ometepe
Island

Solentiname
Archipelago

San Juan River

PACIFIC
OCEAN

Huapí Mts.

Amerrique Mts.

Yolaina Mts.

COSTA RICA

Cape Gracias
a Dios

Bismuna
Lagoon

Páhara
Lagoon

Moskitos
Cays

Wounta
Lagoon

Caribbean
Sea

Man-of-War
Cays

Pearl
Lagoon

Pearl
Cays

Little Corn
Island

Great Corn
Island

Bluefield
Bay

Point Mono

Point
Gorda Bay

MOSQUITO COAST

88°W
86°W
84°W
14°N
12°N

N

the Caribbean, and the southeast/northwest side along the Costa Rican border and Pacific Ocean.

The land naturally divides into three topographic zones: the Pacific Lowlands, the Central Highlands, and the Atlantic Lowlands. The Pacific Lowlands is a band about 75 kilometers (47 miles) wide along the Pacific Ocean between Honduras and Costa Rica. The plain is punctuated by clusters of volcanoes, immediately to the east of which is a long, narrow depression passing along the isthmus from the Gulf of Fonseca in the north to the San Juan River at the bottom of the country. This depression is sometimes called the Nicaraguan Depression. To the northeast are the Central Highlands; this region has the highest

mountains and the coolest temperatures. The sparsely populated Atlantic Lowlands comprise more than half the area of Nicaragua. These lowlands and the Mosquito Coast are the traditional home of the Miskito peoples (after whom the coastal region was named). Tropical rainforest and savannahs dominate this region, crossed by scores of rivers flowing to the Caribbean.

Nicaragua is situated on the Caribbean Tectonic Plate, but just off the country's Pacific coast is the Cocos Tectonic Plate. Frequent earthquakes and volcanic eruptions result from action of the Caribbean and Cocos plates. Nicaragua has hundreds of minor earthquakes and shocks each year and occasionally experiences a serious quake. In 1931 and again in

1972, earthquakes virtually destroyed the capital city of Managua. As of early 2003, central Managua had yet to be rebuilt.

5 ⊕ OCEANS AND SEAS

Seacoast and Undersea Features

Nicaragua has coasts on the Pacific Ocean and on the Caribbean Sea (an extension of the Atlantic Ocean). There are coral reef systems off the eastern coast, including the largest hard-carbonate bank in the Caribbean; however, most of the reefs are not situated near the mainland due to sediment runoff from the many rivers. Closer to the shore, reef systems form four groups of islands: the Moskitos Cays, Man-of-War (Guerrero) Cays, Pearl Cays, and the Corn Islands. The last three of these island groups are inhabited.

Sea Inlets and Straits

The relatively remote and sparsely populated Atlantic Lowlands and Mosquito Coast are periodically interrupted by lagoons and estuaries where major rivers end. From north to south, the largest are Bismuna, Páhara, Karatá, Wounta, and Pearl Lagoons. The Bluefield Bay lies at an inlet just north of Point Mono, while the Point Gorda Bay lies in the curved inlet to the south of Point Mono. There are no significant lagoons along the Pacific Ocean side; the Gulf of Fonseca, however, is located at the northernmost point where the coast turns inland at Point Cosigüina.

Islands and Archipelagos

Scores of large islands dot the huge Lake Nicaragua. Two volcanoes, one at each end, formed the dumbbell-shaped Ometepe Island. Its total area is 276 square kilometers (106 square miles), including the Isthmus of Istián that connects the two sections of the island. At the south end of Lake Nicaragua are thirty-six small islands collectively named the Solentin-

ame Archipelago. Some of the larger islands in this group are Venada, San Fernando, Mancarroncito, and Mancarrón.

Besides islands in the freshwater lakes, there also are a few islands off the Caribbean shore, but none exist on the Pacific side. The two Corn Islands are 70 kilometers (43 miles) off the southern coast; they are just 8 kilometers (5 miles) apart. Great Corn Island is about 8 square kilometers (3 square miles) in area; Little Corn Island is about half that size.

The Moskitos Cays is an offshore island group with associated coral reefs situated 12 kilometers (7.5 miles) from the north shore. The area is home to several endangered species including the Hawksbill turtle, Caribbean manatee, Tucuxi freshwater dolphin, and caiman crocodile.

The two other coralline island groups, the Pearl Cays and the Man-of-War Cays, also sit not far from the mainland. They are sparsely populated with fishing villages.

Coastal Features

The most hospitable, populated coast is the Pacific Ocean side. This coastline is relatively straight with few inlets or peninsulas. Cape Gracias a Dios marks the northern end of the Atlantic coastline; near the south, Point Mono juts out into the sea.

6 ⊕ INLAND LAKES

Lake Nicaragua (Lago de Nicaragua) is the largest freshwater lake in Central and South America; in fact, it is one of the most spectacular bodies of water in all of the Americas. It fills the southern portion of the Nicaragua Depression, which runs parallel to the Pacific Ocean. The lake is 160 kilometers (99 miles) long, 65 kilometers (40 miles) at its widest point, and 32 meters (105 feet) above sea level. It is relatively shallow, however, with an average depth of 20 meters (66 feet), and a maximum depth of 60 meters (197 feet). With a total surface area of 8,000 square kilometers (3,089 square miles), the lake is sprinkled with many islands, including the large Ometepe Island.

Lake Managua connects to Lake Nicaragua by the Tipitapa River. The lake is 52 kilometers (32 miles) long and up to 25 kilometers (16 miles) wide, covering an area of 1,025 square kilometers (396 square miles). It is only 30 meters (98 feet) at its deepest point, however. On the lake's southwest side, the Chiltepe peninsula holds two small crater lakes: Xiloá and Apoyeque.

7 ⊕ RIVERS AND WATERFALLS

Nicaragua has nearly one hundred principal rivers, most of which drain the Central Highlands through the Atlantic Lowlands and empty along the Mosquito Coast. The majority of them are relatively short rivers with a few longer ones, such as Río Grande de Matagalpa. A few rivers feed the Managua and Nicaragua Lakes. Coco River, Nicaragua's longest river, flows 680 kilometers (423 miles) from the northwest highlands to the Caribbean Sea, forming Nicaragua's border with Honduras.

The river that carries the largest volume of water is the San Juan River, which is only 180 kilometers (110 miles) long. It flows from the southeast corner of Lake Nicaragua east to the Caribbean Sea. This deep, navigable river forms the boundary between Nicaragua and Costa Rica.

With many rivers, Nicaragua also has many wetlands. Besides the entire Caribbean coast, which is mostly swampy and marshy land, there are three other areas of particular note. Deltas del Estero Real (816 square kilometers/ 315 square miles) in the Gulf of Fonseca is a natural reserve that is part of the large mangrove systems of the gulf, shared with El Salvador and Honduras. Humedales de San Miguelito is situated near the point at which the San Juan exits Lake Nicaragua. It is home to a diverse species of birds, fish, reptiles, and mammals. Finally, Tisma Lagoon is a small area of lake, marsh, and river ecosystems on the northwest shores of Lake Nicaragua.

8 ⊕ DESERTS

There are no desert regions in Nicaragua.

9 ⊕ FLAT AND ROLLING TERRAIN

Nicaragua has numerous rainforests, some of which are protected as reserves. Ecologically, two exceptional reserves are Reserva Natural Miraflor and Reserva Biológic Indo-Maiz. Miraflor (206 square kilometers/80 square miles) is remarkably pristine and has tropical savannah at lower altitude, pine forest higher up, and cloud forest at its highest elevations. Miraflor also contains a tiny lake at an altitude of 1,380 meters (4,528 feet), as well as a 60-meter (196-feet) waterfall.

Biológic Indo-Maiz covers 3,626 square kilometers (1,400 square miles). In only a few square kilometers within the preserve, a habitat exists for a greater number of species of birds, trees, and insects than are found on

AP Photo/Anita Baca

A toddler takes a nap while her mother washes laundry in Lake Managua.

the entire continent of Europe. Indo-Maiz protects the largest contiguous extent of primary rainforest in Central America, a 7,300-square-kilometer (2,820-square-mile) area that is called the Bosawás Biosphere Reserve.

10 ⊕ MOUNTAINS AND VOLCANOES

Nicaragua has three inland mountain ranges and a chain of volcanoes. Cordillera Isabella runs southwest to northeast, toward the Honduran border. Cordillera Dariense runs nearly west to east, defining the southern edge of the triangular Central Highlands. The rugged mountain terrain in between is composed of ridges from 900 to 1,800 meters (1,968 to 5,905 feet) high. River valleys drain mostly to the Caribbean. Cordillera Los Maribios is the chain of volcanoes, which originates in the northwest. Three smaller mountain ranges cut across the Atlantic Lowlands in the south-

east. From north to south, they are the Huapí Mountains, the Amerrique Mountains, and the Yolaina Mountains. The highest peak in Nicaragua, Mogotón Peak, sits on the Honduran border, about 161 kilometers (100 miles) inland from the Pacific Ocean. The peak rises to a height of 2,438 meters (7,999 feet).

A chain of seventeen volcanoes runs along the Pacific Coast. Six of them have erupted in the last hundred years. The most significant active volcanoes in this chain are Concepción, San Cristóbal, Telica, and Masaya. Concepción Volcano, Nicaragua's second-highest volcano is situated on the north end of Ometepe Island in the middle of Lake Nicaragua. This symmetrical volcano erupted frequently during the twentieth century; in December 2000, it spewed ash over the countryside.

A complex of five volcanoes northwest of Managua is named for its oldest volcano, San Cristóbal (El Viejo), which also is the highest peak of the Maribios Range. Casita, immediately east of San Cristóbal, was the site of a catastrophic landslide in 1998.

Telica, located northwest of the city of León, has erupted frequently since the 1800s. Telica's steep cone is topped by a double crater which is 700 meters (2,300 feet) wide.

Masaya, near Managua, is one of only four volcanoes on earth with a constant pool of lava that neither increases nor recedes. It is the primary tourist attraction within one of Nicaragua's oldest national parks.

11 ⊕ CANYONS AND CAVES

Nicaragua has more than ninety principal rivers running through canyons of various depths. In comparison to mountain ranges in North and South America, and even compared to adjacent Honduras, Nicaragua's highest mountains are modest, so few of its canyons are notably deep.

There are no major caves in Nicaragua.

12 ⊕ PLATEAUS AND MONOLITHS

There are no significant plateau regions in Nicaragua.

13 ⊕ MAN-MADE FEATURES

Several areas in Nicaragua rely on river dams as a source of hydroelectric power. Two of the largest dams are the Mancotal and El Salto Dams. Though both of these structures were damaged during 1998's Hurricane Mitch, reconstruction has taken place with the help of the U.S. Army Corps of Engineers and the

---

DID YOU KN⊕W?

Central America contains the seven nations of Belize, Guatemala, Honduras, El Salvador, Nicaragua, Costa Rica, and Panama. The land area containing these states is often called the Central American Isthmus. An isthmus is a narrow section of land connecting two larger land masses; in this case, the isthmus joins North America (at Mexico) to South America (at Colombia).

U.S. Agency for International Development (USAID).

14 ⊕ FURTHER READING

Books

Glassman, Paul. *Nicaragua Guide: Spectacular and Unspoiled.* Champlain, NY: Travel Line, 1996.

Griffiths, John. *Nicaragua.* Philadelphia: Chelsea House, 1999.

Haverstock, Nathan A. *Nicaragua in Pictures.* Minneapolis: Lerner Publications, 1993.

Kott, Jennifer. *Nicaragua.* New York: Marshall Cavendish, 1995.

Web Sites

Nicaragua Network Environmental Committee. http://environment.nicanet.org/resources.htm (accessed April 17, 2003).

Niger

- **Official name:** Republic of Niger
- **Area:** 1,267,000 square kilometers (489,191 square miles)
- **Highest point on mainland:** Mount Gréboun (1,944 meters/6,378 feet)
- **Lowest point on land:** Sea level
- **Hemispheres:** Northern and Eastern
- **Time zone:** 1 P.M. = noon GMT
- **Longest distances:** 1,845 kilometers (1,146 miles) from east-northeast to west-southwest; 1,025 kilometers (637 miles) from north-northwest to south-southeast

- **Land boundaries:** 5,697 kilometers (3,540 miles) total boundary length; Algeria 956 kilometers (594 miles); Benin 266 kilometers (165 miles); Burkina Faso 628 kilometers (390 miles); Chad 1,175 kilometers (730 miles); Libya 354 kilometers (220 miles); Mali 821 kilometers (510 miles); Nigeria 1,497 kilometers (930 miles)
- **Coastline:** None
- **Territorial sea limits:** None

1 ⊕ LOCATION AND SIZE

Landlocked Niger is the second-largest country in West Africa (surpassed only by Algeria) and the tenth largest on the continent. With a total area of 1,267,000 square kilometers (489,191 square miles), it is nearly twice the size of the state of Texas.

2 ⊕ TERRITORIES AND DEPENDENCIES

Niger has no territories or dependencies.

3 ⊕ CLIMATE

Niger's climate is one of the hottest on Earth. Between February and July, high temperatures on the plateaus in the northeast can hit 50°C (122°F). In January, readings can drop to a low of 8°C (46°F) in the desert regions, which experience both the hottest temperatures and the greatest contrast between highs and lows. The *harmattan* wind blows across the eastern desert for much of the year. Rainfall varies markedly between Niger's Saharan and Sahel regions. Most of Niger receives less than 36 centimeters (14 inches) of rain annually; in fact, almost half the country receives less than 10 centimeters (4 inches). South of the Sahel, however, in the Niger River Valley, the capital city of Niamey receives much more precipitation; yearly rainfall averages about 56 centimeters (22 inches).

4 ⊕ TOPOGRAPHIC REGIONS

Niger is a dry country. Although four-fifths of its land is covered by desert, its remaining topography is diverse, including plains, plateau regions, and mountains. The country can be divided into three major regions: the arid, inhospitable deserts to the north and northeast, a transitional Sahelian region in the center, and a small fertile area in the south, between the Niger River basin in the southwest and the Lake Chad basin in the southeast.

5 ⊕ OCEANS AND SEAS

Niger is landlocked (no access to the sea).

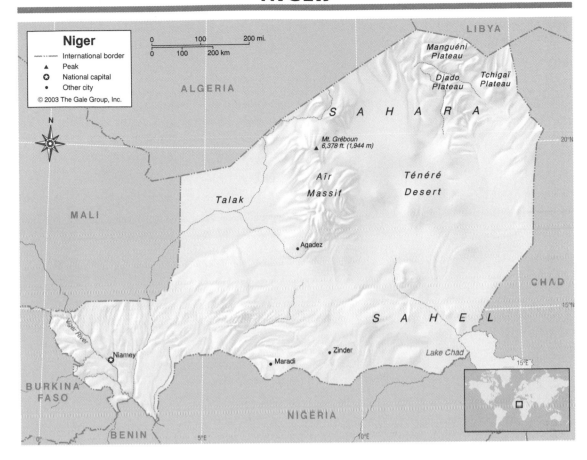

Niger
- – – – International border
- ▲ Peak
- ✪ National capital
- • Other city
- © 2003 The Gale Group, Inc.

ALGERIA

LIBYA

Manguéni Plateau

Djado Plateau

Tchigaï Plateau

S A H A R A

Mt. Gréboun
6,378 ft. (1,944 m)

Aïr Massif

Ténéré Desert

Talak

MALI

20°N

• Agadez

CHAD

15°N

S A H E L

Niger River

• Zinder

Lake Chad

Niamey

• Maradi

15°E

BURKINA FASO

NIGERIA

BENIN

5°E

10°E

6 ⊕ INLAND LAKES

About 2,590 square kilometers (1,000 square miles) of Lake Chad lies within the southeastern tip of Niger. The size of the lake, which Niger shares with Chad and Nigeria, varies greatly from season to season, shrinking to nearly one-third of its maximum size in the dry season. In October, its surface area can exceed 9,950 square miles (28,457 square kilometers); by May, however, it usually has been reduced to roughly 3,000 square miles (8,580 square kilometers).

7 ⊕ RIVERS AND WATERFALLS

The lifeline of the country is the Niger River, which flows year-round across the southwestern corner of the country for about 563 kilometers (350 miles) from northwest to southeast, while its tributaries flow only during the rainy season. In the southeast, the Kamadougou Yobé River drains into Lake Chad, forming part of Niger's border with Nigeria.

8 ⊕ DESERTS

The Ténéré Desert that lies to the east of the mountains and the Talak to the west have vast expanses of shifting sand dunes (called *ergs*) where no vegetation grows, as well as other dunes that are anchored by sparse, scrubby vegetation.

9 ⊕ FLAT AND ROLLING TERRAIN

The southwest region drained by the Niger River is a savannah with low bushes and trees such as the baobab, kapok, bastard mahogany, and tamarind.

10 ⊕ MOUNTAINS AND VOLCANOES

In the north-central region are the mountains of the volcanic Aïr Massif, which belong to the same system as Algeria's Ahaggar Mountains and extend southward more than 400 kilometers (248 miles) from Niger's border with Algeria. The mountains cover an area of approximately 80,000 square kilometers (30,880 square miles), and their average elevation is between 600 to 900 meters (2,000 and 3,000 feet). Their highest summit is Mount Gréboun in north-central Niger, at 1,944 meters (6,378 feet).

11 ⊕ CANYONS AND CAVES

Crystalline rocks have been found in large caves in western Niger.

12 ⊕ PLATEAUS AND MONOLITHS

The Manguéni, Djado, and Tchigaï Plateaus are clustered together in the northeastern corner of the country near the border with Libya. Their average elevation is about 800 meters (2,600 feet). The mountains of the Manguéni Plateau are a continuation of Chad's Tibesti Mountains.

13 ⊕ MAN-MADE FEATURES

The Kennedy Bridge, named after U.S. president John F. Kennedy, is the only bridge that crosses the Niger River at the capital city of Niamey. It is 710 meters (2,330 feet) long and is part of a larger network of roads that connects Niger to Togo, Benin, and Burkina Faso.

14 ⊕ FURTHER READING

Books

Chilson, Peter. *Riding the Demon: On the Road in West Africa.* Athens: University of Georgia Press, 1999.

UNESCO/Pierre Donnaint

Camels are native to desert regions of Niger.

Hollett, Dave. *The Conquest of the Niger by Land and Sea: From the Early Explorers and Pioneer Steamships to Elder Dempster and Company.* Abergavenny, Gwent, Wales, UK: P. Heaton, 1995.

Miles, William. *Hausaland Divided: Colonialism and Independence in Nigeria and Niger.* Ithaca, NY: Cornell University Press, 1994.

Web Sites

Lonely Planet World Guide: Niger. http://www.lonelyplanet.com/destinations/africa/niger/ (accessed April 11, 2003).

Mbendi Information Services: Niger. http://www.mbendi.co.za/land/af/ni/p0005.htm (accessed April 11, 2003).

Nigeria

- **Official name:** Federal Republic of Nigeria
- **Area:** 923,768 square kilometers (356,669 square miles)
- **Highest point on mainland:** Chappal Waddi (2,419 meters/7,936 feet)
- **Lowest point on land:** Sea level
- **Hemispheres:** Northern and Eastern
- **Time zone:** 1 P.M. = noon GMT
- **Longest distances:** 1,127 kilometers (700 miles) from east to west; 1,046 kilometers (650 miles) from north to south

- **Land boundaries:** 4,047 kilometers (2,514 miles) total boundary length; Chad 87 kilometers (54 miles); Cameroon 1,690 kilometers (1,050 miles); Benin 773 kilometers (480 miles); Niger 1,497 kilometers (930 miles)
- **Coastline:** 853 kilometers (530 miles)
- **Territorial sea limits:** 22 kilometers (12 nautical miles)

1 ⊕ LOCATION AND SIZE

Nigeria is located in western Africa, bordering the Gulf of Guinea. The country also shares borders with Chad, Cameroon, Benin, and Niger. With an area of about 923,768 square kilometers (356,669 square miles), the country is slightly more than twice the size of California. Nigeria is divided into thirty-six states and one federal territory.

2 ⊕ TERRITORIES AND DEPENDENCIES

Nigeria has no outside territories or dependencies.

3 ⊕ CLIMATE

The climate in Nigeria varies from equatorial in the south, to tropical in the center, and arid in the north. Inland, the midday temperatures may surpass 38°C (100°F), but the nights are relatively cool, dropping as low as 12°C (54°F). On the Jos Plateau, temperatures are more moderate. Near the coast, temperatures rarely exceed 32°C (90°F), but humidity is high and nights are hot.

Inland, there are two distinct seasons: a wet season from April through October, with generally lower temperatures, and a dry season from November through March, with hotter temperatures. Along the coast, annual rainfall varies from about 180 centimeters (70 inches) in the west to about 420 centimeters (170 inches) in certain parts of the east. Inland, it decreases to around 130 centimeters (50 inches) over most of central Nigeria and only 50 centimeters (20 inches) in the extreme north.

4 ⊕ TOPOGRAPHIC REGIONS

Nigeria sits on the center of the African Tectonic Plate and lies entirely in the tropics, with its southern edge being only a few degrees above the equator and its northern border well below the Tropic of Cancer.

The outstanding geographic feature of the country is the basin of the Niger and Benue Rivers, running east and west through the center of the country. South of the basin, the elevation generally is less than 304 meters

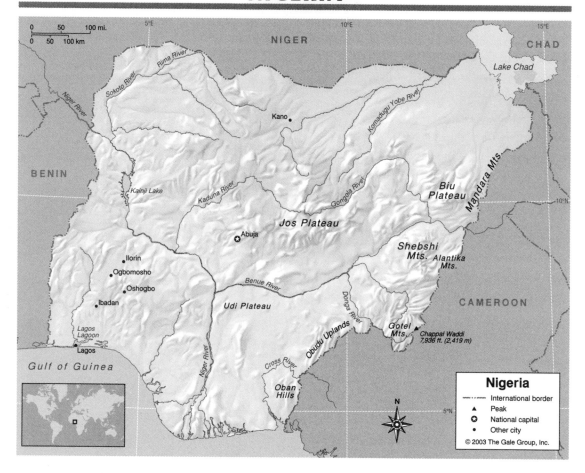

(1,000 feet), except for a few plateau surfaces. To the north of the basin, a broad plateau occupies the country to its northern border with elevations from 304 meters to 1,219 meters (1,000 to 4,000 feet). In the east, the country contains mountainous regions, in which the highest point is located.

5 ⊕ OCEANS AND SEAS

Seacoast and Undersea Features

Nigeria faces the Gulf of Guinea, which is a part of the Atlantic Ocean.

Sea Inlets and Straits

The Bight of Benin is to the west and the Bight of Biafra to the southeast; both of these are in-lets of the Gulf of Guinea. There are a number of lagoons along the westerly coastal areas.

Islands and Archipelagos

Islands of solid ground within the Niger Delta are inhabited. The city of Lagos is located on a group of islands at the western end of Lagos Lagoon.

Coastal Features

Low swampy land, which varies in width up to 32 kilometers (20 miles) or more, is part of the coastal belt extending along the entire Gulf of Guinea coast of West Africa. The outer edge of the coastal area consists of sand spits; it changes to mud as the coast nears the Niger

Delta. Behind the outer spits and lagoons, creeks of varying size parallel the coast and form a continuous waterway from the border with Benin on the west to the tributaries of the Niger Delta in the east.

One of the major features of the West African coastline is the Niger Delta, which projects into the Gulf of Guinea from the southern coast of Nigeria. This great bulge of sedimentary material, deposited by the Niger River, stretches some 120 to 128 kilometers (75 to 80 miles) from its apex below the town of Aba to the sea. It covers an area of about 25,900 square kilometers (10,000 square miles). The water of the Niger flows through this delta in a series of radial tributaries. For navigational purposes, the two most important rivers are the Forcados and the Nun.

The outer edge of the delta is fringed by sand spits and ridges, varying in width from less than one kilometer to more than 16 kilometers (more than 10 miles). Behind these ridges are mangrove swamps covering about 10,360 square kilometers (4,000 square miles); farther inland is an extensive area of freshwater swamps. The delta contains large natural gas and oil deposits.

Mangroves dominate the coast, while freshwater swamp forests with palms, abura, and mahogany predominate throughout the adjacent inland area.

6 ⊕ INLAND LAKES

The largest lake in Nigeria is Lake Chad, which is shared by the neighboring countries of Chad and Niger. The size of the lake varies from season to season depending on rainfall—from 10,360 to 25,900 square kilometers (4,000 to 10,000 square miles)—as it alternately advances and recedes over considerable distances in the flat plains area on the Nigerian side. Between December and January, at the height of the rainy season, the lake may cover up to 25,900 square kilometers (10,000 square miles). During the ensuing months, however, it may diminish to less than half that size, with depths of only 1.2 to 5 meters (4 to 16 feet). At times, the waters recede so much that the entire portion located within Nigeria dries up. Little water is supplied to the lake from rivers in Nigeria. Its principal source is the Chari River in the Republic of Chad. The lake has no outlets. Lake Chad is the largest inland body of water on the Sahel.

In the far western part of the country is Kainji Lake, formed in 1968 by the damming of the Niger River. The lake extends for about 137 kilometers (85 miles) in a section of the Niger River valley from Kainji to a point beyond Yelwa. At maximum level, it covers an area of about 1,243 square kilometers (480 square miles) and has a width of 14 to 24 kilometers (9 to 15 miles)

7 ⊕ RIVERS AND WATERFALLS

The valleys of the Niger and Benue Rivers, which account for most of the country's drainage, form a great east-west arc across the middle of the country. The Niger River valley extends from the border with Benin on the west and the Benue River valley extends from the eastern border with Cameroon. Near Lokoja, in the center of the country, the two rivers join and change course to flow southward to the Gulf of Guinea.

The Niger is the longest river in Nigeria, with a total length of about 4,100 kilometers (2,460 miles). It rises in the Fouta Djallon of Guinea and travels in a wide arc through Mali, Niger, and Benin before crossing the border into Nigeria. Inside Nigeria, the river travels approximately 1,175 kilometers (730 miles) before it empties into the Gulf of Guinea.

UNESCO

*The landscape around the Sukur cultural site features villages
in the valleys with terraced fields and ruins of iron mining.*

The Benue, which rises in Cameroon, flows about 796 kilometers (495 miles) inside Nigeria to its confluence with the Niger River.

The most important river outside this system is the Cross River in the southeast. The Cross originates in southern Cameroon and enters the country through the Eastern Highlands. It was a major transportation route for the slave trade in the eighteenth and nineteenth centuries.

South of the Western High Plains, several rivers flow directly into the Gulf of Guinea or its fringe lagoons. In the north from the Jos Plateau radiate rivers that flow toward Lake Chad or into the Niger-Benue system, including the Sokoto, Kaduna, Rima, Komadugu, Yobe, and Gongola rivers.

8 ⊕ DESERTS

Though there are no true desert regions in Nigeria, the northern part of Nigeria lies within the region known as the Sahel. Sahel is an Arabic word that means "shore." It refers to the 5,000-kilometer (3,125-mile) stretch of savannah that forms the shore or edge of the Sahara Desert. The Sahel spreads west to east from Mauritania and Senegal to Somalia.

9 ⊕ FLAT AND ROLLING TERRAIN

Many of the low-lying plains are covered in wetlands. Most of these wetlands are found along the Niger Delta, the Niger River flood plains, and in the Lake Chad basin. On the northern edges of the coastal lagoons, many smaller rivers lose themselves in freshwater swamps. Open flood plains extend between

Yelwa and Jebba in the Niger River valley. Eastward from Jebba, to the confluence of the Niger and Benue Rivers, extensive swampy plains spread up to 80 kilometers (50 miles) wide. Extremely low gradients in the Lake Chad basin impede river flow so that during much of the year, the flood plains are swampy.

Beyond the tropical belt to the north grow tall grasses and deciduous trees of small stature, characteristic of the savannah. The Western High Plains are covered largely with savannah parkland and grass.

The uppermost levels of the Obudu Uplands and the Oban Hills, westward extensions of the Bamenda Highlands, are covered grasslands.

Tropical rain forests form a belt roughly 130 kilometers (80 miles) wide across the southern zone, with trees such as African mahogany, irokol, African walnut, and obeche reaching heights of 60 meters (200 feet). These forests are found in the Obudu Uplands and the Oban Hills in the east as well as in the plains in Western State. The central and western sections of Mid-Western State, with gentle slopes and elevations mostly less than 122 meters (400 feet), contain extensive and luxuriant forest areas in protected reserves.

10 ⊕ MOUNTAINS AND VOLCANOES

Nigeria's boundary with Cameroon contains about 804 kilometers (500 miles) of mountainous country. The northern part of the highlands consists of several hill groups, with peaks around 1,097 meters (3,600 feet). To the south of these are the Mandara Mountains, a dissected plateau with a general elevation of about 1,219 meters (4,000 feet) encompassing an area of some 482 kilometers (300 miles) in length with an average width of about 32 kilometers (20 miles).

The central part of the border region consists of the Adamawa Highlands, a discontinuous series of mountain ranges and high plateau surfaces situated between the Benue River valley and the Donga River valley. They include the Alantika Mountains along the border and the Shebshi Mountains. The Shebshi Mountains, generally at an elevation of 1,066 meters (3,500 feet), are a dissected plateau with highly eroded lower slopes. The highest surveyed point in the country, Chappal Waddi, at a height of 2,419 meters (7,936 feet), is located in these hills. To the southwest of the Adamawa Highlands lies the Nigerian section of the Bamenda Highlands at 1,219 meters (4,000 feet) in elevation. The Gotel Mountains rise up along the southeastern border with Cameroon.

11 ⊕ CANYONS AND CAVES

There are no significant caves or canyons in Nigeria.

12 ⊕ PLATEAUS AND MONOLITHS

With the exception of the coastal plains and the Niger-Benue valley, Nigeria consists mostly of high plains and plateaus. Directly to the east of the Lower Niger Valley are the Udi and Igala Plateaus and the Akwa-Orlu Uplands. The general elevation of these plateaus is about 304 meters (1,000 feet), with escarpments rising considerably higher. Between the low western coastal plains and the Niger-Benue River valley lie the Western High Plains, or Plateau of Yorubaland, part of the belt of high plains that extends through West Africa. Plateau surfaces here vary in elevation from about 228 meters to 372 meters (750 feet to 1,200 feet), with some dome-shaped hills attaining a height of 609 meters (2,000 feet).

North of the Niger-Benue valley lies a broad plateau, the Northern High Plains or the High Plains of Hausaland. The central section of the plateau extends for about 482 kilometers (300 miles) from east to west, with stepped plains ranging from about 183 meters (600 feet) at the outer edge to roughly 914 meters (3,000 feet) in the area surrounding the Jos Plateau. The Jos Plateau covers an area of about 7,770 square kilometers (3,000 square miles), separated from the surrounding area by pronounced escarpments. The area's general elevation is above 1,219 meters (4,000 feet), and some hills in its eastern section attain heights of over 1,767 meters (5,800 feet). The Jos Plateau contains tin and other metals that have made the region economically important.

The Biu Plateau to the east of the Gongola River basin covers about 5,180 square kilometers (2,000 square miles). The upper level of the plateau, from 609 to 914 meters (2,000 to 3,000 feet), is separated from the Northern High Plains by a pronounced escarpment. Inactive volcanic cones are found in the northern part of this area.

13 ⊕ MAN-MADE FEATURES

Kainji Lake was developed as a combined hydroelectric power and river navigation project. A dam built on the Niger River created the lake.

14 ⊕ FURTHER READING

Books

Achebe, Chinua. *Anthills of the Savannah.* New York: Doubleday, 1987.

Africa South of the Sahara, 2002. Nigeria. London: Europa, 2001.

Floyd, Barry. *Eastern Nigeria: A Geographical Review.* London: Macmillan, 1969.

Grove, Alfred Thomas. *The Changing Geography of Africa.* Oxford: Oxford University Press, 1989.

Udo, Reuben K. *Geographical Regions of Nigeria.* London: Heinemann, 1970.

Web Site

Nigeria Today. http://www.nigeriatoday.com (accessed June 18, 2003).

DID YOU KN⊕W?

The Tropics is the name given to the region of the world that lies between the Tropic of Cancer and the Tropic of Capricorn. The Tropic of Cancer is the parallel of latitude located at 23°30′ north of the equator. The Tropic of Capricorn is located at the parallel of latitude that is 23°30′ south of the equator. These imaginary lines mark the boundaries of an area in which the Sun will appear to be directly overhead, or at a 90° angle from Earth, at noon. North or south of these lines, the angle of the Sun at noon appears to be less than 90°. The lines were named for the constellations that the Sun crosses during the solstices (Capricorn on December 21 or 22 and Cancer on June 21 or 22).

Norway

- **Official name:** Kingdom of Norway
- **Area:** 324,220 square kilometers (125,182 square miles)
- **Highest point on mainland:** Galdhøpiggen (2,469 meters/8,100 feet)
- **Lowest point on land:** Sea level
- **Hemispheres:** Northern and Eastern
- **Time zone:** 1 P.M. = noon GMT
- **Longest distances:** 1,752 kilometers (1,089 miles) from north-northeast to south-southwest, 430 kilometers (267 miles) from east-southeast to west-northwest

- **Land boundaries:** 2,515 kilometers (1,562 miles) total boundary length; Finland 729 kilometers (453 miles); Sweden 1,619 (1,006 miles kilometers); Russia 167 kilometers (104 miles)
- **Coastline:** 21,925 kilometers (13,594 miles)
- **Territorial sea limits:** 7 kilometers (4 nautical miles)

1 ⊕ LOCATION AND SIZE

Norway is located on the Scandinavian peninsula in northern Europe, west of Sweden and east of the North Sea and the Norwegian Sea. The country also shares borders with Russia and Finland. Almost one-third of the country sits north of the Arctic Circle. With a total area of about 324,220 square kilometers (125,182 square miles), the country is slightly larger than the state of New Mexico. Norway is divided into nineteen counties.

2 ⊕ TERRITORIES AND DEPENDENCIES

Norway has claimed four island dependencies. Bouvet Island is located in the South Atlantic Ocean between Africa and Antarctica. Peter I Island is also located off the Antarctic coast. Jan Mayen Island is located in the Arctic Ocean northeast of Iceland. All three of these islands are uninhabited.

The Svalbard Archipelago, located north of Norway in the Arctic Ocean, is at the center of a maritime border dispute between Norway and Russia.

In addition to the four islands, Norway also has a territorial claim in Antarctica.

3 ⊕ CLIMATE

The warm waters of the Gulf Stream and prevailing westerly winds keep the climate of Norway mild, even though the country is so far north. Along the west and southwest coast, high temperatures average 3°C (38°F) in January and 19°C (66°F) in July. The climate is more extreme and temperature ranges are broader in Norway's interior. The arctic north is much colder than the south, but even here the Gulf Stream keeps temperatures relatively warm and the coast ice-free. Oslo, in the southern interior, has an average high temperature of 28°C (82°F) in July and 5°C (41°F) in January.

The coastal areas of the west receive almost year-round rainfall. Some areas average 330

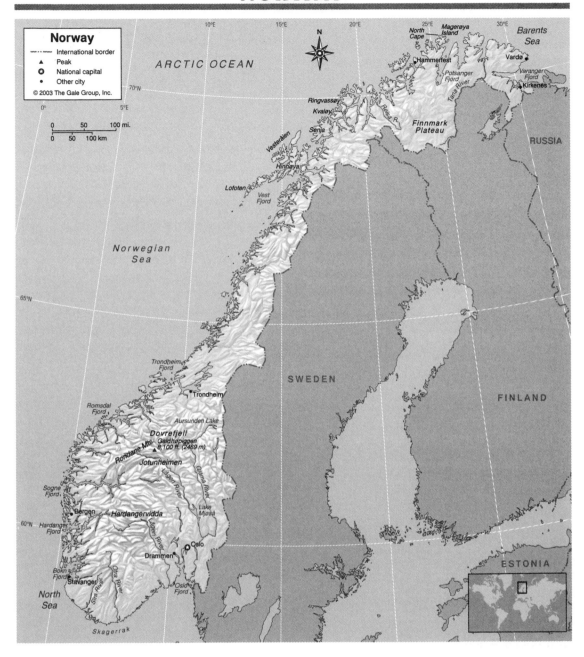

centimeters (130 inches). Precipitation is not as great in the interior. Oslo, in the southern interior, averages 76 centimeters (30 inches) of precipitation a year.

4 ⊕ TOPOGRAPHIC REGIONS

Norway consists of five geographic regions. The West Country (Vestlandet) is an area carved by glaciers and features majestic fjords and the abrupt slope of the western Scandinavian Mountains toward the North Sea. Connected to the West Country by numerous valleys, the East Country (Ostlandet) contains rolling hills and valleys that contain some of the country's richest agricultural soil. The Trondheim (Trøndelag) Depression forms a natural boundary between the northern and southern halves of the country. It is a region of hills, valleys, and fjords north of the high mountain ranges. Farther to the north is North Norway (Nord Norge), which is marked by fjords, mountains, vast snowfields, and some of Europe's largest glaciers. In the far south is an area of agricultural lowlands known as South Country (Sorlandet).

5 ⊕ OCEANS AND SEAS

Seacoast and Undersea Features

Most of the western coast of Norway lies on the Norwegian Sea. Part of the southwest coastline borders the North Sea. Both seas are extensions of the Atlantic Ocean. The northernmost coast of the country borders the Barents Sea, an extension of the Arctic Ocean.

Sea Inlets and Straits

On the southernmost coast of Norway, the Skagerrak Strait separates the country from Denmark.

Most of the Norwegian coastline is cut with countless fjords, for which the country is most famous. High plateaus often surround these fjords, forming breathtaking natural harbors.

Islands and Archipelagos

Except in the southwest and the far north, the Norwegian coast has a stretch of islands called the Skjaergard. Containing roughly fifty thousand islands, this island zone reaches its broadest width of over 60 kilometers (37 miles) at the southern approaches to the Trondheim Fjord. The outer islands, protruding from relatively

> ## DID YOU KN⊕W?
>
> Scandinavia is the region of northwestern Europe that lies on the peninsula bordered by the Atlantic Ocean (in the form of the Norwegian Sea and the North Sea), the Baltic Sea, and the Gulf of Bothnia. Even though Norway and Sweden are the only two countries that lie directly on this peninsula, the countries of Denmark, Iceland, and Finland also are usually considered to be Scandinavian countries in a cultural context.

shallow waters, rarely exceed 30 meters (100 feet) in height, while the inner islands may rise to 305 meters (1,000 feet). These islands are characterized by a series of rock terraces known as strandflats.

The Lofoten and Vesterålen Islands off the northwestern coast are the country's most extensive island chains. They are formed from glaciers that covered the tops of partially submerged ancient volcanic ranges. The larger islands of Hinnøya, Kvaløy, Senja, and Ringvassøy also lie off the northwest coast.

The Svalbard archipelago, a dependency that includes the Spitzbergen archipelago, North-East Island, Edge Island, and Barents Island, is located north of Norway in the Arctic Ocean. The island group covers an area of 62,700 square kilometers (24,208 square miles). Although ice sheets and permafrost blanket most of the islands, they are the sites of the northernmost permanent settlements in Europe.

EPD Photos/©2002 Peter Wolff

A road stretches across the West Country of Norway.

Bouvet Island was claimed for Norway in 1927. It is located in the South Atlantic Ocean between Africa and Antarctica. It is uninhabited and is almost completely covered by ice. Additionally, Norway has claimed Peter I Island, off the Antarctic coast.

Coastal Features

Except in the southernmost part of the country, Norway's coastline is extremely irregular. Deep fjords extend far into the interior of the country in many places. Glaciers carved these troughs into the interior plateau. The longest and deepest fjord is Sogne Fjord (Sognafjorden). It is approximately 204 kilometers (127 miles) long, with walls rising sharply from the coast to elevations of 1,500 meters (5,000 feet)

in some places. Other major fjords in the south include Oslo Fjord, Hardanger Fjord, Bokn Fjord, and Romsdals Fjord. In the middle of the country, the Trondheim Fjord extends 126 kilometers (78 miles) into the interior. Arctic fjords such as Tana, Porsangen, and Varanger tend to be broader and somewhat shorter.

In the far north of Norway, on Magerøya Island, is North Cape (Nordkap). This is the northernmost point in all of Europe.

6 ⊕ INLAND LAKES

Glacial lakes abound in Norway. Nearly one-twelfth of the country is under fresh water. Lake Mjøsa, at 363 square kilometers (140 square miles) in area and 452 meters (1,982 feet) in depth, is by far the largest lake. Most of the other larger lakes are 122 meters (400 feet) above the sea; these elevated lakes perhaps were once heads of fjords that have since been sealed off from the ocean.

7 ⊕ RIVERS AND WATERFALLS

Norway has numerous glacier-fed rivers. Most are swift and turbulent, rushing through steep valleys and rocky gorges. The only navigable rivers are the Glåma and the Dramselva. The Glåma is the longest river in Scandinavia, at 563 kilometers (350 miles) long. It rises more than 610 meters (2,000 feet) above sea level at Aursunden Lake and flows south into the Skagerrak. Many lakes widen the stream, and the river is famous for its waterfalls. The Dramselva River rises in the central part of the country and also flows south, entering Oslo Fjord at Drammen. Other major rivers in the south are the Otra, Sira, and the two Lågen Rivers. The Reisa and the Tana Rivers are situated in the extreme north.

8 ⊕ DESERTS

There are no desert regions in Norway.

9 ⊕ FLAT AND ROLLING TERRAIN

The East Country contains rolling hills and valleys that support most of the agriculture of the country. Only 3 percent of Norway's land is considered arable, however, and there are no regions of permanent pasture. The Trondheim Depression forms a natural boundary between the northern and southern halves of the country.

10 ⊕ MOUNTAINS AND VOLCANOES

Norwegian mountain ranges are roughly divided into three groups. In the north, the Kjølen range forms a natural barrier between Norway and Sweden and extends northward toward the border with Finland. Further south is the Dovrefjell chain, which abuts the Trondheim Depression in the south; together, the mountains and valleysplit the country into its northern and southern areas.

Norway's highest mountain range, the Langfjell, lies south of the Trondheim Depression and the Dovrefjell. This range, comprised of sharp peaks called *fjells* and high plateaus called *vidder*, runs southwest to northeast and divides the West and East countries. The Rondane Mountains and the Jotunheimen are part of this range. Galdhøpiggen, Scandinavia's highest mountain at 2,469 meters (8,100 feet), belongs to the Jotunheimen.

The Beerenberg volcano (2,277 meters/ 7,470 feet), the world's northernmost active volcano, created the uninhabited dependency of Jan Mayen Island in the Arctic Ocean northeast of Iceland. Jan Mayen has an area of 373 square kilometers (144 square miles). Beerenberg erupted most recentlyin 1970.

11 ⊕ CANYONS AND CAVES

The movements of glaciers created most of the cave areas in Norway. Svarthammergrotta has the largest chamber of any cave in Norway. "Glacier Hall," as the chamber is called, has

DID YOU KN⊕W?

Known as the "land of the midnight sun," the far northern region of Norway has 24-hour daylight from May through July. Oslo and the rest of the southern region have summer daylight from about 4 A.M. to 11 P.M. Conversely, from November to the end of January, the sun never rises above the horizon in the north.

a width of 30 to 50 meters (98 to 164 feet), a height of 5 to 10 meters (16 to 33 feet), and a length of 200 meters (656 feet). Ice samples taken from the cave have been dated to approximately 1,200 A.D.

12 ⊕ PLATEAUS AND MONOLITHS

Glaciers of the Ice Age carved countless plateaus into the Norwegian landscape, some of them very large. The Norwegian Plateau includes the western and eastern vidders in the high mountains of the central region. Other major plateaus are the Finnmark Plateau in the far north and the Hardangervidda in the south. The Hardangervidda has an elevation of 1,830 meters (6,004 feet) and an area of 6,474 square kilometers (2,500 square miles), with steep sides scarred and grooved by waterfalls and valleys.

Most of the northern end of the Norwegian Plateau in the country's central region is covered by icecaps. The Jostedalsbreen glacier is found in this area. It is the largest glacier in Europe at 1,502 square kilometers (580 square miles) in area and possibly 457 meters (1,500 feet) thick. The Folgefonn glacier is also found here. The top of this glacier is over 1,524 meters (5,000 feet) above sea level.

Norway's northern extremes, including the Finnmark Plateau, are also heavily glaciated. Other large snowfields include Hallinskarvet in the Hardangervidda, Snohetta in the Dovrefjell, Seiland near Hammerfest, and Oksfjordjokel near Kvanangen.

13 ⊕ MAN-MADE FEATURES

There are no significant man-made structures affecting the geography of Norway.

14 ⊕ FURTHER READING

Books

Blashfield, Jean F. *Norway*. New York: Children's Press, 2000.

Charbonneau, Claudette. *The Land and People of Norway*. New York: HarperCollins, 1992.

Norway in Pictures. Minneapolis: Lerner Publications, 1992.

Vanberg, B. *Of Norwegian Ways*. New York: Harper & Row, 1984.

Zickgraf, Ralph. *Norway*. Broomall, PA: Chelsea House, 1999.

Web Site

Visit Norway. http://www.visitnorway.com (accessed June 18, 2003).

Oman

- **Official name:** Sultanate of Oman
- **Area:** 212,460 square kilometers (82,031 square miles)
- **Highest point on mainland:** Jabal Sham (3,035 meters/9,957 feet)
- **Lowest point on land:** Sea level
- **Hemispheres:** Northern and Eastern
- **Time zone:** 4 P.M. = noon GMT
- **Longest distances:** 972 kilometers (604 miles) from northeast to southwest; 513 kilometers (319 miles) from southeast to northwest

- **Land boundaries:** 1,374 kilometers (854 miles) total boundary length; Yemen 288 kilometers (179 miles); Saudi Arabia 676 kilometers (420 miles); United Arab Emirates 410 kilometers (255 miles)
- **Coastline:** 2,092 kilometers (1,300 miles)
- **Territorial sea limits:** 22 kilometers (12 nautical miles)

1 ⊕ LOCATION AND SIZE

The sultanate of Oman is located in the extreme southeastern corner of the Arabian Peninsula and is the second-largest country on the peninsula. It includes a small enclave at the tip of the Musandam Peninsula, on the Strait of Hormuz, that is separated from the rest of Oman by the United Arab Emirates. With an area of 212,460 square kilometers (82,031 square miles), Oman is nearly as large as the state of Kansas.

2 ⊕ TERRITORIES AND DEPENDENCIES

Oman has no territories or dependencies.

3 ⊕ CLIMATE

Oman's climate is arid subtropical. The climate differs somewhat from one region to another, however. The interior is generally very hot, with temperatures reaching 54°C (129°F) in the hot season from May to October. The coastal areas are hot and humid from April to October. The prevailing summer wind, the *Gharbi*, makes the heat more oppressive. In the south, the Dhofar (Zufar) region has a more moderate climate.

Average annual precipitation is 5 to 10 centimeters (2 to 4 inches), depending on the region and the prevailing summer wind. While the mountain areas receive more plentiful rainfall, some parts of the coast, particularly those areas near the island of Maşīrah, sometimes receive no rain at all. Yearly rainfall totals of up to 64 centimeters (25 inches) have been recorded in the rainy season from late June to October. An unusual feature of Oman's weather is that part of the eastern coast regularly has dense fog.

4 ⊕ TOPOGRAPHIC REGIONS

Oman has a diverse topography with a number of different regions and subregions. The major regions are the narrow Al Bātinah coastal plain to the north, bordering the Gulf of Oman; the Al Hajar mountain range that stretches south-

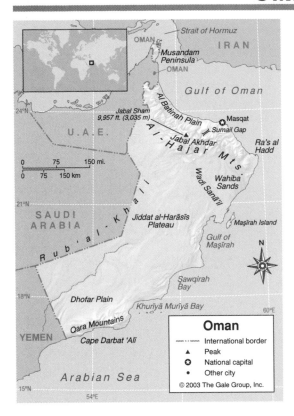

Strait of Hormuz
OMAN
IRAN
Musandam
Peninsula
OMAN
Gulf of Oman
Al Bāṭinah Plain
Jabal Sham
9,957 ft. (3,035 m)
Masqat
Sumail Gap
Jabal Akhḍar
U.A.E.
Ra's al
Hadd
Al - Hajar Mts
Wadi Sanā'īl
Wahiba
Sands
SAUDI
ARABIA
Jiddat al-Harāsīs
Plateau
Maṣīrah Island
Rub' al - Khālī
Gulf of
Maṣīrah
Sawqirah
Bay
Dhofar Plain
Khurīyā Murīyā Bay
Qara Mountains
YEMEN
Cape Darbat 'Alī
Arabian Sea

Oman
International border
▲ Peak
✪ National capital
● Other city
© 2003 The Gale Group, Inc.

eastward paralleling the northern coast; an interior plateau that stretches southwestward toward the desert; the Rub'al Khālī desert, which Oman shares with Saudi Arabia and Yemen; the barren plain of Jalaan, which borders the Arabian Sea on the east; and the southern Dhofar region, which includes both mountainous highlands and a fertile coastal strip that constitutes the southernmost part of Oman. In addition, Oman encompasses an isolated strip of land at the tip of the Musandem Peninsula.

5 ⊕ OCEANS AND SEAS

Oman borders the Arabian Sea and the Gulf of Oman, the latter of which separates the Arabian Peninsula from the rest of the Middle East.

Sea Inlets and Straits

Inlets (*khors*) in the Al Bātinah plain often have stands of mangroves. An extremely rug-

ged area exists where two inlets, the Elphinstone and Malcom, cut into the coastline south of the Strait of Hormuz.

Islands and Archipelagos

Along the Arabian Sea coastline and separated from it by about 16 kilometers (10 miles) is the barren and virtually uninhabited island of Maṣīrah,

Coastal Features

The northern coastline is smooth, while the shore along the Arabian Sea is more jagged and indented, forming several bays and capes (including the Ra's al Hadd, which separates the Gulf of Oman from the Arabian Sea) and the Gulf of Maṣīrah near Maṣīrah Island.

6 ⊕ INLAND LAKES

There are no lakes in Oman, but the country has two large areas of salt flats, one in the west-central region and another opposite Maṣīrah Island, off the eastern coast.

7 ⊕ RIVERS AND WATERFALLS

There are no perennial rivers in Oman. A small number of *wadis* (shallow watercourses) are found in the Al Hajar Mountains and their foothills, however.

8 ⊕ DESERTS

Situated mainly in Saudi Arabia but occupying a portion of western Oman, the Rub'al Khālī, or Empty Quarter, is one of the largest sand deserts in the world and one of the driest places on earth. The Wahiba Sands, in Oman's interior, are the largest areas of lithified (changed into solid rock) sand dunes in the world. Its surface dunes can reach heights of 100 meters (328 feet).

9 ⊕ FLAT AND ROLLING TERRAIN

The Al Bātinah coastal plain to the north, scored along its length by *wadis*, is cultivated

ARAMCO/Tor Eigeland

Mountains of Musandam in northern Oman.

with the aid of irrigation. The sandy plain of Jalaan to the east is barren and inhospitable, while the narrow coastal strip of the Dhofar region in the south is lush and fertile. The valleys and foothills immediately south of the Al Hajar Mountains are considered the country's heartland.

10 ⊕ MOUNTAINS AND VOLCANOES

The Al Hajar (the Rock) Mountains—the highest in the eastern part of the Arabian peninsula—form two ranges: the Hajar al-Gharbi, or Western Hajar, and the Hajar al-Shargi, or Eastern Hajar. They are divided by the Wadi Sanā'il, a valley that forms the traditional route between Masqat and the interior. The general elevation is about 4,000 feet (1,219 meters). In the southern Dhofar region, a semicircular band of mountains rises to around 1,500 meters (5,000 feet).

11 ⊕ CANYONS AND CAVES

There are many caverns in Oman. One of the largest in the world, Teyq Cave, is 250 meters (820 feet) deep and 300 cubic meters (10,595 cubic feet) in volume.

12 ⊕ PLATEAUS AND MONOLITHS

The foothills of the Al Hajar Mountains in the north give way to a plateau with an average height of about 300 meters (1,000 feet). It is mostly stony and waterless, arable only at oases, extending to the sands of the Rub'al Khālī Desert. In the central part of Oman, in the Al-Wusta region, this plateau narrows to the Jiddat al-Harāsīs, bordered by the Rub'al Khālī desert to the west and the plain of Jalaan to the east.

OMAN

ARAMCO/Tor Eigeland

Wave-like dunes are found in Oman's Rub'al Khālī Desert.

13 ⊕ MAN-MADE FEATURES

There are three forts in Muscat that have remained essentially unchanged since the 1580s.

14 ⊕ FURTHER READING

Books

Chatty, Dawn. *Mobile Pastoralists: Development Planning and Social Change in Oman.* New York: Columbia University Press, 1996.

Kay, Shirley. *Enchanting Oman.* Dubai, United Arab Emirates: Motivate Publishing, 1988.

Newcombe, Ozzie. *The Heritage of Oman: A Celebration in Photographs.* Reading, Berkshire, U.K.: Garnet Publishing, 1995.

Oman: People & Heritage. Oman: Oman Daily Observer, 1994.

Web Sites

Middle East & Islamic Studies Collection. http://www.library.cornell.edu/colldev/ mideast/universi.htm (accessed March 10, 2003).

Ministry of Information: Sultanate of Oman. http://www.omanet.com/ (accessed March 10, 2003).

Natural History of Oman & Arabia. http://www.oman.org/nath00.htm (accessed May 10, 2003).

Pakistan

- **Official name:** Islamic Republic of Pakistan

- **Area:** 803,940 square kilometers (310,403 square miles)

- **Highest point on mainland:** K2 (Mount Godwin-Austen) (8,611 meters/28,251 feet)

- **Lowest point on land:** Sea level

- **Hemispheres:** Northern and Eastern

- **Time zone:** 5 P.M. = noon GMT

- **Longest distances:** 1,875 kilometers (1,165 miles) from northeast to southwest; 1,006 kilometers (625 miles) from southeast to northwest

- **Land boundaries:** 6,774 kilometers (4,209 miles) total boundary length; China 523 kilometers (325 miles); India 2,912 kilometers (1,809 miles); Iran 909 kilometers (565 miles); Afghanistan 2,430 kilometers (1,510 miles)

- **Coastline:** 1,046 kilometers (650 miles)

- **Territorial sea limits:** 22 kilometers (12 nautical miles)

1 ⊕ LOCATION AND SIZE

Pakistan is located in South Asia between the Himalaya Mountains and the Arabian Sea—west of India, east of Iran and Afghanistan, and south of China. The nation is almost two times the size of California, and is divided up into four provinces and one territory.

2 ⊕ TERRITORIES AND DEPENDENCIES

Since their creation as independent countries in 1947, India and Pakistan have disputed ownership of the northern region of Jammu and Kashmir. The simmering tension has erupted into fighting between the neighbors in 1948, 1965, and 1971; the dispute continues to be a source of sporadic conflict in the early 2000s.

3 ⊕ CLIMATE

Pakistan is in the temperate zone and varies greatly in weather conditions—from the humid coast to the dry, hot desert interior to the icy mountains in the north. Four seasons are experienced in the country: winter from December through February; a hot, dry spring from March through May; the arrival of the southwest monsoon from June through September; and the northeast monsoon from October through November. In the north and west, the rainy season occurs during the winter

The northern capital, Islamabad, has average temperatures ranging from a low of 2°C (35°F) in January to a high of 40°C (104°F) in June. The southern port of Karachi has average temperatures varying from a low of 13°C (55°F) in winter to a high of 34°C (93°F) in summer.

Arid conditions prevail in most of Pakistan, which misses the full force of the monsoons. Punjab has had major fluctuations in monsoon rainfall, with droughts in some years and floods in others. On Pakistan's plains, the

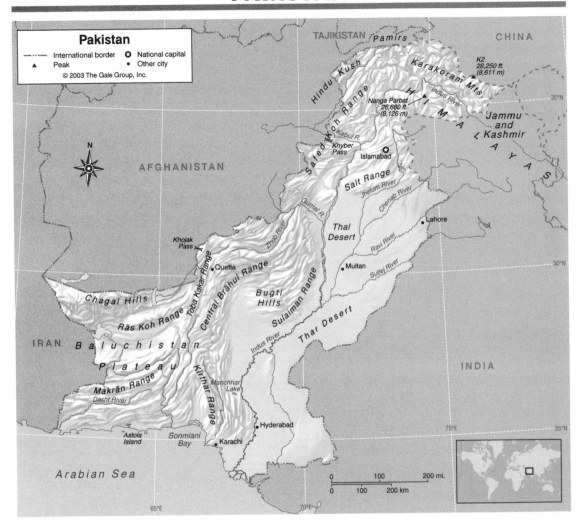

Pakistan

- ----- International border
- ▲ Peak
- ⊕ National capital
- • Other city

© 2003 The Gale Group, Inc.

TAJIKISTAN — Pamirs — CHINA

Hindu Kush — Karakoram Mts — K2 28,250 ft. (8,611 m)

Safed Koh Range — HIMALAYAS

Nanga Parbat 26,660 ft. (8,126 m)

Indus River

Jammu and Kashmir

35°N

AFGHANISTAN

Kabul R.
Khyber Pass
Islamabad

Salt Range

Jhelum River
Chenab River

Thal Desert

Lahore

Khojak Pass

Qumal R.

Zhob River

Quetta

Ravi River

30°N

Central Brahui Range

Bugti Hills

Sulaiman Range

Multan

Sutlej River

Chagai Hills

Rās Koh Range

Toba Kakar Range

Baluchistan Plateau

Indus River

Thar Desert

INDIA

Makrān Range

Kirthar Range

Dasht River

Manchhar Lake

75°E

IRAN

Sonmiani Bay

Astola Island

Karachi

Hyderabad

25°N

Arabian Sea

65°E

70°E

0   100   200 mi.
0   100   200 km

average annual rainfall is a mere 13 centimeters (5 inches), while in the highlands it is 89 centimeters (35 inches). Hailstorms are common, and snow falls in the north in winter. The lofty mountains of the north are permanently cloaked in snow and ice.

4 ⊕ TOPOGRAPHIC REGIONS

Pakistan can be divided into three major geographic areas: the northern highlands, the Indus River plain, and the Baluchistan Plateau. About one-third of the Pakistan-India border is also the cease-fire line in the Jammu and Kashmir region, disputed between the two countries since their independence.

Pakistan lies at the border of three tectonic plates: the Arabian, Indian, and Eurasian. The Arabian Plate meets with the Eurasian Plate at the coastline in southeastern Pakistan. On Pakistan's eastern and northeastern border, the Eurasian Plate collides with the Indian Plate; as a result, seismic activity is high along this border. The region surrounding Quetta is also prone to frequent and devastating earthquakes.

Mohanis fishermen catch herons in the Indus River. They sneak up on unsuspecting birds by wearing headgear made from dead herons as a decoy. Birds are caught for food, as well as for sale and to be trained.

5 ⊕ OCEANS AND SEAS

Seacoast and Undersea Features

The coastline of Pakistan meets the Arabian Sea of the northern Indian Ocean.

Sea Inlets and Straits

There are no notable sea inlets or straits in Pakistan.

Islands and Archipelagos

Pakistan's only major offshore island is Astola (Haft Talar), about 25 kilometers (15 miles) south of Baluchistan in the Arabian Sea, with an area of 50 square kilometers (19 square miles). Astola is a turtle-nesting area and a bird and reptile habitat.

Coastal Features

Baluchistan's Ormara Turtle Beaches, about 10 kilometers (6 miles) along the western coast, are a habitat for endangered sea turtles; mud volcanoes also sputter along this shore. The central coast is indented by Sonmiani Bay. The coast has few settlements, except for Pakistan's largest city, the port of Karachi. The city's beaches are badly polluted by oil spills, sewage, and industrial toxic waste, all of which pours directly into the ocean.

6 ⊕ INLAND LAKES

In Pakistan's southeast is Manchhar Lake, once a large body of fresh water (roughly 259 square kilometers/100 square miles) and a major habitat for birds and fish. Pollution and water diversion have shrunk the lake dramatically, however, and made its waters increasingly saline. Other lakes in the lower Indus region face extinction, including Kerjhar Lake and Hammal Lake. Kinjhar (Kalri) Lake, Haleji Lake, and Drigh Lake are wildlife sanctuaries in this region. Further north are the Khabbaki, Uchali and Jahlar Lakes. The far-northern basin known as Snow Lake is a massive snowbed, comprising the Sim Gang Glacier and a frozen glacial lake with ice more than 15 kilometers (9 miles) thick.

7 ⊕ RIVERS AND WATERFALLS

The Indus River is an irrigation lifeline for much of the country. The Indus rises in the Tibetan Himalayas. After crossing the Indian-administered portion of Jammu and Kashmir, it enters Pakistan and flows southwest for 1,609 kilometers (1,000 miles) to the Arabian Sea. At Attock, the Indus receives the waters of the Kabul River from the west. After being joined by the Gumal River, the Indus continues south to Mithanhot, where it is joined by its major tributary, the Panjnad. The short Panjnad River, about 121 kilometers (75 miles) long, is actually the combined input of the "five rivers of the Punjab": the Jhelum, Chenab, Ravi, Beas, and Sutlej. The principal river of Baluchistan is the Zhob, running along the southern slopes of the Toba Kakar Range and north into the Gumal River. In southern Baluchistan, several minor rivers flow into the Arabian Sea; these include the Dasht, Mashkai, Nal, and Porali.

8 ⊕ DESERTS

Pakistan's Thal Desert is south of the Salt Range, between the Indus and Jhelum Rivers. The Thar Desert (Cholistan Desert) lies south of the Sutlej River along the Pakistan-India border. Both these Pakistani desert regions are extensions of India's Thar Desert.

The Baluchistan Plateau is largely a desert area with erosion, sand dunes, and sandstorms. There is also a dry region in the northern Chilas-Gilgit area. In addition to existing deserts, the environmental change called desertification is occurring across Pakistan, with more than one-third of the country considered at risk. Deforestation, depletion of soil, and water shortages are causing desertification as vegetation is cut and stripped away.

9 ⊕ FLAT AND ROLLING TERRAIN

The upper Indus River plain, in Punjab, varies from about 152 to 304 meters (500 to 1,000 feet) in elevation. The lower Indus Plain, generally corresponding to the province of Sind, is lower in altitude. On the Indus plain, grasslands called *doabs* provide grazing on the strips of land between rivers.

Coniferous and deciduous forests, scrub woods, mangrove forests, and tree plantations grow in Pakistan. Some 40 percent of the forests are conifer or scrub woods, found mainly in mountain watershed areas. Pakistan's forest cover has been reduced to less than four percent of the land area. Deforestation in northern Pakistan has caused severe erosion.

The Margalla Hills, 610 to 914 meters (2,000 to 3,000 feet) high, are foothills of the northern mountains that overlook Islamabad, the capital. The Swat and Chitral Hills in the northwest have heights of 1,524 to 1,829 meters (5,000 to 6,000 feet).

10 ⊕ MOUNTAINS AND VOLCANOES

The northern highlands are a convergence of some of the most rugged mountains in the world. The Himalayas stretch from northeast India to the northeast corner of Pakistan, where they merge into the Karakoram and Pamirs mountain ranges. West of the Pamirs are the heights and steep valleys of the Hindu Kush.

In the northern mountains, virtually all elevations are higher than 2,438 meters (8,000 ft) above sea level. More than fifty peaks are above 6,705 meters (22,000 feet). The soaring summits of K2 (Mount Godwin Austen) in the Karakoram Range, the world's second-highest mountain (8,611 meters/28,251 feet), and Nanga Parbat (8,126 meters/26,660 feet) in the Himalayan range, have posed often-deadly challenges to climbing expeditions. Enormous glaciers sprawl across this region, including Baltoro and Pasu, each of which is longer than 50 kilometers (31 miles).

The Safed Koh range south of the northern highlands and west of the Indus River plain reaches 4,761 meters (15,620 feet) in its extension to the Afghanistan border. This area includes the strategic Khyber Pass, which connects the Peshawar Valley to Afghanistan. South of the Safed Koh and near the border are the mountains of Waziristan. Beyond them, the Toba Kakar range, with an average elevation of about 2,743 meters (9,000 feet), extends from northern Baluchistan to the Khojak Pass. The Rās Koh range, west of the city of Quetta, and the Chagai Hills extending further west complete the western highlands.

11 ⊕ CANYONS AND CAVES

Northern Pakistan has many narrow, twisting canyons, particularly in Hunza. The Indus River rushes through the steep Attock Gorge near the Khyber Pass.

12 ⊕ PLATEAUS AND MONOLITHS

The Baluchistan Plateau, at an elevation of 914 to 1,219 meters (3,000 to 4,000 feet), is an arid tableland of approximately 350,945 square kilometers (135,000 square miles). The Potwar Plateau, at the foot of the mountains south of Islamabad, is a dry, eroded area where most of Pakistan's oil is located.

13 ⊕ MAN-MADE FEATURES

Pakistan has two major river dams. In northern Punjab, near Kashmir, the Mangla Dam sits on the Jhelum River. The Tarbela Dam is situated on the Indus near Taxila. Dams on the Indus River, built for hydropower or agricultural water diversion, have been extremely controversial. The provincial governments of Sind and Baluchistan believe that Punjab Province is diverting too much water from the Indus. Intensive irrigation has led to a crisis of water-logging and salinity throughout the farmlands of the Indus Basin. In this geological syndrome, salty water seeps from canals into surrounding soil, which the salt renders useless for farming as the water evaporates.

14 ⊕ FURTHER READING

Books

Britton, Tamara L. *Pakistan*. Edina, MN: Abdo, 2003.

Deady, Kathleen. *Pakistan*. Mankato, MN: Bridgestone Books, 2001.

Schofield, Victoria. *Kashmir in Conflict: India, Pakistan, and the Unfinished War*. New York: I.B. Taurus, 2000.

Web Sites

Islamic Republic of Pakistan. http://www. pak.gov.pk (accessed March 6, 2003).

Pakistan News Service. http://www.paknews.com (accessed March 6, 2003).

Palau

- **Official name:** Republic of Palau
- **Area:** 458 square kilometers (177 square miles)
- **Highest point on mainland:** Mount Ngerchelchauus (242 meters/794 feet)
- **Lowest point on land:** Sea level
- **Hemispheres:** Northern and Eastern

- **Time zone:** 8 P.M. = noon GMT
- **Longest distances:** Not available
- **Land boundaries:** None
- **Coastline:** 1,519 kilometers (944 miles)
- **Territorial sea limits:** 6 kilometers (3 nautical miles)

1 ⊕ LOCATION AND SIZE

Palau is the westernmost archipelago of the Caroline Island chain in the portion of the North Pacific Ocean that is often called Oceania. The country lies southeast of the Philippines and consists of six island groups totaling more than two hundred islands that are oriented roughly north to south. With a total area of about 458 square kilometers (177 square miles), the country is slightly more than two-and-one-half times the size of Washington, D.C. Palau is divided into eighteen states.

2 ⊕ TERRITORIES AND DEPENDENCIES

Palau has no outside territories or dependencies.

3 ⊕ CLIMATE

Located near the equator, Palau has a maritime tropical climate, characterized by very little seasonal or diurnal (day/night) variation. The yearly mean temperature is 28°C (82°F) in the coolest months.

Palau experiences relatively high humidity of 82 percent, with heavy rainfall from May to November. Short, torrential rainfall produces up to 381 centimeters (150 inches) of precipitation annually. Although outside of the main typhoon path, damaging storms can occur in the months from June through November.

4 ⊕ TOPOGRAPHIC REGIONS

The islands include four types of topographical formations: volcanic, high limestone, low platform, and coral atoll. Palau's volcanic and limestone islands sustain distinctly different vegetation.

5 ⊕ OCEANS AND SEAS

Seacoast and Undersea Features

The Palau islands border the North Pacific Sea on the southeast and the Philippine Sea to the northwest.

Sea Inlets and Straits

The Pkurengel Komebail Lagoon stretches across an area of 1,267 square kilometers (489 square miles) on the western side of the islands. It is enclosed by the enormous barrier reef that encircles most of the islands.

Islands and Archipelagos

Babelthuap is the largest island, with an area of 397 square kilometers (153 square miles). It is also the second-largest island in

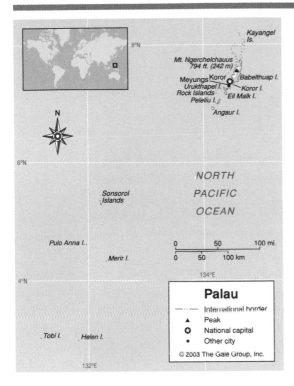

Micronesia after Guam. The second-largest island in Palau is Urukthapel. Koror Island, containing the capital and most of the country's population, has an area of 18 square kilometers (7.1 square miles). Other islands include Eil Malk; the islands of Pelcliu and Angaur, which are low-platform reefs; and Sonsorol and Hatohobei, the two smallest islands. Kayangel is a coral atoll.

Palau is also home to the world-famous Rock Islands. The Rock Islands are a cluster of more than two hundred rounded knobs of forest-capped limestone that plunges steeply into the sea.

Coastal Features

The Palau barrier reef encircles the Palau islands, except for Angaur Island and the Kayangel atoll. The dramatic marine environment of extensive coral rock formations, caves, and reefs, and the abundance of sea life surrounding Palau make it a prime spot for snorkeling as well as for scientific research. The waters are warm year-round, and many of the islands have beautiful white sandy beaches that attract tourists and scuba divers from around the world.

6 ⊕ INLAND LAKES

There are around eighty saltwater lakes in Palau, all of which are generally very small. The lakes were formed by erosion of the limestone terrain of the islands. Some of the lakes have simple, but unique marine life. Jellyfish Lake is located on Eil Malk. This marine lake has been cut off from the ocean for millions of years. Because of this isolation, and the lack of natural predators, the jellyfish that live in the lake have evolved without the venomous sting that is associated with jellyfish that live in the open ocean.

Ngardok Lake, located near the town of Melekeok on Babelthuap Island, is the largest freshwater lake on Palau. It is about 720 meters (2362 feet) long, 180 meters (591 feet) wide, and 2.7 meters (9 feet) deep. Besides receiving water from several small rivers, it is also the largest rainwater catchment area in the country.

7 ⊕ RIVERS AND WATERFALLS

There are no major rivers in Palau, but several smaller rivers and streams run throughout the islands. Ngermeskang River and Tabecheding River are both located on Babelthuap.

Mangrove forests exist in coastal areas and the lower portions of many of the country's rivers. Swamp forests are found in low-lying areas, just inland of mangroves and above tidal areas.

8 ⊕ DESERTS

There are no desert regions in Palau.

EPD/Tom Till

This beach is part of Rock Islands National Park in Palau.

9 ⊕ FLAT AND ROLLING TERRAIN

Most of the islands are covered with rock or tropical forest; grasslands cover large areas of Babelthuap, however, where forests have been cleared.

10 ⊕ MOUNTAINS AND VOLCANOES

The highest point in Palau, Mount Ngerchelchauus, is 242 meters (794 feet) above sea level. The peak is located on the main island of Babelthuap, which, compared to the rest of the islands comprising Palau, is high and mountainous. Many of the other islands are low coral atolls.

11 ⊕ CANYONS AND CAVES

There are a great number of underwater caves and caverns throughout the reefs surrounding Palau. One of the most popular for divers is Chandelier Cave. Located underneath the island of Ngarol, this four-chamber cave has an opening that is 4.6 meters (15 feet) underwater. Divers can enter this opening, then surface into the cave's air-filled chambers to view its large stalactites.

12 ⊕ PLATEAUS AND MONOLITHS

On the eastern coast of Ngarchelong stands a series of thirty-seven stone monoliths known as Badrulchau. According to local legend, the gods placed the basalt monoliths

DID YOU KN🌐W?

Oceania refers to the islands in the region that covers the central and southern Pacific Ocean and its adjacent seas. The boundaries for the region are the Tropic of Cancer in the north and the southern tip of New Zealand. Micronesia is a division of Oceania that includes the islands east of the Philippines and north of the equator. These include the Caroline Islands (of which Palau is a part), the Marshall Islands, the Mariana Islands, and the Gilbert Islands.

here as columns for a *bai*, or meeting house. Archaeologists believe Portuguese or other native ancestors erected the stones some time between 90 and 1665 A.D.

13 🌐 MAN-MADE FEATURES

Besides the monoliths described above, there are no other significant man-made features affecting the geography of Palau.

14 🌐 FURTHER READING

Books

Brower, Kenneth. *1944-With Their Islands Around Them*. New York: Holt, Rinehart and Winston, 1974.

Dahl, Arthur L. *Review of the Protected Areas System in Oceania*. Gland, Switzerland: International Union for Conservation of Nature and Natural Resources, Commission on National Parks and Protected Areas, in collaboration with the United Nations Environment Programme, 1986.

Faulkner, Douglas. *This Living Reef*. New York: Quadrangle-New York Times Book Co., 1974.

Web Sites

"Palau: Paradise of the Pacific," *Living Edens*. http://www.pbs.org/edens/palau (accessed May 2, 2003).

United Nations Environmental Programme. http://www.unep-wcmc.org/sites/ wetlands/ngradok.htm (accessed May 2, 2003).

Panama

- **Official name:** Republic of Panama
- **Area:** 78,200 square kilometers (30,193 square miles)
- **Highest point on mainland:** Volcán Barú (3,475 meters/11,401 feet)
- **Lowest point on land:** Sea level
- **Hemispheres:** Northern and Western
- **Time zone:** 7 A.M. = noon GMT
- **Longest distances:** 772 kilometers (480 miles) from east to west; 185 kilometers (115 miles) from north to south

- **Land boundaries:** 555 kilometers (345 miles) total boundary length; Colombia 225 kilometers (140 miles); Costa Rica 330 kilometers (205 miles)
- **Coastline:** 2,490 kilometers (1547 miles)
- **Territorial sea limits:** 22 kilometers (12 nautical miles)

1 ⊕ LOCATION AND SIZE

Panama is an isthmus in Central America, a narrow strip of land that connects the larger land masses of Costa Rica and Colombia. The country lies between the Caribbean Sea and the Pacific Ocean. With a total area of about 78,200 square kilometers (30,193 square miles), the country is slightly smaller than the state of South Carolina. Panama is administratively divided into nine provinces and one territory.

2 ⊕ TERRITORIES AND DEPENDENCIES

Panama has no outside territories or dependencies.

3 ⊕ CLIMATE

Panama has a tropical climate with temperate areas at the higher elevations of 700 to 1,500 meters (2,297 to 4,921 feet). There are two seasons: a rainy "winter" from May through December, when humidity is 90 percent to 100 percent, and a drier "summer" from January through April, when the northeast trade winds arrive. Panama's average temperature is 29°C (84°F) on the coasts and 18°C (64°F) in the highlands.

Rainfall patterns are different on Panama's Caribbean and Pacific coast regions. The Caribbean coast and mountain slopes get rain throughout the year, receiving from 150 to 355 centimeters (59 to 140 inches) annually. The Pacific coast experiences a more distinct dry season and has annual rainfall of 114 to 229 centimeters (45 to 90 inches).

From year to year, Panama has considerable variation in the amount of rainfall, since the country is affected by El Niño and La Niña weather patterns. Panama is not in the path of Caribbean hurricanes.

4 ⊕ TOPOGRAPHIC REGIONS

Panama, an *S*-shaped isthmus, divides the Pacific and Atlantic Oceans. The country's narrowest point is just 48 kilometers (30 miles) across, and its widest is 185 kilometers (115 miles).

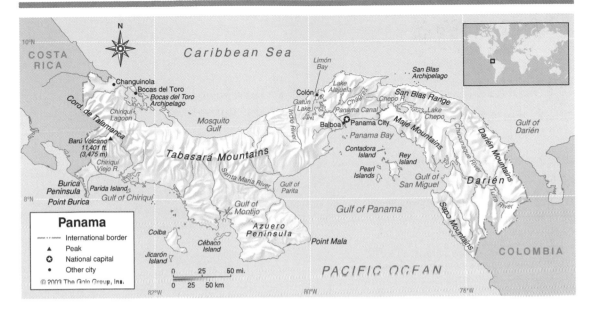

Two parallel mountain ranges traverse Panama; between the mountains are valleys and plains. The highest lands are toward the Costa Rican border; the interior of the country, where the Panama Canal is found, has the lowest elevation.

Panama is seated on the Caribbean Tectonic Plate, but just offshore there are three other plates that bump into the Caribbean Plate: the Cocos Plate to the west, the Nazca Plate to the south, and the South American Plate to the southeast. During the Miocene Epoch, these plates collided, causing the Isthmus of Panama to rise out of the ocean. As the plates kept pushing against one another, the mountain ranges and volcanoes of Panama also rose. Today, the continued interaction of the Cocos, Nazca, and Caribbean Plates causes frequent earthquakes in Panama. Its volcanoes, however, have not erupted in hundreds of years.

5 ⊕ OCEANS AND SEAS

Seacoast and Undersea Features

The Pacific Ocean lies to the south of Panama while the Caribbean Sea (an extension of the Atlantic Ocean) is to the north. Coral reefs are found along the coastlines; one notable example is the protected coral reef at Isla Bastimentos National Park of Bocas del Toro. This reef, located off the northwestern coast, serves as a nesting site for sea turtles. Panama claims the seabed of the continental shelf, which has been defined by the country to extend to the 500-meter submarine contour.

The waters of Panama's Pacific coast, especially within the Gulf of Panama and the Gulf of Chiriquí, are extremely shallow (with depths less than 180 meters/590 feet), with extensive mud flats. Because of this, the tidal range in this area is extreme. The tidal range (the difference in sea level between high and low tide) on the Pacific coast exceeds 700 centimeters (275 inches), while on the Caribbean coast it is only 70 centimeters (27 inches).

Sea Inlets and Straits

The Caribbean coastline is marked by several good natural harbors; however, Cristóbal, near the Panama Canal, is the only one with significant traffic. The major port on the Pacific is Balboa.

Sea turtles find a suitable nesting site in the waters off Bocas del Toro, Panama.

From the Costa Rica border to the west, Panama's Caribbean coastline is indented by the Chiriquí Lagoon, and then by the broad Mosquito Gulf, before curving north to the city of Colón and the port of Cristobal on Limon Bay, which is the Caribbean entrance to the Panama Canal. Past the Canal, this coast sweeps south to the Gulf of Darién (Golfo del Darién) and the border of Colombia.

On Panama's Pacific coast, the Gulf of Chiriquí lies between the southwest Point Burica on the Burica Peninsula and the Azuero Peninsula (Peninsula de Azuero). The Gulf of Panama, the largest of the country's Pacific inlets, contains Panama Bay at its apex. There, the capital, Panama City, marks the Pacific entrance to the Panama Canal. The Gulf of Panama is indented on the west by the Gulf of Parita, and on the east by the Gulf of San Miguel, where rivers flow down from the highlands of Darién.

Islands and Archipelagos

On the Caribbean side, the 366-island San Blas Archipelago stretches for more than 160 kilometers (100 miles) down the eastern Panama coast. The Bocas del Toro Archipelago extends along the west of Panama to the border of Costa Rica.

The Pacific coast has many more offshore islands than the Caribbean. Within the Gulf of Panama are the Pearl Islands, Isla Del Ray, and Contadora Island. Coiba, Panama's largest island at 271 square kilometers (104 square miles), sits in the Gulf of Chiriquí along with Jicarón Island, Cébaco Island, Parida Island, and hundreds of much smaller islands and islets.

As much as 30 percent of Panama's land is under some degree of official protection—as forest reserves, national parks, or wildlife refuges. Darién National Park is an UNESCO World Heritage Site and Biosphere Reserve extending along most of Panama's border with Colombia. The park's 5,970 square kilometers (2,305 square miles) of mountains and river basins are covered with primary and secondary tropical rainforests, dwarf and cloud forests, and wetlands. Darién National Park is home to jaguars, ocelots, giant anteaters, tapirs, howler monkeys, and many other wildlife species.

Coastal Features

The Burica Peninsula is located at the western edge of the Pacific coastline. The Azuero Peninsula juts out into the Pacific and separates the Gulf of Chiriquí from the Gulf of Panama. Point Malta is located on the southeast corner of the Azuero Peninsula.

6 🌐 INLAND LAKES

Gatún Lake, formed by damming the Chagres River, is Panama's largest lake, with an area of 418 square kilometers (161 square miles). Located in the center of Panama at 26 meters (85 feet) above sea level, Gatún Lake is an important bird habitat and includes the Barro Colorado wildlife refuge. Gatún Lake and Lake Alajuela (also known as Lake Madden) are supplied by rainwater and provide the water for the Panama Canal and the drinking water for Panama City. Lake Chepo is another large reservoir in central Panama.

7 🌐 RIVERS AND WATERFALLS

Panama has more than five hundred rivers, most of which are quite short. Rivers flowing into the Pacific include two of equal length that both are the longest rivers on the country. The Chucunaque and the Chepo are each 215 kilometers (134 miles) long. The Chepo has been dammed to produce hydroelectric power. Other rivers with Pacific outlets are the Santa Maria (168 kilometers/104 miles), Chiriquí Viejo (161 kilometers/100 miles), and the Tuira (127 kilometers/79 miles).

More than 150 rivers draining into the Caribbean, including the Chagres (125 kilometers/78 miles), Changuinola (110 kilometers/68 miles), Indio (92 kilometers/ 57 miles), and Cricamola (62 kilometers/38 miles). There is a hydroelectric dam on the Chagres, which has its source in mountain cloud forest. The Chagres waters run into Lakes Gatún and Alajuela.

8 🌐 DESERTS

There are no desert regions in Panama.

9 🌐 FLAT AND ROLLING TERRAIN

Some regions of natural savannahs exist on Panama's Pacific coast. There are also cattle ranches on the country's central plains, where most of the pastureland is located. Invasive grass species have taken hold in areas deforested by burning and in abandoned pastures.

In Panama, there are three sites that have been designated as Wetlands of International Importance under the Ramsar Convention on Wetlands. Punta Patino in Darién (where there are extensive swamps) is a private nature reserve on a coastal plain with mangroves, salt flats, and reefs; it also is a seabird habitat.

EPD/Saxifraga/Wiel Poelmans

The copper mines at Cerro Colorado may prove to be among the best in the world.

The Golfo de Montijo on the Pacific coast is a complex of coastal marshes, mangrove forests, and seasonally flooded grassland. San San-Pond Sak, in Bocas del Toro on the Costa Rican border, is a river basin complex of shallow lakes, mangrove forests, and peat bogs. It is an important bird habitat.

Hills dominate Chiriquí Province in the west, particularly in the Boquete district, where coffee is grown on the hillsides. The Azuero Peninsula and much of the country's center are hilly and are occupied by farming communities.

10 ⊕ MOUNTAINS AND VOLCANOES

A spine of mountains formed by an undersea volcanic chain divides Panama into its Pacific and Caribbean (Atlantic) regions. These two main ranges are the Serrianía de Tabasará in Panama's west and the Cordillera de San Blas in the east. A gap between them in the center of the country is where the Panama Canal was built. A third mountain system, Cordillera Talamanca on the Costa Rican border, contains Volcán Barú (formerly known as Volcán Chiriquí). It is the highest point in Panama at 3,475 meters (11,401 feet). The peak of Barú, a long-extinct volcano, has views of both the Pacific and Caribbean on clear days. In the east, there are three other smaller mountain ranges. The Majé Mountains run parallel to the Gulf of Panama shore. Entering Panama from Colombia along the Pacific and Caribbean coasts, respectively, are the Sapo Mountains and the Darien Mountains.

The tropical rainforests on the Caribbean region mountain slopes, particularly in the Darién region near Colombia, have an extremely high level of biodiversity, with species from both North and South America. In addition to the rainforests, there also are dwarf forests and cloud forests in the mountains.

11 ⊕ CANYONS AND CAVES

The rugged terrain of western Panama contains narrow river canyons. Erosion has carved gorges in Darién, the thickly forested region in the east.

Though not fully explored, the Cerro Colorado copper mine in Chiriquí Province has the potential to be one of the largest copper mines in the world. Another copper mine is located west of Panama City in Petaquilla.

12 ⊕ PLATEAUS AND MONOLITHS

The El Santuario Plateau rises 400 meters (1,212 feet) in the Boquete district of Chiriquí Province, near the border with Costa Rica.

13 ⊕ MAN-MADE FEATURES

Since its opening in 1914, the Panama Canal has been an extremely important link between the Pacific and the Atlantic Oceans. Before the canal was built, ships carrying passengers and goods between the western coasts of North and South America and Europe had to travel all the way around the coast of South America to reach their destination. French and American companies built the canal, beginning its construction in 1881. The Panama Canal route shortens a boat trip from New York to San Francisco by an incredible 7,872 miles.

The canal channel is 82 kilometers (51 miles) long, with entrances at Limón Bay on the Atlantic side and the Bay of Panama on the Pacific side. A ship entering Limón Bay is raised by a set of three locks (known as the Gatún Locks) to an elevation of 25.9 meters (85 feet) above sea level. It then crosses Gatún Lake and a stretch known as the Gaillard (formerly Culebra) Cut before reaching the Pedro Miguel Lock, which lowers the ship into Miraflores Lake. Once across Miraflores, a set of two locks (known as the Miraflores Locks) lowers the ship to sea level. On the return trip, the ship undergoes the same process in reverse. It takes about eight to ten hours for a ship to complete its passage through the canal.

A number of dams have been constructed in order to regulate the flow of water through and around the canal. The Gatún Dam on the Chagres River created Lake Gatún. The dam was built with soil and rock that was excavated as the canal was being built. The two Miraflores Dams created Miraflores Lake. One of them is an earth-fill dam. The other was made of concrete. An earth-fill dam near the Pedro Miquel Lock helps to regulate the water used in its operation.

The United States government owned and operated the canal and the area surrounding it (known as the Canal Zone) until December 31, 1999. On that date, the U.S. government turned over the entire operation to Panama.

14 ⊕ FURTHER READING

Books

Espino, Ovidio Diaz. *How Wall Street Created a Nation: J.P. Morgan, Teddy Roosevelt and the Panama Canal.* New York: Four Walls Eight Windows, 2001.

Friar, William. *Adventures in Nature: Panama.* Emeryville, CA: Avalon Travel Publishing, 2001.

Rau, Dana Meachen. *Panama.* New York: Children's Press, 1999.

Ventocilla, Jorge, et al. *Plants and Animals in the Life of the Kuna.* Austin: University of Texas Press, 1995.

Web Sites

Canal Museum Online. http://www.canalmuseum.com (accessed May 6, 2003).

Smithsonian Tropical Research Institute. http://www.stri.org (accessed May 6, 2003).

Papua New Guinea

- **Official name:** Independent State of Papua New Guinea

- **Area:** 462,840 square kilometers (178,704 square miles)

- **Highest point on mainland:** Mount Wilhelm (4,509 meters/14,793 feet)

- **Lowest point on land:** Sea level

- **Hemispheres:** Southern and Eastern

- **Time zone:** 10 P.M. = noon GMT

- **Longest distances:** 2,082 kilometers (1,294 miles) from north-northeast to south-southwest, 1,156 kilometers (718 miles) from east-southeast to west-northwest

- **Land boundaries:** 820 kilometers (510 miles) total boundary length, all with Indonesia

- **Coastline:** 5,152 kilometers (3,201 miles)

- **Territorial sea limits:** 22 kilometers (12 nautical miles)

1 ⊕ LOCATION AND SIZE

The territory of Papua New Guinea includes the eastern half of the island of New Guinea and a group of offshore islands, all located in the southwest Pacific between the Coral Sea and the South Pacific Ocean. The country shares a land border with Indonesia. With a total area of about 462,840 square kilometers (178,704 square miles), the country is slightly larger than the state of California. Papua New Guinea is divided into twenty provinces.

2 ⊕ TERRITORIES AND DEPENDENCIES

Papua New Guinea has no outside territories or dependencies.

3 ⊕ CLIMATE

Papua New Guinea is a tropical country, but it has two main seasons and two transition periods: December through March brings the northwest monsoon, April is a transition month, May through October brings the southeast monsoon, and November is a transition month. Average lowland temperatures range from 21°C to 32°C (70°F to 90°F) while the Highlands have temperatures as cold as

3°C (37°F). Lowland humidity averages 75 percent to 90 percent, and Highland humidity averages 65 percent to 80 percent.

Most of Papua New Guinea gets its rain from the northwest monsoon from December through March, but some areas, such as Lae and the Trobriand Islands, get their main rainfall from May through October. The Solomon Islands and the Louisiade Archipelago are out of the monsoon pattern, so rainfall occurs there year-round.

Port Moresby receives less than 127 centimeters (50 inches) of rain per year. Rainfall is heaviest in the island of New Guinea's western river basin region, averaging up to 584 centimeters (230 inches) a year. The average annual rainfall for all of Papua New Guinea is 203 to 254 centimeters (80 to 100 inches). Snow and ice cover the highest mountain peaks.

4 ⊕ TOPOGRAPHIC REGIONS

The island of New Guinea, the second-largest in the world (820,003 square kilometers/ 316,605 square miles), is divided in half between Papua New Guinea and the Indonesian

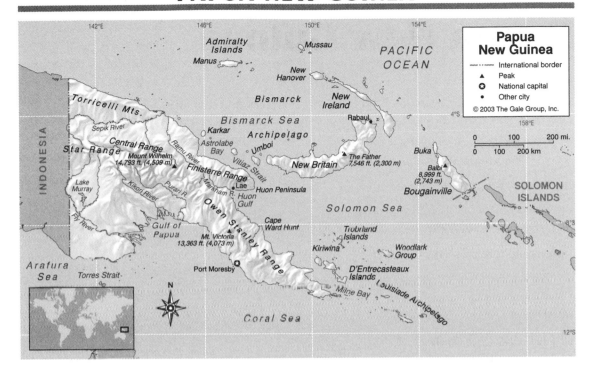

province of Papua (formerly Irian Jaya.) The border between the two is a nearly straight north-south line. The island of New Guinea was formed by the colliding Australian and Pacific Tectonic Plates. New Guinea's mountains have isolated the surrounding regions from one another, producing diversity in languages, customs, and wildlife. The mountains form chains crossing the island, with riverine plains interspersed. Hundreds of smaller volcanic and coral islands lie off the eastern shore to complete the nation of Papua New Guinea, but 85 percent of the total land area is on the island of New Guinea itself.

5 ⊕ OCEANS AND SEAS

Seacoast and Undersea Features

The seas surrounding New Guinea all belong to the Pacific Ocean. The Bismarck Sea is to the north of the main island of New Guinea and is encircled by the Bismarck Archipelago. To the east of New Guinea is the Solomon Sea, which is enclosed by New Britain, Bougainville, and the Solomon and Trobriand Islands. The Coral Sea is south of New Guinea and north of Australia.

About 40,000 square kilometers (15,444 square miles) of coral reefs, rich in marine life, lie close to the shore of New Guinea. The Ontong Java Plateau, one of the world's largest ocean lava platforms, is to the northeast of New Guinea. The Eastern and Papuan Plateaus lie beneath the Coral Sea.

Sea Inlets and Straits

The D'Entrecasteaux Islands enclose Milne Bay at the southeastern end of New Guinea. The Gulf of Papua is an inlet of the Coral Sea on Papua New Guinea's southern coast. The coast indents at Astrolabe Bay near the town of Madang. The Torres Strait separates New Guinea from the northern tip of Australia and leads to the Arafura Sea of Indonesia. The Vitiaz Strait flows between the Huon Peninsula and New Britain. The natural harbor of Port Moresby, the nation's capital, is situated on the south side of the arm of southeast New Guinea.

Islands and Archipelagos

Papua New Guinea includes more than fourteen hundred islands besides New Guinea itself. Off the north coast of New Guinea are the volcanic Manam, Karkar, Long, and Umboi Islands. To the east of New Guinea are the islands of the Bismarck Sea and Solomon Sea. A chain of volcanoes formed New Britain Island, in the western Bismarck Archipelago. New Ireland, also in the western Bismarck Archipelago, contains limestone mountains. New Hanover and Mussau are smaller islands in the same area. Further west in the Bismarck Archipelago is Manus. Manus and the surrounding coral atolls form the Admiralty Islands.

The two largest islands in Papua New Guinea are the mountainous, mineral-rich Bougainville, which is 204 kilometers (127 miles) long and 80 kilometers (50 miles) wide; and Buka, which is 56 kilometers (35 miles) long and 14 kilometers (9 miles) wide. These two land masses are part of the chain of islands known as the Solomon Islands (not to be confused with the country of that same name). There are also many small atolls near these islands.

Many of the twenty-two small islands comprising the Trobriand Group in the Solomon Sea are low coral types. They include Kaileuna, Kiriwina, Kitava, and Vakuta. Other island groups in the Solomon Sea include the D'Entrecasteaux Group, the Louisiade Archipelago, and the Woodlark Group.

Coastal Features

The northern coast of Papua New Guinea slopes to the southeast from the Indonesian border along Cape Moem and the outlets of the Sepik and Ramu Rivers. In the southeast, the Huon Peninsula protrudes above the Huon Gulf, an indentation of the Solomon Sea. Cape Ward Hunt extends southeast from the Huon Gulf, leading into the long arm of southeast New Guinea, formed by the Owen Stanley Range.

6 ⊕ INLAND LAKES

The largest lake in the country is Lake Murray. It is a 647-square-kilometer (250-square-mile) freshwater lake that connects with the Strickland River in western New Guinea. The lake and river both are badly polluted with chemicals from nearby mining operations. Lake Kutubu, in the southern Highlands, has been designated a Wetland of International Importance under the Ramsar Convention on Wetlands. The 49-square-kilometer (19-square-mile) site includes the pristine lake and adjacent swamp forest. The lake contains ten unique fish species.

The Muruk Lakes are a group of freshwater lakes and saltwater lagoons in the Sepik River region with mangrove forests around them. Also in the Sepik region are the Blackwater Lakes and the Chambri Lakes, a 216-square-kilometer (83-square-mile) system of linked shallow lakes and swamps.

7 ⊕ RIVERS AND WATERFALLS

The Fly, Purari, and Kikori Rivers all flow southward into the Gulf of Papua. The Sepik, Markham, and Ramu Rivers flow northward into the Pacific. The Fly River and Sepik River are crucial transportation routes. Rising in the Star Mountains, the twisting Fly River is navigable for 805 kilometers (500

The Sepik River is one of Papua New Guinea's most important transportation routes.

miles). It is 80 kilometers (50 miles) wide at its entry to the Gulf of Papua. The Fly forms a 1,200-kilometer-long (746-mile-long) river system with the Ok Tedi and Strickland Rivers, creating the largest river network in the country. The Sepik River, which is 1,126 kilometers (698 miles) long, has its source in the Victor Emmanuel Mountains. It is wide and navigable throughout its entire length and has no real delta.

Savannahs, mixed with scrub woods and swamps, stretch from the Fly and Sepik Rivers into Indonesian Papua. These coastal grasslands flood during the rainy season.

8 ⊕ DESERTS

There are no desert regions in Papua New Guinea.

9 ⊕ FLAT AND ROLLING TERRAIN

Tonda Wildlife Management Area is also a Ramsar Wetland of International Importance. It is located near the Indonesian Papua border and covers an area of about 5,900 square kilometers (2,278 square miles). The site includes coastal plains that flood seasonally as well as grasslands and mangroves, all of which are waterbird habitat.

Tropical rainforest covers as much as 77 percent of Papua New Guinea. These forests are a wealth of biodiversity. Papua New Guinea has an estimated 11,000 plant species, 250 mammal species, and 700 bird species.

The steep mountains of the Highlands have very few foothills. Hill areas of the island of New Guinea include the upper Sepik region and the countryside surrounding Port Moresby.

EPD/Cynthia Bassett

A view from the Highlands of Papua New Guinea.

The valleys in the central Highlands have grasslands that were produced by burning forests to clear land for agriculture. Alpine grasslands exist at elevations above 3,353 meters (11,000 feet), where there is a moist, cool climate.

10 ⊕ MOUNTAINS AND VOLCANOES

The island of New Guinea is rugged, with many high peaks. At the center of the island are the Highlands, which include the Bismarck Range. Papua New Guinea's highest peak, Mount Wilhelm (4,509 meters/14,793 feet), is in the Bismarck Range. The second-highest summit, also in the central mountain complex, is Mount Giluwe, an extinct volcano at an elevation of 4,367 meters (14,327 feet). Another major mountain range, the Owen Stanley, is found in the southeast. The highest peak there is Mount Victoria (4,073 meters/13,363 feet). The Finisterre, Sarawat, and Rawlinson ranges line the northeast coast. They are made of coral limestone and extend into New Guinea from the sea. In the west of New Guinea, near the Indonesian Papua border, the Star, Hindenburg, and Victor Emmanuel ranges also are made of limestone.

Many of the islands in Papua New Guinea are volcanic in origin, with rugged terrain and peaks above 1,524 meters (5,000 feet). The Father, on New Britain, rises to 2,300 meters (7,546 feet), but the tallest peak on the outer islands is Balbi (2,743 meters/8,999 feet), located on Bougainville.

Most of the active volcanoes are on the southeastern arm of New Guinea, the large island of New Britain, and other islands.

DID YOU KN🌐W?

The Ok Tedi mine is a major producer of copper concentrate for the world smelting market. It is located on Mount Fubilan in the Star Mountains of western New Guinea. An average of 80,000 metric tons of material are mined each day. In 2001, Ok Tedi Mining Limited exported 694,900 dry metric tons of copper concentrate. This mixture contained 203,762 tons of copper, 455,222 ounces of gold, and 1,150,031 ounces of silver. At this rate of production, the mine will be depleted of its resources by 2010.

11 ⊕ CANYONS AND CAVES

Numerous canyons, gorges, and ravines slice through the rugged mountain terrain of New Guinea. The upper Fly River has many deep gorges. The region between the northeastern coastal mountains and the central Highlands, where the Sepik and Markham Rivers and their tributaries flow, is known as the Central Depression.

In the west of New Guinea, the Star, Hindenburg, and Victor Emmanuel ranges contain many deep limestone caves.

12 ⊕ PLATEAUS AND MONOLITHS

The Great Papuan Plateau is in the central mountains, rising 1,500 to 2,000 meters (4,921 to 6,562 feet) above sea level. It is a limestone formation, with many caves and petroleum deposits. The Oriomo Plateau rises in the west. Nine rivers run through it from east to west into Indonesian Papua. Tabubil Plateau, also in the west, is the site of the enormous Ok Tedi copper and gold mine. Sogeri Plateau, on the outskirts of Port Moresby, is 800 meters (2,625 feet) in elevation and is home to many bird species.

13 ⊕ MAN-MADE FEATURES

There are no significant man-made structures affecting the geography of Papua New Guinea.

14 ⊕ FURTHER READING

Books and Periodicals

Fox, Mary. *Papua New Guinea*. Chicago: Children's Press, 1994.

Salak, Kira. *Four Corners: Into the Heart of New Guinea*. New York: Counterpoint Press, 2001.

Sillitoe, Paul. *A Place Against Time: Land and Environment in the Papua New Guinea Highlands*. New York: Routledge, 1996.

Theroux, Paul. "The Spell of the Trobriand Islands." *National Geographic*, July 1992, 117-136.

Web Sites

Papua New Guinea Eco-Forestry Forum. http://www.ecoforestry.org.pg (accessed April 10, 2003).

Wantoks Communications, Limited: Papua New Guinea. http://www.niugini.com (accessed April 10, 2003).

Paraguay

- **Official name:** Republic of Paraguay
- **Area:** 406,750 square kilometers (157,047 square miles)
- **Highest point on mainland:** Cerro Pero (842 meters/2,762 feet)
- **Lowest point on land:** Junction of Paraguay River and Paraná River (46 meters/151 feet)
- **Hemispheres:** Southern and Western
- **Time zone:** 8 A.M. = noon GMT

- **Longest distances:** 491 kilometers (305 miles) from east-northeast to west-southwest; 992 kilometers (616 miles) from north-northwest to south-southeast
- **Land boundaries:** 3,920 kilometers (2,436 miles) total boundary length; Argentina 1,880 kilometers (1,168 miles); Bolivia 750 kilometers (466 miles); Brazil 1,290 kilometers (802 miles)
- **Coastline:** None
- **Territorial sea limits:** None

1 ⊕ LOCATION AND SIZE

Located in the south-central interior of South America and bisected laterally by the Tropic of Capricorn, Paraguay is separated from Argentina on the west by the Pilcomayo and Paraguay Rivers and on the south by the Alto Paraná River. On the east, it is separated from Argentina and Brazil by the higher reaches of the Alto Paraná. On the north and northwest, its border with Bolivia is marked by small streams and by surveyed boundary lines. Paraguay is seventh in size among the South American nations and one of only two land-locked countries on the continent (the other is Bolivia). With an area of 406,750 square kilometers (157,047 square miles), Paraguay is almost as large as the state of California.

2 ⊕ TERRITORIES AND DEPENDENCIES

Paraguay has no territories or dependencies.

3 ⊕ CLIMATE

Most of the Eastern Paraguay region lies south of the Tropic of Capricorn and thus has a subtropical climate. The Chaco region to the west, which lies mostly between the Tropic of Cancer and the Tropic of Capricorn, has a tropical climate. There are basically two seasons: summer (October through March) and winter (May through August), with April and September serving as transitional months. Average summer temperatures range from about 25°C (77°F) to 38°C (100°F). Summer highs in the east usually do not rise much above 32°C (90°F), whereas highs in the west can top 43°C (109°F). Average winter temperatures are usually between about 16°C (60°F) and 21°C (70°F). Rainfall is heaviest on the Paraná Plateau in the east, where it averages over 152 centimeters (60 inches) annually, decreasing to about 127 centimeters (50 inches) in the lowlands east of the Paraguay River, and about 76 centimeters (30 inches) in the Chaco region west of the river. Most of the rain falls in the summer months, but rainfall is generally irregular.

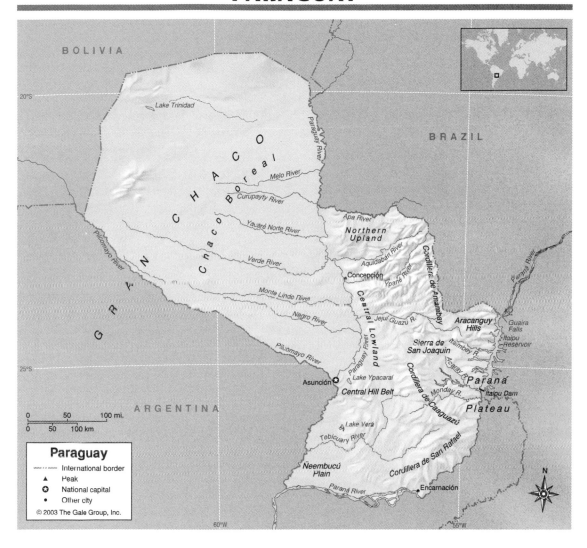

4 ⊕ TOPOGRAPHIC REGIONS

Flowing south from Brazil, the Paraguay River divides the country into two contrasting regions. The three-fifths of Paraguay north and west of the river is the Chaco, a hot, flat, semiarid plain with little vegetation and few inhabitants. The two-fifths of the country to the south and east is called Eastern Paraguay, sometimes referred to as Paraguay Proper. Its lush and diverse landscape is home to nearly the entire population of the country. The east-ernmost part of this region forms the western end of the Paraná Plateau, which also extends into Brazil and Argentina.

5 ⊕ OCEANS AND SEAS

Paraguay is landlocked.

6 ⊕ INLAND LAKES

The largest freshwater lakes are the shallow Lake Ypacaraí in the Central Hill Belt and Lake Ypoá on the Ñeembucú Plain.

AP Photo/Walter Astrada

A man carries a cayman (type of South American crocodile) in a field near a lagoon northeast of Asuncion. Thousands of caymans in the area are threatened because the small lakes are drying up due to drought and the rerouting of water from the Pilcomayo River for crop irrigation.

The cayman is a type of crocodile native to Central and South America. Thousands of caymans in Paraguay are threatened because the small lakes are drying up. The lake and lagoon habitats of the caymans began to dry up when water from the Pilcomayo River was rerouted so that farmers could use it to irrigate their crops. The government is experimenting with a program to move the caymans to another location.

7 ⊕ RIVERS AND WATERFALLS

The Paraguay and Alto Paraná Rivers and their tributaries define most of the country's frontiers.

Rising in the Mato Grosso of Brazil, the Paraguay River borders or passes through the country along a southward course of about 1,128 kilometers (700 miles). The Paraná River flows some 804 kilometers (500 miles) from the Brazilian frontier at the Guaira Falls, where it becomes known as the Alto Paraná River, to its juncture with the Paraguay River. The third-largest river, the Pilcomayo, is a tributary of the Paraguay and enters it near Asunción after following the entire length of the frontier between the Chaco and Argentina. The Verde and Monte Lindo Rivers also enter the Paraguay River from the Chaco. Major tributaries of the Paraguay River entering it from Eastern Paraguay include the Apa, Ypané, and Jejuí-Guazú. Some sixteen rivers—including Acaray, Monday, and Itaimbey—enter the Alto Paraná above Encarnación.

8 ⊕ DESERTS

Paraguay has no deserts.

9 ⊕ FLAT AND ROLLING TERRAIN

Between the two westward extensions of the Paraná Plateau lies the Central Lowland, which slopes gently upward toward the plateau and is covered largely with savannah. Its most conspicuous features are flat-topped, forested hills projecting 6 to 9 meters (20 to 30 feet) above the grassy plain and covering areas ranging from a few acres to several square miles. They are called *islas de monte* (mountain islands).

The Chaco region is part of the South American Gran Chaco, which extends from Argentina to the fringes of Bolivia and Brazil. Its eastern border is the Paraguay River and its southwestern edge is the Pilcomayo River. Except for low hills in the northeast, the featureless landscape is virtually flat, broken by intermittent rivers and streams and by extensive swamps in the south. In the southwestern part of Paraguay's eastern region lies the Ñeembucú Plain, an alluvial flatland bisected by the Tebicuary River.

10 ⊕ MOUNTAINS AND VOLCANOES

The mountains of the Paraná Plateau include the Cordillera de Amambay, which extends southward from Brazil along the border with Paraguay, and, to the southeast, the Cordillera de San Rafael, which contains the country's highest peak.

11 ⊕ CANYONS AND CAVES

The pre-Columbian caves in the Cerro Corá National Park are among the country's major historical and natural attractions.

12 ⊕ PLATEAUS AND MONOLITHS

The heavily wooded Paraná Plateau occupies one-third of Eastern Paraguay. At its western edge is an escarpment that descends from an altitude of about 457 meters (1,500 feet) in

---

DID YOU KN⊕W?

The prairies and swamps of Paraguay's Chaco region, while nearly uninhabited by humans, provide a habitat for a diverse array of wildlife, including such unusual species as anteaters, armadillos, tapirs, peccaries, and the capybara, the world's largest rodent, which can grow to a length of over 1 meter (4 feet).

---

the north to about 183 meters (600 feet) at its southern extremity. Eroded extensions of the Paraná Plateau further divide Eastern Paraguay into sub-regions.

13 ⊕ MAN-MADE FEATURES

The Itaipu Dam, located on Paraguay's border with Brazil, supplies more than three-fourths of Paraguay's electrical power. Built jointly with Brazil and completed in the 1980s, it is the largest hydroelectric generation facility ever built. It is 196 meters (643 feet) high and 7.8 kilometers (4.8 miles) long.

14 ⊕ FURTHER READING

Books and Periodicals

Argentina, Uruguay and Paraguay. Berkeley, CA: Lonely Planet, 2003.

Jacobs, Mark. *The Liberation of Little Heaven and Other Stories*. New York: Soho Press, 1999.

"Public Saves Park." *American Forests*: 106 (winter 2001): 12.

Web Sites

Paraguay. Lonely Planet World Guide. http://www.lonelyplanet.com/destinations/south_america/paraguay/ (accessed March 25, 2003).

Paraguay.com. http://www.paraguay.com/ (accessed March 12, 2003).

Peru

- **Official name:** Republic of Peru
- **Area:** 1,285,220 square kilometers (496,226 square miles)
- **Highest point on mainland:** Nevado Huascarán (6,768 meters/22,205 feet)
- **Lowest point on land:** Sea level
- **Hemispheres:** Southern and Western
- **Time zone:** 7 A.M. = noon GMT
- **Longest distances:** 1,287 kilometers (800 miles) from southeast to northwest; 563 kilometers (350 miles) from northeast to southwest

- **Land boundaries:** 5,536 kilometers (3,440 miles) total boundary length; Bolivia 900 kilometers (559 miles); Brazil 1,560 kilometers (969 miles); Chile 160 kilometers (99 miles); Colombia 1,496 kilometers (930 miles); Ecuador 1,420 kilometers (882 miles)
- **Coastline:** 2,414 kilometers (1,500 miles)
- **Territorial sea limits:** 370 kilometers (200 nautical miles)

1 ⊕ LOCATION AND SIZE

Peru is located on the western coast of South America, just south of the equator. It is the third-largest country in South America and shares borders with Ecuador, Colombia, Brazil, Bolivia, and Chile. With a total area of about 1,285,220 square kilometers (496,226 square miles), the country is slightly smaller than the state of Alaska. Peru is divided into twenty-four departments and one constitutional province.

2 ⊕ TERRITORIES AND DEPENDENCIES

Peru has no territories or dependencies.

3 ⊕ CLIMATE

Peru has two seasons that correspond to rainfall rather than to temperature. Summer is from January through March and winter is during the remainder of the year. Because of extremes in topography, average temperatures vary greatly between regions.

In the La Sierra region, temperatures average 8°C (47°F) all year. To the east in the *montaña* forests, the temperature is warmer but still fairly moderate. To the south, in La Selva and the jungles of the Amazon Basin, temperatures average 20°C (68°F) and can soar as high as 35°C (95°F) during the hottest months. The Coast (La Costa) is also warm all year, averaging 20°C (68°F). Despite being a desert area, these relatively moderate temperatures are credited to nearly constant cold air movement. The Peru (Humboldt) Current is a wind blowing from the very cold waters, located in the Peru-Chile Trench of the Pacific Ocean, toward the equator.

In addition to the chilly Peru Current, Peru is affected by a second weather phenomenon: El Niño. Every four to ten years, El Niño presents the strongest climate-changing phenomenon on Earth. El Niño is a warm current originating from the central Pacific Ocean along the coasts of Peru and Ecuador that, among other effects,

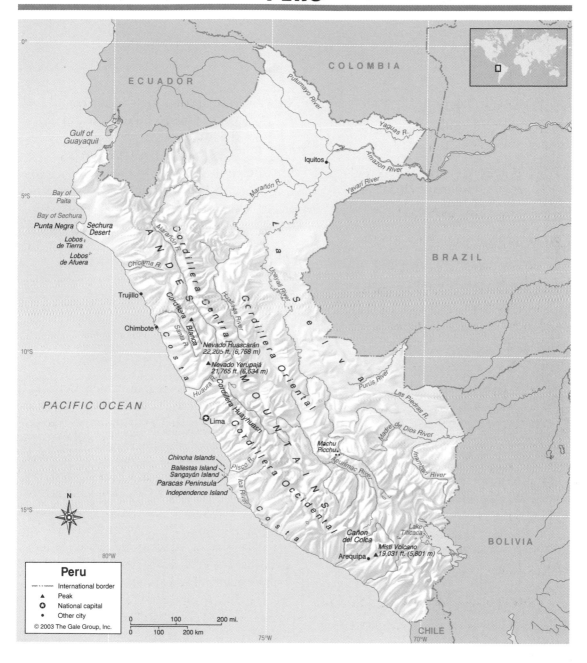

brings flooding rains and unusually warm temperatures to Peru. Peruvian fishermen chose the name El Niño, which refers to the infant Christ, because the weather system begins near Christmas. El Niño has strong worldwide effects on climate, as well as on fishing, agriculture, and animal and plant life.

Most rain and moisture originates from trade winds to the east, blowing across the Amazon Basin. Because the mountains trap nearly all the rains, the coastal plain is relatively dry year-round, averaging less than 2.5 centimeters (one inch) of annual rainfall in Lima. During the winter season, however, a nearly constant mist, the *garua*, shrouds the coast. In extreme contrast, the eastern forests receive an average annual rainfall of 245 centimeters (100 inches); in some years, these areas are inundated with up to 350 centimeters (140 inches).

4 ⊕ TOPOGRAPHIC REGIONS

Peru is a country of geographic extremes. Consider, for example, that two canyons in Peru are each twice as deep as the Grand Canyon in the United States. Peru also has the highest navigable lake in the world and has some of the world's highest and most spectacular mountains. Off the Pacific Ocean shoreline is a trench as deep as the Andes Mountains are high, and the driest desert on earth is located in Peru.

Peru has three major topographic regions running from north to south: La Costa, La Sierra, and La Selva. La Costa, bordering the Pacific Ocean, is a 2,414-kilometer- (1,500-mile-) long desert; it is only 16 kilometers (10 miles) wide at one point, but it widens to about 160 kilometers (100 miles) in both the north and the south. La Sierra is the Peruvian portion of the Andes, a vast mountain range crossing Peru and parts of Bolivia, Chile, and Ecuador. La Selva covers roughly 60 percent of Peru. It is the rainforest region of the Amazon Basin, between the mountains of La Sierra and the eastern foothills.

Peru has occasional volcanic activity and earthquakes from the effect of the offshore Nazca Tectonic Plate moving under the South American Plate, on which Peru sits.

5 ⊕ OCEANS AND SEAS
Seacoast and Undersea Features

The western border of Peru is the Pacific Ocean. Offshore, the ocean floor drops quickly into the Peru-Chile Trench, a trench that is 1,770 kilometers (1,100 miles) long and averages a depth of 5,000 meters (16,400 feet), as deep as the Andes Mountains are tall. Cold water rising in the underwater trench generates the chilly coastal winds named the Peru Current.

Sea Inlets and Straits

A section of the north coast near Ecuador has two inlets: Bahía de Paita (Paita Bay) and the larger Bahía de Sechura (Sechura Bay).

Islands and Archipelagos

The Islas de los Uros, in the Peruvian part of Lake Titicaca, may be the most unique inhabited islands in South America. The Uros are made of reeds that float; consequently, they are also called Islas Flotantes. The largest islands in the group are Toranipata, Huaca Huacani, and Santa Maria. Lake Titicaca also surrounds more than thirty normal islands on each side of the Peru/Bolivia border. On the Peruvian side, two important islands, both to the east of Islas de los Uros, are Isla Taquile and Isla Amantani; the latter contains Inca ruins. A third, Isla Esteves, is connected to the mainland town of Puno by a causeway.

Because the ocean floor is so steep, few islands appear off the Pacific coast of Peru, and those that do are relatively small. Starting from the north, a few kilometers from the shore of the Sechura Desert, are Isla Lobos de Tierra and Islas Lobos de Afuera, the latter of which actually is composed of two tiny islands. Much further south, near the mouth of the Pisco River within Reserva Nacional

EPD/Wilko Gijsbertsen

The Urubamba River flows through El Valle Sagrado.

de Paracas, are several islands notable for the rare sea animals and birds that live there, including the most northern habitat of penguins. From north to south they are the Chincha Islands, Islas Ballestas, Islas de Sangayán, and Isla de la Independencia.

Coastal Features

The coastline is somewhat featureless, with few ports, bays, or dramatic points. The Pacific coast begins at the border with Ecuador in the Gulf of Guayaquil. Punta Negra on the northern coast separates Bahía de Paita and Bahía de Sechura. Further south, the Paracas Peninsula juts out below Lima near the town of Pisco.

6 ⊕ INLAND LAKES

Dozens of small lakes filled by milky-blue glacial water speckle the Peruvian Andes. One notably large lake, Lake Titicaca, is by far the largest lake in the country. At 3,856 meters (12,650 feet) above sea level, Titicaca is the world's highest navigable lake. It is situated in the mountains, in Peru's southeastern corner on the border with Bolivia. The lake is nearly equally shared between the two countries. Titicaca is 220 kilometers (136 miles) long and 60 kilometers (37 miles) at its widest. Its surface covers a total area of 8,320 square kilometers (3,212 square miles) and its maximum depth is 360 meters (1,181 feet).

In 1998, the especially severe El Niño created Peru's newest lake. It is located in the northern desert district of Piura and was formed from rainfall and drainage off the western mountains. It has become the second-largest lake in Peru, but it has not yet been named. Experts expect the lake will dry out in a few years unless another El Niño occurs.

7 ⊕ RIVERS AND WATERFALLS

About sixty rivers flow generally westward through the coastal plains to empty into the Pacific. They are relatively short and low-volume. The rivers swell during the few rainy months, then diminish or even dry up during the arid season. Rio Santa is an exception. It is larger in volume than the other rivers flowing into the Pacific and flows mostly from north to south for 160 kilometers (100 miles). Other rivers that empty into the Pacific include the Chicama, the Huaura, the Pisco, and the Ica Rivers.

Scores of rivers flow eastward into the Amazon Basin. Because of heavy rainfall, these rivers carry a tremendous volume of water. Many of these rivers are tributaries that create the Amazon. The Amazon is the second-longest river in the world with a total length of about 6,570 kilometers (4,080 miles). In 2000, a National Geographic

EPD/Wilko Gijsbertsen

Southwest Peru, near the Cañon del Colca.
The region provides habitat for the large bird, the Andean condor.

expedition established the precise source of the Amazon to be a stream running from Nevado Mismi, an 5,597-meter (18,363-foot) mountain in the Cordillera del Chila of the central-south Andes. It is the farthest point from which water flows year-round into the Amazon. Less than one-tenth, or a total of 592 kilometers (368 miles), of the Amazon flows through Peru, however. The river flows through Colombia and Brazil before reaching the Atlantic Ocean. It has eighteen major tributaries, including ten that are larger than the Mississippi River. The river is also known as having the world's largest flow of water, emptying about 80 million gallons of water per second into the Atlantic Ocean. The Amazon Basin is home to the world's largest tropical rainforest area.

Major northeastern Peruvian rivers that contribute to the Amazon include the Marañón, the Ucayali, and the Yavarí. The Marañón flows northeast from the Andes and the Ucayali flows north from central Peru; both tributaries join the Amazon in the northeast. The Marañón has many tributaries of its own, including the Napo, Mantaro, Huallaga, Tigre, and Pastaza. Rivers that feed into the Ucayali include the Urubamba and the Apurímac. The Urubamba River flows through El Valle Sagrado (The Sacred Valley), beside and below the ancient city of Machu Picchu. The Yavarí River flows somewhat parallel and to the east of the Urubamba and makes up most of Peru's border with Brazil. The Putumayo River, which forms the border with Colombia, later joins the Amazon in Brazil.

In southeastern Peru, there are several important rivers. The Purús, Río de las Piedras, Madre de Dios, and Inambari drain the region north of Lake Titicaca. They all flow northeast and join the Amazon thousands of miles later, in Brazil.

DID YOU KN⊕W?

The Nazca lines, created by the ancient Nazca people of southern Peru, continue to mystify archaeologists. The elegant lines are really a series of over three hundred pictures or drawings of animal and plant figures (called biomorphs) and geometric figures (also called geoglyphs) that were created in the desert plains on the southern coast of Peru, about 400 kilometers south of Lima. Since the lines of the pictures extend for hundreds of meters, the images are only completely recognizable from the air; because of this, they were not discovered until the 1920s as airplanes began to fly over the area. The Nazca people created the lines by moving aside the dark stones of the desert to reveal the lighter-colored sands beneath.

Since the climate there is very dry and relatively windless, the pictures have remained for centuries. Archaeologists have not yet agreed on why the Nazca people drew the pictures. One theory indicates that the images were created as part of rituals involving the worship of sky gods and ancient astronomy or astrology practices.

Besides various estuaries, one remote large wetland in the northeast Selva region is especially interesting. Reserva Pacaya Samiria (20,800 square kilometers/8,031 square miles) is a complex expanse of alluvial terraces and floodplains covered by tropical rainforest. It contains two river basins, permanent freshwater lakes, and seasonally flooded, forested wetlands.

8 ⊕ DESERTS

The western side of Peru, bordering the Pacific Ocean, is desert. One particularly inaccessible area in the far northwest is the Sechura Desert. This desert consists of shifting sand dunes and borax lakes. It is a national reserve area.

The driest area anywhere on Earth is at Peru's far south near the Chilean border. This region marks the beginning of the Atacama Desert, an area that virtually never receives rain and is measurably drier than the Sahara Desert.

9 ⊕ FLAT AND ROLLING TERRAIN

Some of the world's most spectacular forests are in Peru. An enormous band of tropical cloud forests (*montaña*) form a natural border between the Andes and the Amazon Basin to the east. Starting at about 2,500 meters (8,200 feet) and below, the mountain vegetation changes from grasses to bushes, shrubs, and then trees. This transition in vegetation is sharply noticeable, hence the Spanish name for it: *ceja de la montaña* (eyebrow of the forest). Further east and south, toward Brazil, is La Selva, the lowland forest and rainforest region of Peru. Over some areas of this region, the forest is so dense that access to it exists only along the rivers.

10 ⊕ MOUNTAINS AND VOLCANOES

The Andes Mountains (Cordillera de los Andes) is the world's longest continuous mountain chain. At about 8,045 kilometers (5,000 miles) long, it stretches down the entire western coast of South America, from Venezuela to the Tierra del Fuego of Argentina. The Andes is the second-highest mountain range in the world, with some peaks rising more than 6,096 meters (20,000 feet).

Covering the greater part of the country, the Andes Mountains in Peru are subdivided into three main parallel ranges. From west to east, they are the Cordillera Occidental, the Cordillera Central, and the Cordillera Oriental. The Cordillera Occidental is further divided into the adjacent Cordillera Blanca and Cordillera Huayhuash. Nevado Huascarán, Peru's highest mountain, towering to 6,768 meters (22,205 feet), is in the Cordillera Blanca about 97 kilometers (60 miles) inland from the coastal city of Chimbote. The Cordillera Huayhuash is lower but includes Nevada Yerupajá at 6,634 meters (21,765 feet) and Cerro Jyamy at 5,197 meters (17,050 feet). In the south are two of the highest volcanoes in the world: Volcán Misti, which rises to 5,801 meters (19,031 feet) at the edge of Arequipa, and the slightly shorter Volcán Yucamani, which reaches 5,444 meters (17,860 feet).

11 ⊕ CANYONS AND CAVES

Cañon del Colca (Colca Canyon), in southwest Peru, is 3,182 meters (10,607 feet) deep, twice as deep as the United States' Grand Canyon. Unlike the Grand Canyon, however, parts of Colca Canyon are inhabited. The canyon attracts visitors who not only want to view the magnificent canyon itself, but also wish to watch the Andean condors, which hunt and nest in the canyon. Only recently has the canyon been fully traversed. Nearby Cañon del Cotahuasi is less explored. Some observers think that Cotahuasi is deeper than Colca, and ultimately may prove to be the world's deepest canyon.

12 ⊕ PLATEAUS AND MONOLITHS

The Altiplano (meaning "high plain") is a high plateau within the Andes that is shared by Peru and Bolivia. Lake Titicaca is located here. The high level plain is densely populated. Open land is used mainly as pasture for sheep, goats, alpacas, and llamas. The Mato Grosso plateau extends from Brazil into southeast Peru and northwest Bolivia. This is a sparsely populated area of forests and grasslands.

13 ⊕ MAN-MADE FEATURES

Peru's Valley of the Pyramids, or the Pyramids of Tucume, is the most significant artificial geographic feature. The Valley of the Pyramids is located between the cities of Chiclayo and Trujillo. Twenty-six step-type pyramids, built sometime before 1,100 A.D., serve as tombs for ancient Peruvians. One pyramid honors the Lord of Sipan, believed to have been a revered leader of the Moche people, who were prominent from about 3 A.D. to 700 A.D. Archaeologists have discovered artifacts of gold, silver, copper, and semi-precious stones in his tomb, as well as several sets of human remains. Scientists speculate these remains were unfortunate subjects of the king, who may have been entombed alive at the time the pyramid was closed for the king's burial.

14 ⊕ FURTHER READING

Books

Barrett, Pam. *Insight Guide: Peru.* London: Geocenter International, 2003.

Pearson, David, and Beletsky, Les D. *Peru: The Ecotravellers' Wildlife Guide.* Burlington, MA: Academic Press, 2000.

Landau, Elaine. *Peru.* New York: Children's Press, 2000.

Lyle, Gary. *Peru.* Broomall, PA: Chelsea House, 1998.

Wright, Ruth M, and Alfredo Valencia Zegarra. *The Machu Picchu Guidebook: A Self-Guided Tour.* Boulder, CO: Johnson Books, 2001.

Web Sites

Virtual Peru. http://www.virtualperu.net (accessed April 3, 2003).

The Philippines

- **Official name:** Republic of the Philippines
- **Area:** 300,000 square kilometers (115,800 square miles)
- **Highest point on mainland:** Mount Apo (2,954 meters/9,692 feet)
- **Lowest point on land:** Sea level
- **Hemispheres:** Northern and Eastern
- **Time zone:** 8 P.M. = noon GMT
- **Longest distances:** 1,851 kilometers (1,150 miles) from south-southeast to north-northwest, 1,062 kilometers (660 miles) from east-northeast to west-southwest

- **Land boundaries:** None
- **Coastline:** 36,289 kilometers (22,499 miles)
- **Territorial sea limits:** Determined by treaty and irregular in shape, extending up to 185 kilometers (100 nautical miles) from shore in some locations

1 ⊕ LOCATION AND SIZE

The Philippines is an archipelago in southeastern Asia, located between the South China Sea and the Pacific Ocean. With an area of about 300,000 square kilometers (115,800 square miles), the country is slightly larger than the state of Arizona. The Philippines is divided into seventy-three provinces.

2 ⊕ TERRITORIES AND DEPENDENCIES

The Philippines has no outside territories or dependencies.

3 ⊕ CLIMATE

The Philippines has a tropical maritime climate with two seasons. From November through April, the northeast monsoon brings rain, and from May through October, the southwest monsoon brings cool, dry weather. The average temperature is 27°C (80°F) with a range between 23°C and 32°C (73°F and 90°F). Humidity averages 77 percent.

The annual average rainfall varies from 96 to 406 centimeters (38 to 106 inches). The northern islands are often heavily affected by seasonal typhoons, which cause destructive winds and flooding rains.

4 ⊕ TOPOGRAPHIC REGIONS

The very complex and volcanic origin of most of the Philippine islands is visible in their varied and rugged terrain. A number of the volcanoes are still active. Mountain ranges divide most of the island surfaces into narrow coastal strips and low-lying interior plains or valleys. The islands are subject to flooding and destructive earthquakes.

5 ⊕ OCEANS AND SEAS

Seacoast and Undersea Features

All of the waters surrounding the Philippines are branches of the Pacific Ocean. The eastern coast of the Philippines faces the Philippine Sea, where the Philippine Trough (Emden Deep) plunges to 10,430 meters (34,219 feet).

THE PHILIPPINES

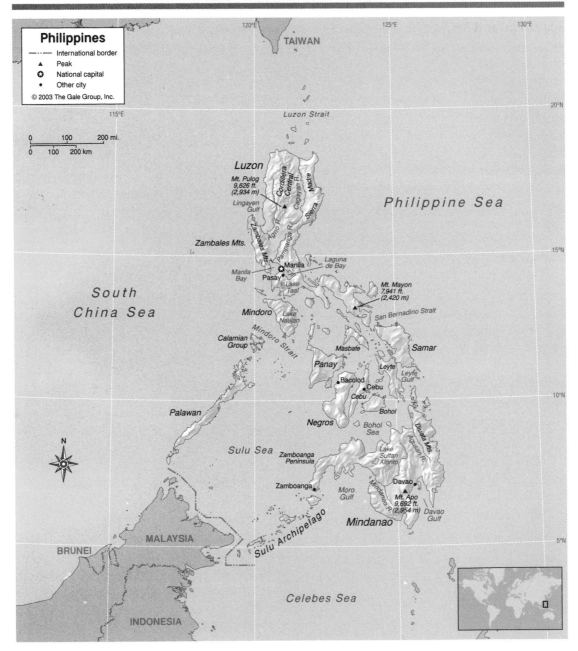

Philippines

- - - - International border
▲ Peak
✪ National capital
• Other city

© 2003 The Gale Group, Inc.

TAIWAN

Luzon Strait

Luzon

Mt. Pulog
9,626 ft.
(2,934 m)

*Lingayen
Gulf*

*Cordillera
Central*

Cagayan R.

*Sierra
Madre*

Philippine Sea

Zambales Mts.

Zambales Mts.

Agno R.

Pampanga R.

*South
China Sea*

Manila
*Manila
Bay*

Pasay

*Laguna
de Bay*

*Lake
Taal*

Mt. Mayon
7,941 ft.
(2,420 m)

San Bernadino Strait

Mindoro

*Lake
Naujan*

*Calamian
Group*

Mindoro Strait

Masbate

Samar

Panay

Leyte

*Leyte
Gulf*

Bacolod

Cebu

Cebu

Bohol

Palawan

Negros

*Bohol
Sea*

Sulu Sea

*Zamboanga
Peninsula*

*Lake
Sultan
Alonto*

Diuata Mts.

Agusan R.

Zamboanga

*Moro
Gulf*

Mindanao R.

Davao

Mt. Apo
9,692 ft.
(2,954 m)

*Davao
Gulf*

Sulu Archipelago

Mindanao

MALAYSIA

BRUNEI

Celebes Sea

INDONESIA

The northwest coast faces the South China Sea. The southwest surrounds the Sulu Sea on three sides. The Celebes (Sulawesi) Sea is in the south, between the island of Mindanao and the Indonesian island of Sulawesi. The Bohol Sea is to the north of Mindanao. The Visayan Sea is encircled by Panay, Masbate, Cebu, Negros, and other islands. The Sibuyan Sea meets southern Luzon and eastern Mindoro. The Camotes Sea lies between Cebu, Leyte, and Bohol. The Samar Sea is between Samar and Masbate.

Sea Inlets and Straits

There are countless straits between the Philippine islands. Principal among them are the San Bernadino Strait and Verde Island Passage, both of which permit ocean travel across the northern part of the archipelago. The Surigao Strait allows travel between the Pacific and the Bohol Sea in the south. The Mindoro Strait lies between Mindoro and the Calamian Group of islands. A number of channels north of the country make up the Luzon Strait, separating that island from Taiwan.

Islands and Archipelagos

The Philippine Archipelago contains about 7,100 islands and extends over 1,609 kilometers (1,000 miles) from north to south. Only 154 of the islands exceed 13 square kilometers (5 square miles) in area. The two largest islands, Luzon in the north and Mindanao in the south, comprise about 65 percent of the total land area of the archipelago.

The largest of the Philippine islands, Luzon, has an area of 104,687 square kilometers (40,420 square miles). The main part of the island is roughly 402 kilometers (250 miles) in length and has a width from between 120 and 160 kilometers (75 and 100 miles).

Just south of Luzon lies Mindoro. This island is largely mountainous and has high peaks rising above 2,438 meters (8,000 feet). Coastal lowlands lie to the east and northeast of the mountain zone.

Southwest of Mindoro is the Calamian Group of islands, with the long, narrow island of Palawan beyond them. Over eleven hundred smaller islands and islets surround Palawan.

Over half of the islands that make up the country belong to the Visayan group, forming a rough circular pattern around the Visayan Sea. They include the seven large, populated islands of Masbate, Samar, Bohol, Cebu, Leyte, Panay, and Negros, plus numerous islets. The long narrow island of Cebu is the site of the country's largest copper mine and also produces low-grade coal and limestone used for cement.

Mindanao, the second largest of the Philippine Islands, has an area of 94,630 square kilometers (36,537 square miles). In the east of the island, the Agusan River runs between two mountain ranges. To the southwest of those ridges, several rivers meet in the Cotabato Basin and mountain peaks lead to the Bukidnon-Lanao Plateau. West of the Plateau, the island narrows to an isthmus ten miles wide, from which the long Zamboanga Peninsula protrudes to the southwest. The peninsula is covered largely with mountains and possesses limited coastal lowlands.

Southwest of the Zamboanga Peninsula of Mindanao is the Sulu Archipelago, a string of smaller islands of volcanic and coral origin protruding from a submarine ridge. The Sulu Archipelago stretches for about 322 kilometers (200 miles) and has over eight hundred islands. Its three principal islands are Basilan, Jolo, and Tawi-Tawi.

Coastal Features

Lingayen Gulf indents Luzon's western coast. Further south is Manila Bay, which is surrounded by the Bataan Peninsula. The capital city of Manila is located on the eastern shore of Manila Bay. Tayabas Bay and Ragay Gulf surround the Bondoc Peninsula of Luzon's southern coastline. The southeastern extension of Luzon ends in the Sorsogon Peninsula. North of the peninsula on the east coast is Lamon Bay; further north are Dingalan Bay and Escarpada Point.

Mindanao's very irregular shape is characterized by a number of sizable gulfs and bays and several large peninsulas that give

EPD/Saxifraga/Wiel Poelmans

Mount Katanglad National Park on Mindanao.

it an extremely long coastline. Mindanao's northernmost point is the Surigao Peninsula, with Butuan Bay to its west. Iligan Bay makes a deep indentation, creating a narrow isthmus that connects the large Zamboanga Peninsula to the rest of Mindanao. Sibuguey and Baganian Peninsulas protrude from the south coast of the Zamboanga Peninsula on Moro Gulf, with Pagadian Bay on the south of the isthmus and Illana Bay continuing the southwest coast. Sarangani Bay indents the coast just above its southernmost part, Tinaca Point. North of that point is Davao Gulf, defined by Cape San Agustin.

Among the Visayan Islands there are two large gulfs: Leyte in the southeast and Panay in the west.

6 ⊕ INLAND LAKES

The largest lake in the Philippines is the freshwater Laguna de Bay, located on Luzon, south-east of Manila Bay. It has a water surface of 922 square kilometers (356 square miles). Lake Taal , which has an active volcano in its center, lies a few miles to the southwest of Laguna de Bay. Other crater lakes are Lake Danao and Lake Balinsasayan in southeast Negros.

On Mindanao, atop the Bukidnon-Lanao Plateau, is Lake Sultan Alonto (formerly Lake Lanao). The second-largest lake in the country, it covers 347 square kilometers (134 square miles). The shallow Lake Buluan is in Mindanao, south of the Plateau. The lowland of Mindoro contains Lake Naujan, one of the country's larger lakes, home to many fish and bird species.

7 ⊕ RIVERS AND WATERFALLS

In general, the larger rivers of the Philippines are navigable for only short distances. Most main streams and their tributaries are subject to extensive and damaging floods during the heavy rainfall of typhoons and the monsoon seasons.

The Cagayan River is located in the Cagayan Valley of northern Luzon. It flows northward and empties into the sea at Aparri. A network of rivers and streams interlaces the low-lying Central Luzon Plain. Two of the plain's more important rivers are the Agno, which flows northward into Lingayen Gulf, and the Pampanga, which empties into Manila Bay. The short Pasig River flows through the city of Manila.

Two large rivers are found on Mindanao. The Agusan River is the longest in the country, with a length of 386 kilometers (240 miles). It flows northward through the Agusan Valley into the Bohol Sea. The Mindanao River and its tributaries drain the Cotabato Lowland, emptying into Moro Gulf.

On Palawan, the St. Paul Underground River is a popular destination for adventurous tourists. At its mouth lies a small bay connecting it to the ocean. Accessible only by canoe, the river flows through a large cavern inhabited by bats and filled with stalagtites.

8 ⊕ DESERTS

There are no desert regions in the Philippines.

9 ⊕ FLAT AND ROLLING TERRAIN

The Central Luzon Plain, barely above sea level, has extensive swamps along the north of Manila Bay and the Candaba Swamp.

The low Ragay Hills overlook Ragay Gulf on the Bicol Peninsula of southeastern Luzon. To the south on Samar, the terrain is broken up by rocky hills, which are 152 to 305 meters (500 to 1,000 feet) high. In central Bohol there is a 52-square-kilometer (20-square-mile) area known as the Chocolate Hills. There are 1,268 individual mounds in the Chocolate Hills, each one between 50 and 200 meters (164

DID YOU KN⊕W?

There are four "Wetlands of International Importance" in the Philippines, as designated under the Ramsar Convention on Wetlands. These are: Agusan Marsh Wildlife Sanctuary, which includes rare swamp forest and peat forest; Olango Island Wildlife Sanctuary, a shorebird habitat; Naujan Lake National Park; and Tubbataha Reefs National Marine Park.

The mountain rice terraces of northern Luzon's Cordillera are an UNESCO World Heritage site. Built by the indigenous Ifugao people over the last two millennia, the terraces follow mountain contours over 1,000 meters (3,281 feet) high, creating an agricultural landscape that is both productive and harmonious with nature.

and 656 feet) high; these hills are covered in grass, which turns brown in the dry season. Although their origin has not been determined; scientists speculate they were formed from eroded coral limestone. Hill areas also exist on Panay and nearby Guimaras, as well as on Masbate, Tablas, and Romblon.

Savannahs, mixing grasslands and scrub woods, are found in Luzon's Cagayan Valley, and amid the hills of Mindoro, Negros, and Masbate, as well as on Panay, and on Mindanao's Bukidnon-Lanao Plateau.

EPD/Saxifraga

Palawan Cave in St. Paul's National Park on Palawan.

10 ⊕ MOUNTAINS AND VOLCANOES

All of the Philippine Islands are volcanic in origin. As a result, the country is very mountainous. The northern part of Luzon Island is extremely rugged. Luzon's highest peak, Mount Pulog, rises to 2,934 meters (9,626 feet). The island has three mountain ranges that run roughly parallel in a north-south direction. A range in the east, the Sierra Madre, runs so close to the island's eastern shore that there is hardly any coastal lowland. The valley of the Cagayan River separates this eastern range from a large mountain complex to the west, the Cordillera Central. On the west, the Zambales Mountains extend southward and terminate at Manila Bay. Southeastern Luzon consists of a large peninsula. It is a mountainous and volcanic area containing the active volcano, Mount Mayon (2,420 meters/7,941 feet).

The large island of Mindanao has five major mountain systems, some of which were formed by volcanic action. The eastern edge of Mindanao is highly mountainous; this region includes the Diuata Mountains, with several elevations above 1,828 meters (6,000 feet), and the southeastern ranges, which reach a high point of 2,804 meters (9,200 feet). In central Mindanao there is a broad mass of rugged mountain ranges, one of which bisects the island from north to south. This range contains Mount Apo (2,954 meters/9,692 feet), the highest peak in the country, which overlooks Davao Gulf.

Most of the islands are located on the Eurasian Tectonic Plate, but a major fault line extends along the eastern part of the archipelago, aligned over the boundary with the Philippine Plate. As part of the western-Pacific

"Ring of Fire," the Philippines have thirty-seven volcanoes, of which eighteen are active.

11 ⊕ CANYONS AND CAVES

Many of the Philippines's rivers have carved canyons through the mountains. Particularly deep canyons cut through the Bukidnon-Lanao Plateau of Mindanao. Pagsanjan Gorge National Park, southeast of Manila on Luzon, is a river gorge with each of its steep faces towering to a height of 91 meters (300 feet).

12 ⊕ PLATEAUS AND MONOLITHS

The central mountain complex of Mindanao extends into the northwest corner of the island, terminating in the Bukidnon-Lanao Plateau. At approximately 609 meters (2,000 feet) in elevation, the plateau is interspersed with extinct volcanic peaks. On southeast Negros, the volcanic rock Tablas plateau rises 152 to 305 meters (500 to 1,000 feet.)

13 ⊕ MAN-MADE FEATURES

There are no major man-made structures affecting the geography of the Philippines.

14 ⊕ FURTHER READING

Books

Broad, Robin, and John Cavanagh. *Plundering Paradise: The Struggle for the Environment in the Philippines.* Berkeley: University of California Press, 1994.

Davis, Leonard. *The Philippines: People, Poverty, and Politics.* New York: St. Martin's Press, 1987.

Olesky, Walter G. *The Philippines.* New York: Children's Press, 2000

Wernstedt, Frederick. *The Philippine Island World.* Berkeley: University of California Press, 1967.

Web Sites

VolcanoWorld: Tectonics and Volcanoes of the Philippines. http://volcano.und.nodak.edu/ (accessed April 28, 2003).

Poland

- **Official name:** Republic of Poland
- **Area:** 312,685 square kilometers (120,728 square miles)
- **Highest point on mainland:** Mount Rysy (2,499 meters/8,199 feet)
- **Lowest point on land:** Raczki Elblaskie (2 meters/6.6 feet below sea level)
- **Hemispheres:** Northern and Eastern
- **Time zone:** 1 P.M. = noon GMT
- **Longest distances:** 689 kilometers (428 miles) from east to west; 649 kilometers (403 miles) from north to south

- **Land boundaries:** 2,888 kilometers (1,794 miles) total boundary length; Russia 206 kilometers (128 miles); Lithuania 91 kilometers (57 miles); Belarus 605 kilometers (376 miles); Ukraine 428 kilometers (266 miles); Slovakia 444 kilometers (276 miles); Czech Republic 658 kilometers (409 miles); Germany 456 kilometers (283 miles)
- **Coastline:** 491 kilometers (305 miles)
- **Territorial sea limits:** 22 kilometers (12 nautical miles)

1 ⊕ LOCATION AND SIZE

Poland is an unbroken plain in Eastern Europe extending from the shore of the Baltic Sea to the Carpathian Mountains. It covers an area of 312,685 square kilometers (120,728 square miles), or slightly less than the state of New Mexico.

2 ⊕ TERRITORIES AND DEPENDENCIES

Poland has no territories or dependencies.

3 ⊕ CLIMATE

Poland's continental climate is modified by westerly winds. Summers are generally cool, with only the southern portions of the country experiencing notable humidity. Winters can be frigid. Average temperatures are –6°C to –1°C (21–30°F) in January and 13°C –24°C (55°F –75°F) in July. Annual average precipitation ranges from 50 centimeters (20 inches) in the lowlands to 135 centimeters (53 inches) in the mountains. For the country as a whole, the average annual precipitation is 64 centimeters (25 inches).

4 ⊕ TOPOGRAPHIC REGIONS

Differences in climate and terrain occur in bands that extend from east to west. The coastal area lacks natural harbors except those at Gdansk-Gdynia and Szczecin. The vast plains south of the coast and its adjoining lake district have more fertile soil, a longer growing season, and a denser population than the northern regions. The southern foothills and mountains contain most of the country's mineral wealth and much of this land has attracted the greatest concentration of industry and people.

5 ⊕ OCEANS AND SEAS

Poland is bordered by the Baltic Sea to the north.

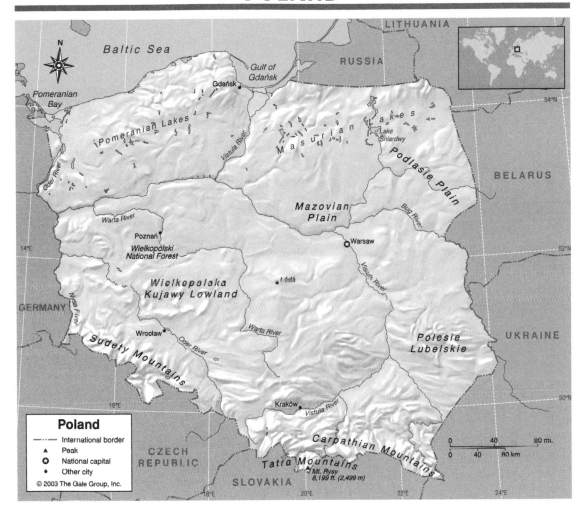

Poland
- - - - International border
▲ Peak
◉ National capital
• Other city
© 2003 The Gale Group, Inc.

Sea Inlets and Straits

The major ocean inlets bordering the Polish coast are the Pomeranian Bay in the west and the Gulf of Gdansk in the east.

Coastal Features

Poland's coastline is a narrow lowland dotted with bays, lakes, and promontories (high rocky cliffs).

6 ⊕ INLAND LAKES

The lake district of northeast Poland is subdivided into two smaller regions. The Pomeranian district has over four thousand lakes,

occupying over 115,000 hectares (290,000 acres); the Masurian district has over twenty-five hundred lakes, which cover almost 142,000 hectares (355,000 acres). Most of the lakes are small and shallow; nearly a dozen, however, including some very small ones, have depths exceeding 50 meters (164 feet).

7 ⊕ RIVERS AND WATERFALLS

By far the greatest portion of the country drains northwestward to the Baltic Sea by way of the Vistula (Wisla) and Oder (Odra) Rivers. Most other rivers in Poland join the Vistula and Oder systems. The Vistula and its tributaries

EPD/Saxifraga/Jan van der Straaten

The central lowlands are the largest region in Poland.

drain the country's largest basin, an area that includes practically all of the southeastern and east-central regions and much of the northeast as well. The Vistula rises in the Tatra Mountains in the south, flows northward, and drains into the Baltic Sea at the Gulf of Gdansk (Danzig). One of its tributaries, the Bug, forms about 280 kilometers (174 miles) of Poland's eastern border. The Oder, which together with the Neisse (Nysa) River forms most of the border between Poland and Germany, is fed by several other rivers and streams, including the Warta, which drains a large section of central and western Poland. The Oder reaches the Baltic Sea through the harbors and bays north of Szczecin.

8 ⊕ DESERTS

There are no deserts in Poland.

9 ⊕ FLAT AND ROLLING TERRAIN

Poland's average elevation is 173 meters (567 feet); more than 90 percent of the country lies below 300 meters (984 feet). The single largest region is the central lowlands area, which ac-

counts for three-fourths of Poland's territory. Extending over the entire country in an east-west band, it is narrow in the west but expands to both the north and the south as it extends eastward. At the eastern border, it includes nearly all the terrain from the northeastern tip of the country to about 200 kilometers (124 miles) from the southeastern corner.

When the most recent glacier receded several millennia ago, it left behind the hills, forests, and lakes north of the central lowlands. The effects of glaciation dominate the terrain for about 200 kilometers (124 miles) inland from the Baltic Sea in the western part of the country, but for a much shorter distance in the east. There are large areas of swampland in the northern lake district because of poor drainage, and land here has been hard to reclaim.

The foothills of the Tatra Mountains and Sudeten Mountains to the south of the central lowlands blend into the other mountains in the extreme south and in the southwestern corner of the country.

10 ⊕ MOUNTAINS AND VOLCANOES

Mount Rysy, the country's highest peak at 2,499 meters (8,199 feet), is in the Tatra (Tatry) range of the Carpathian Mountains. Six other peaks in the Polish portion of the Tatras reach 1,900 meters (6,233 feet) or more. The Sudeten Mountains are lower, with only one peak exceeding 1,600 meters (5,249 feet). Most of the more rugged slopes are in the Tatra Mountains; many slopes in the Sudeten range are gentle and have been cultivated or used as meadows and pastures on dairy farms.

11 ⊕ CANYONS AND CAVES

Over twenty-five hundred caves have been identified in Poland, most clustering in the south-central part of the country, in the western Tatra Mountains and the Kraków region.

12 ⊕ PLATEAUS AND MONOLITHS

Only 3 percent of Poland's terrain rises above 500 meters (1,640 feet). These small highland areas in the Carpathian and Sudeten (Sudety) Mountains extend across the country parallel to the southern border in a belt roughly 90 to 120 kilometers (55 to 74 miles) wide.

13 ⊕ MAN-MADE FEATURES

Gdansk is known for its historic gateways, including the landmark sixteenth-century Green Gate and High Gate and the fifteenth-century Crane Gate, which was rebuilt following World War II (1939–45).

DID YOU KN⊕W?

In 98 A.D., the Roman historian Tacitus recorded the name of Poland's longest river, the Vistula. One of the early Germanic tribes who had settled in the region, the Goths, gave the river its name.

14 ⊕ FURTHER READING

Books

McLachlan, Gordon W. *Off the Beaten Track: Poland.* Old Saybrook, CT: Globe Pequot Press, 1995.

Salter, Mark. *Poland: The Rough Guide.* New York: Penguin Books, 1996.

Stephenson, Jill, and Alfred Bloch. *Poland.* New York: Hippocrene Books, 1993.

Web Sites

Polish Home Page. http://www.fuw.edu.pl/ PHe.html (accessed April 22, 2003).

Warsaw Travel Guide. http://www. hotelspoland.com/guide/wa1/ index.html (accessed April 22, 2003).

Portugal

- **Official name:** Portuguese Republic
- **Area:** 92,391 square kilometers (35,672 square miles)
- **Highest point on mainland:** Estrela (1,991 meters/6,532 feet)
- **Highest point in territory:** Ponta do Pico (2,351 meters/7,714 feet)
- **Lowest point on land:** Sea level
- **Hemispheres:** Northern and Eastern
- **Time zone:** Noon = noon GMT

- **Longest distances:** 218 kilometers (135 miles) from east to west; 561 kilometers (349 miles) from north to south
- **Land boundaries:** 1,214 kilometers (754 miles) total boundary length, all with Spain
- **Coastline:** 1,793 kilometers (1,114 miles)
- **Territorial sea limits:** 22 kilometers (12 nautical miles)

1 ⊕ LOCATION AND SIZE

Portugal is located at the westernmost edge of continental Europe. It occupies approximately one-sixth of the Iberian Peninsula, which it shares with Spain. There are few natural frontiers between the two nations; many of Portugal's geographical features are continuations of those in Spain. With a total area of 92,391 square kilometers (35,672 square miles), Portugal is almost as large as the state of Indiana.

2 ⊕ TERRITORIES AND DEPENDENCIES

Portugal has jurisdiction over two autonomous island groups in the Atlantic—the Azores and Madeira. The Madeiran archipelago, located about 960 kilometers (600 miles) west of mainland Portugal, consists of the islands of Madeira and Porto Santo, and the uninhabited Desertas and Selvagens islets. The Azorean archipelago, about 1,300 kilometers (800 miles) west of mainland Portugal, is a volcanic mountain chain of nine islands divided into three groups: São Miguel and Santa Maria to the east; Terceira, Pico, Faial, São Jorge, and Gra-

ciosa in the center; and Flores and Corvo to the northwest. Thermal springs are features on the largest island, São Miguel.

3 ⊕ CLIMATE

Proximity to the Atlantic Ocean keeps Portugal's climate generally temperate, with variations from north to south. The northwest has a maritime climate, with short, cool summers and mild winters. In the northeast the climate is more continental, with sharper contrasts between the seasons. The central part of the country has hot summers and mild, rainy winters, and the south has a dry climate with long, hot summers. Average temperatures in Lisbon are about 24°C (75°F) in July and about 4°C (40°F) in January. Average annual rainfall ranges from over 305 centimeters (120 inches) in the northwestern grape-growing region to 51 centimeters (20 inches) on the southern coast. Average annual rainfall in Lisbon is 69 centimeters (27 inches).

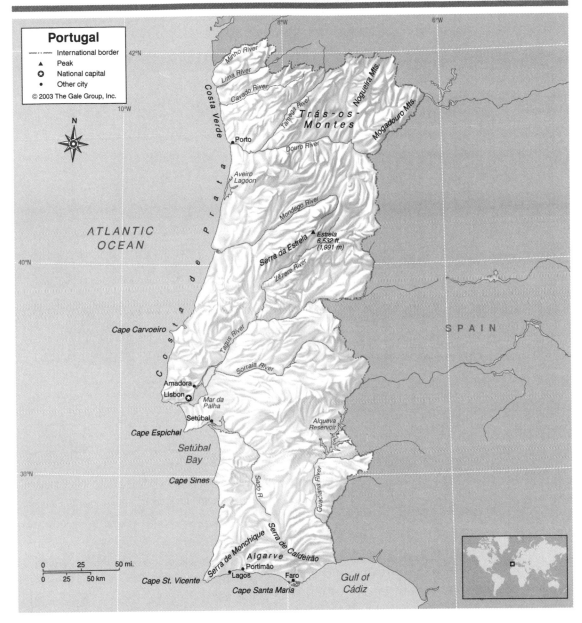

Portugal

- - - - International border
- ▲ Peak
- ✪ National capital
- • Other city

© 2003 The Gale Group, Inc.

ATLANTIC OCEAN

Costa Verde

Minho River
Lima River
Cavado River
Tamega River
Noguiera Mts.
Trás-os-Montes
Mogadouro Mts.
Porto
Douro River
Aveiro Lagoon
Mondego River
Serra da Estrela
▲ Estrela
6,532 ft.
(1,991 m)
Lézere River

Costa de Prata

Cape Carvoeiro

Tagus River
SPAIN
Sorraia River
Amadora
Lisbon
Mar da Palha
Setúbal
Alqueva Reservoir
Cape Espichel
Setúbal Bay
Cape Sines
Sado R.
Guadiana River
Serra de Monchique
Serra de Caldeirão
Algarve
Portimão
Cape St. Vicente
Lagos
Faro
Cape Santa Maria
Gulf of Cádiz

0   25   50 mi.
0   25   50 km

4 ⊕ TOPOGRAPHIC REGIONS

Portugal's major topographical dividing lines are the Douro and Tagus Rivers, which flow across the country, and the centrally located Serra da Estrela mountain range. The Tagus River forms a dividing line between the upland regions of the north and the rolling plains of the south. The Minho region in the northwest is bounded by several mountain ranges on the east and by the Minho and Douro Rivers to the north and south, respectively. Trás-os-Montes (literally, "across the mountains") is the northeasternmost area of Portugal, bounded to the north and east by Spain, to the south by the

EPD/Saxifraga/Marijke Verhagen

The southern coast of Portugal is known as the Algarve.

Douro River, and to the west by the mountains that separate it from the Minho.

The central area south of the Douro and north of the Tagus is the Beiras, a transitional region between the north and the south. The Serra da Estrela divide the region in two. Coastal Beira, known as Beira Litoral, consists of rolling, sandy hills. The northern part, known as Beira Baixa, is a dry and windswept region similar to Trás-os-Montes. The west-central region of Estremadura includes the Tagus estuary, the capital city of Lisbon, and the Tagus valley area known as Ribatejo. The Alentejo region to the south is a vast area of gently rolling hills commonly divided into two subregions: Alto Alentejo and Baixo Alentejo. The Algarve, the southernmost region, is separated from the Alentejo by two mountain ranges: the Serra de Monchique in the west and the Serra de Caldeirao in the east.

5 ⊕ OCEANS AND SEAS

Portugal is bordered on the west and south by the North Atlantic Ocean.

Sea Inlets and Straits

The southeastern part of Portugal's coast is on the Gulf of Cadiz.

Coastal Features

Most of Portugal's coastline is smooth, but there are indentations at the mouths of the major rivers. The major harbors are at the mouths of the Tagus and Sado Rivers. The forested northern part of the coast, which is famous for its vineyards, is called the Costa Verde, or "green coast." The midsection of the coast is called the Costa de Prata, or "silver coast." The Beira coastal plain has salt marshes, alluvial deposits, and stretches of sand dunes.

EPD/Saxifraga/Jan van der Straaten

The plains in the central region make up Portugal's agricultural heartland.

Several capes jut out into the Atlantic in the southern half of the coast, including Cape Carvoeiro, Cape Espichel, Cape Sines, Cape São Vicente, and Cape Santa Maria. The Mar da Palha, the estuary of the Tagus River, is one of the world's great natural harbors.

6 ⊕ INLAND LAKES

The construction of the Alqueva Dam in southern Portugal between 2002 and 2006 is expected to create the largest artificial lake in Europe, with an area of 250 square kilometers (96 square miles).

7 ⊕ RIVERS AND WATERFALLS

Of the ten major rivers in Portugal, five have their origins in Spain, and five lie entirely within Portugal. The major river in northern Portugal is the Douro. The total length of this river is 940 kilometers (584 miles), of which 740 kilometers (460 miles) are situated in Spain and 200 kilo-meters (124 miles) in Portugal. The Tagus is the longest river in both Portugal and on the Iberian Peninsula; its total length is 999 kilometers (621 miles), 228 kilometers (142 miles) of which traverses Portugal. (This river is also called the Tejo in Portugal, and the Tajo in Spain.)

8 ⊕ DESERTS

There are no true deserts in Portugal, but the Alentejo region is semiarid.

9 ⊕ FLAT AND ROLLING TERRAIN

The Alentejo region accounts for one-third of the country's total area. Its undulating land is generally about 183 meters (600 feet) above sea level, but in some places it rises to between 274 and 457 meters (900 and 1,500 feet). The Minho region in the northwest is also hilly.

10 ⊕ MOUNTAINS AND VOLCANOES

The most mountainous part of Portugal is the northern region known as Trás-os-Montes, or "across the mountains." Its ranges are part of the same system as the Cantabrian Mountains of Spain. Portugal's most important single mountain range, however, is the Serra da Estrela in the central part of the country, which includes the country's highest peak, also called Estrela (1,991 meters/6,532 feet). (Ponta do Pico, 2,351 meters/7,714 feet in elevation, lies on Ilha do Pico in the Azores.)

11 ⊕ CANYONS AND CAVES

The six caves that make up the Grutas de Santo-Adriao in northeast Portugal were formerly marble quarries.

12 ⊕ PLATEAUS AND MONOLITHS

At over 7 meters (23 feet) tall, the Menhir of Meada is among the loftiest monoliths on the Iberian Peninsula. It is thought to be at least five thousand years old.

13 ⊕ MAN-MADE FEATURES

The Alqueva Dam on the Guadiana River, whose floodgates opened in early 2002, is intended to provide irrigation for farmlands in Portugal's dry southern region as well as drinking water and electricity. The project was opposed by environmentalists, however. They claimed that construction of the dam destroyed the habitat of several endangered animal species, flooded significant Roman

DID YOU KN⊕W?

The name *Madeira*, taken from the Portuguese word for wood, comes from the dense forests on the islands of this group.

and prehistoric ruins, and swept away one million trees.

The 10-mile (17-kilometer) Vasco da Gama Bridge spans the Tagus River in Lisbon, allowing north-south travelers to bypass the city. It officially opened March 31, 1998.

14 ⊕ FURTHER READING

Books

Proper, Datus C. *The Last Old Place: A Search Through Portugal*. New York: Simon & Schuster, 1992.

Saramago, Josi. *Journey to Portugal: In Pursuit of Portugal's History and Culture*. Translated by Amanda Hopkinson and Nick Caistor. New York: Harcourt, 2001.

Symington, Martin. *Essential Portugal*. Lincolnwood, IL: Passport Books, 1994.

Web Sites

Ideamen's Links to Portugal. http://www.well.com/user/ideamen/Portugal.html (accessed April 3, 2003)

Puerto Rico

- **Official name:** Commonwealth of Puerto Rico
- **Area:** 9,104 square kilometers (3,515 square miles)
- **Highest point on mainland:** Cerro de Punta (1,338 meters/4,390 feet)
- **Lowest point on land:** Sea level
- **Hemispheres:** Northern and Western
- **Time zone:** 8 A.M. = noon GMT

- **Longest distances:** 179 kilometers (111 miles) from east to west; 58 kilometers (36 miles) from north to south
- **Land boundaries:** None
- **Coastline:** 501 kilometers (313 miles)
- **Territorial sea limits:** 22 kilometers (12 nautical miles)

1 ⊕ LOCATION AND SIZE

Puerto Rico, a commonwealth of the United States of America, is located at the eastern end of the Greater Antilles archipelago, between the Atlantic Ocean and the Caribbean Sea. It is 1,609 kilometers (1,000 miles) southeast of the U.S. mainland, between the island of Hispaniola to the west and the Virgin Islands to the east. In addition to its main island, Puerto Rico also includes three smaller ones: Vieques and Culebra to the east and Mona to the west.

2 ⊕ TERRITORIES AND DEPENDENCIES

Puerto Rico has no territories or dependencies.

3 ⊕ CLIMATE

Trade winds from the northeast moderate Puerto Rico's tropical climate. Temperatures year-round generally stay between 21°C and 27°C (70°F and 80°F), although more extreme temperatures are possible in lower inland areas and on the southern coast. The mean temperature in San Juan is 24°C (75°F) in January and 27°C (81°F) in July. Hurricanes are a hazard between August and October. Average annual rainfall varies from 91 centimeters (36 inches) in the south, to 152 centimeters (60 inches) at San Juan, to as much as 457 centimeters (180 inches) in the mountains. Rainfall is distributed fairly evenly throughout the year.

4 ⊕ TOPOGRAPHIC REGIONS

Puerto Rico's main island, rectangular in shape, has a hilly and mountainous interior ringed by a narrow coastal plain. The major mountain system is the Cordillera Central, which bisects the western and central parts of the island.

5 ⊕ OCEANS AND SEAS

Puerto Rico is bordered on the north by the rough, cold waters of the Atlantic Ocean and on the south by the warmer, calmer Caribbean Sea.

Seacoast and Undersea Features

The waters just off the coast are shallow, but a few miles to the north the ocean floor drops to a depth of 1,829 meters (6,000 feet). Some 64 kilometers (40 miles) farther north lies the Puerto Rico Trench. At its western end is the Milwaukee Depth, where the ocean floor plunges more than 8,380 meters (27,493 feet)—

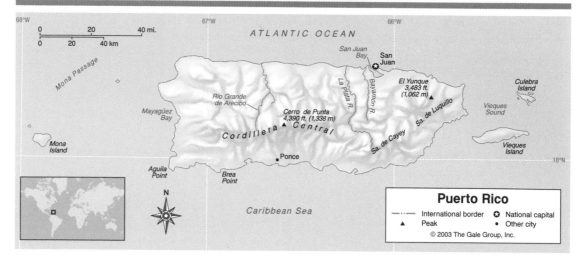

among the deepest ocean trenches in the world, and the greatest known depth in the Atlantic.

Sea Inlets and Straits

Puerto Rico is separated from the island of Hispaniola to the west by the Mona Passage, and from the Virgin Islands to the east by both the Vieques Sound and the Virgin Passage.

Islands and Archipelagos

Vieques, Puerto Rico's largest island aside from the main island, has an area of about 135 square kilometers (52 square miles), much of it occupied by a U.S. naval training facility. Culebra, which also lies to the east of the main island, is an archipelago consisting of a largely flat main island surrounded by twenty islets. Mona Island, to the west, has an area of 52 square kilometers (20 square miles).

Coastal Features

Puerto Rico's coastline is moderately indented at most points. San Juan Bay is in the northeast, and Mayagüez Bay marks the western end of the island. Águila Point and Brea Point are in the southwest. The shore has both rocky and sandy beaches.

6 ⊕ INLAND LAKES

There are no natural lakes in Puerto Rico, but there are more than a dozen artificial ones.

7 ⊕ RIVERS AND WATERFALLS

The major rivers flow northward over the mountains to the coast. These waterways include the La Plata River (the longest), the Río Grande de Loíza (the widest), the Bayamón River, and the Río Grande de Arecibo. The rivers in the south are fewer, shorter, and smaller in volume.

8 ⊕ DESERTS

There are no deserts in Puerto Rico.

9 ⊕ FLAT AND ROLLING TERRAIN

Puerto Rico's steep mountains descend to foothills before giving way to the coastal plains that ring the island. They span 24 kilometers (15 miles) at their widest point, and the strip of plain on the north is only 8 kilometers (5 miles) wide. The Turabo Valley, a largely agricultural area, lies between three mountain chains in the eastern part of the island.

David Boyer/National Geographic Image Collection

A man stands in the mouth of one of the many caves
that lie under Puerto Rico's northwest region.

10 ⊕ MOUNTAINS AND VOLCANOES

Steep mountain slopes cover nearly one-fourth of the island. The highest and longest mountain range is the Cordillera Central, which extends 97 kilometers (60 miles) across the center of the island and reaches elevations of over 914 meters (3,000 feet). Puerto Rico's highest peak, Cerro de Punta (1,338 meters/4,390 feet), is part of this system, which rises rapidly from the southern coast and ascends more gradually in the north. The other major mountain system is the Sierra de Luquillo in the east, where the country's most famous peak, El Yunque (1,062 meters /3,483 feet) is located. A third mountain range—the Sierra da Cayey—is found in the southeast.

11 ⊕ CANYONS AND CAVES

Numerous cliffs, caves, sinkholes, and tunnels have been carved by rainwater into the limestone of Puerto Rico's karst region in the northwest. The subterranean caves at the Camuy River form one of the largest cave systems in the world. The largest single cave, Cueva Clara, is 210 meters (695 feet) long.

DID YOU KN⊕W?

The Camuy River cave system is home to a rare species of fish that is completely blind.

12 ⊕ PLATEAUS AND MONOLITHS

Puerto Rico's karst region in the interior northwest of the island lies on a plateau ranging in elevation from 30 to 213 meters (100 to 700 feet).

13 ⊕ MAN-MADE FEATURES

Dams built on all but one of Puerto Rico's major rivers have created more than a dozen reservoirs. Lakes Guayabal, Guajataca, Dos Bocas, and La Plata are among the largest of these reservoirs.

14 ⊕ FURTHER READING

Books

Luxner, Larry. *Puerto Rico.* Boston: Houghton Mifflin, 1995.

Marino, John. *Puerto Rico: Off the Beaten Path.* Guilford, CT: Globe Pequot Press, 2000.

Pariser, Harry S. *The Adventure Guide to Puerto Rico.* Edison, NJ: Hunter Publications, 1996.

Web Sites

Welcome to Puerto Rico! http://welcome.topuertorico.org/ (accessed March 12, 2003).

Sol Boricua Web Site. http://www.solboricua.com/index.htm (accessed March 12, 2003).

Qatar

- **Official name:** State of Qatar
- **Area:** 11,437 square kilometers (4,416 square miles)
- **Highest point on mainland:** Qurayn Abu al Bawl (103 meters/338 feet)
- **Lowest point on land:** Sea level
- **Hemispheres:** Northern and Eastern
- **Time zone:** 3 P.M. = noon GMT
- **Longest distances:** 160 kilometers (100 miles) from north to south; 90 kilometers (55 miles) from east to west

- **Land boundaries:** 60 kilometers (37 miles) total boundary length, all with Saudi Arabia
- **Coastline:** 563 kilometers (350 miles)
- **Territorial sea limits:** 22 kilometers (12 nautical miles)

1 ⊕ LOCATION AND SIZE

Qatar consists of a tiny peninsula projecting northward into the Persian Gulf from the larger Arabian Peninsula. With an area of 11,437 square kilometers (4,416 square miles), Qatar is almost as large as the state of Connecticut.

2 ⊕ TERRITORIES AND DEPENDENCIES

Qatar has no territories or dependencies.

3 ⊕ CLIMATE

Qatar has a desert climate that is characterized by extremely hot and dry summers, from May to October, and mild winters. Mean temperatures in June are 42°C (108°F), dropping to 15°C (59°F) in winter. Average annual precipitation is less than 8 centimeters (3 inches). Most of the rainfall occurs during the winter months, sometimes only in localized heavy downpours. Humidity along the coast frequently reaches 90 percent during summer.

4 ⊕ TOPOGRAPHIC REGIONS

Qatar's terrain is mostly a flat and barren desert covered with loose sand and gravel, with some low hills and a central limestone plateau.

5 ⊕ OCEANS AND SEAS

Qatar borders the Persian Gulf on the north, east, and southeast and the Gulf of Bahrain on the west.

Seacoast and Undersea Features

A notable feature of the coastal area is the prevalence of salt pans, which are shallow depressions made up of salt flats (*sabkhas*). Their presence at the base of the peninsula suggests that Qatar was an island at one time. Coral reefs impede navigation in the coastal seas surrounding Qatar, as does the shallowness of these waters.

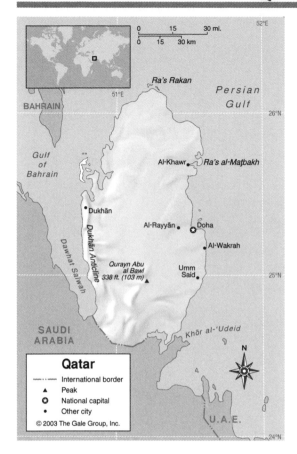

Coastal Features

The coastline of Qatar is part of a regional low desert plain, and it contains two natural harbors. The capital of Doha is located on a sizable, though shallow, port. Umm Said also provides a commercial harbor. Qatar also has two important capes: Ra's Rakan at its northernmost point and Al-Maṭbakh, which juts into the Persian Gulf just north of Al-Khawr. The inlet known as Khōr al-'Udeid (the Inland Sea) is surrounded by extensive sand dunes.

6 ⊕ INLAND LAKES

Limited natural freshwater resources have increased Qatar's dependence on large-scale desalination facilities.

7 ⊕ RIVERS AND WATERFALLS

Though Qatar has no perennial rivers, there are rainwater-draining basins in the north and central areas of the country.

8 ⊕ DESERTS

Qatar is an extension of the Arabian Peninsula's Rub'al-Khali (Empty Quarter) desert, which reaches northward from Saudi Arabia and the United Arab Emirates. Massive sand dunes surround Khōr al-'Udeid in the south of Qatar.

9 ⊕ FLAT AND ROLLING TERRAIN

Qatar is mostly flat, with scanty vegetation. Hills and sand dunes reach an altitude of 40 meters (131 feet) in the western and northern parts of the country.

10 ⊕ MOUNTAINS AND VOLCANOES

There are no mountains in Qatar.

11 ⊕ CANYONS AND CAVES

Qatar's karst limestone topography includes at least ten large caves. Many of the depressions in Qatar's terrain are actually collapsed caverns.

Sea Inlets and Straits

In the southeast there is a jagged inlet of the Persian Gulf that is known as Khōr al-'Udeid (the Inland Sea). Along the southwest coast lies the Dawhat Salwah, an inlet of the Gulf of Bahrain.

Islands and Archipelagos

Qatar includes a few islands in addition to the main peninsula. The most important island is Halul, which lies about 90 kilometers (60 miles) east of Doha and has an area of only about 1.5 square kilometers (0.6 square miles). It is used for storing oil found in offshore wells and loading it onto ships for trade.

12 ⊕ PLATEAUS AND MONOLITHS

A low central limestone plateau, which contains a number of shallow wadis, rises from the east and north. There are elevated limestone formations, called the Dukhān anticline, along the west coast; underneath them lies the Dukhān oil field.

13 ⊕ MAN-MADE FEATURES

Except for the harbors at Doha and Umm Said, all of Qatar's ports are artificial, created by digging channels to deepen Qatar's shallow coastal waters. Among these man-made ports are those at Al-Khawr and Al-Wakrah.

14 ⊕ FURTHER READING

Books

Ferdinand, Klaus. *Bedouins of Qatar.* New York: Thames and Hudson, 1993.

Vine, Peter. *The Heritage of Qatar.* London: IMMEL Publications, 1992.

Winckler, Onn. *Population Growth, Migration and Socio-Demographic Policies in Qatar.* Tel Aviv: Moshe Dayan Center for Middle Eastern and African Studies, 2000.

Web Sites

ArabNet: Qatar. http://www.arab.net/qatar/qatar_contents.html (accessed May 7, 2003).

AP Photo/Kamran Jebreili

A couple takes a walk on a foggy morning in Doha.

Energy Information: Qatar. http://www.eia.doe.gov/cabs/qatar2.html (accessed May 7, 2003).

Library of Congress Country Studies: Qatar. http://lcweb2.loc.gov/frd/cs/qatoc.html (accessed May 7, 2003).

Romania

- **Official name:** Romania
- **Area:** 237,500 square kilometers (91,699 square miles)
- **Highest point on mainland:** Moldoveanu (2,544 meters/8,346 feet)
- **Lowest point on land:** Sea level
- **Hemispheres:** Northern and Eastern
- **Time zone:** 2 P.M. = noon GMT
- **Longest distances:** 789 kilometers (490 miles) from east to west; 475 kilometers (295 miles) from north to south

- **Land boundaries:** 2,508 kilometers (1,558 miles) total boundary length; Bulgaria 608 kilometers (378 miles); Hungary 443 kilometers (275 miles); Moldova 450 kilometers (279 miles); Ukraine (east) 169 kilometers (105 miles); Ukraine (north) 362 kilometers (225 miles); Serbia and Montenegro 476 kilometers (296 miles)
- **Coastline:** 225 kilometers (140 miles)
- **Territorial sea limits:** 22 kilometers (12 nautical miles)

1 ⊕ LOCATION AND SIZE

The southeastern European country of Romania is the largest country on the Balkan Peninsula. It shares borders with Ukraine, Moldova, Bulgaria, Serbia and Montenegro, and Hungary. It also has a very short southeastern coastline on the Black Sea. With a total area of about 237,500 square kilometers (91,699 square miles), the country is slightly smaller than the state of Oregon. Romania is administratively divided into forty counties and one municipality.

2 ⊕ TERRITORIES AND DEPENDENCIES

Romania has no outside territories or dependencies.

3 ⊕ CLIMATE

Romania has a transitional continental climate with moderating influences from the Black Sea and variations due to altitude. In general, winters are cold and summers are warm. Temperatures are lower in the more elevated Transylvanian Plateau in the northwest.

Temperature extremes are greater in the plains of the east and south, where the continental influence is strongest. Average temperatures in the capital city of Bucharest are -3°C (27°F) in January and 23°C (73°F) in July. Average annual rainfall ranges from about 38 centimeters (15 inches) in the eastern lowland region of Dobruja to 125 centimeters (50 inches) or more in the Carpathian Mountains.

4 ⊕ TOPOGRAPHIC REGIONS

The Carpathian Mountains, Romania's major physical feature, define the country's overall topographical pattern. Roughly forming an arc in the center of the country, their various branches separate the Transylvanian Plateau in the center from a wide band of lowlands on the edges, extending to the country's eastern, southern, and western borders.

Romania is traditionally divided into several distinct regions. Transylvania, which forms a large wedge in the north and northwest and makes up one-third of Romania, is by far

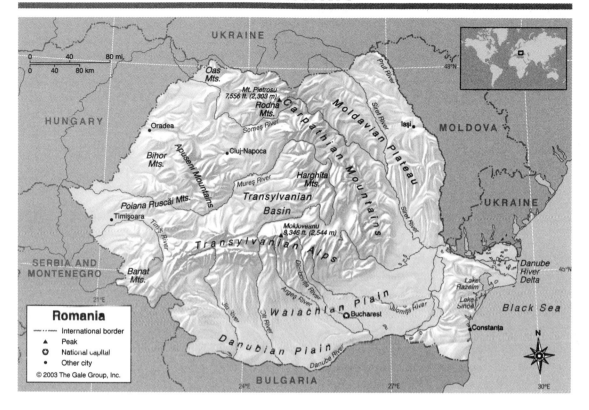

the largest region. It encompasses the central Transylvanian Plateau, all of the Carpathian Mountains except for the most southeastern section, and the hilly terrain in the northwestern part of the country. Walachia, which curves around Transylvania in the south and southeast, is the country's major lowland region, encompassing the plains of the Danube River to the south of the Transylvanian Alps. The part of Walachia west of the Olt River is a subregion known as Oltenia. Dobruja occupies the southeastern corner of Romania, bounded by the path of the Danube where the river flows northward for about 160 kilometers (100 miles) before it again turns to the east for its final passage to the sea. Moldavia, in the northeast, constitutes about one-fourth of the country's area. Much of this region is hilly or mountainous, and it is heavily forested. To the southwest, in the opposite corner of the country from Dobruja, is the Banat region.

Romania is located on the Eurasian Tectonic Plate.

5 ⊕ OCEANS AND SEAS

Seacoast and Undersea Features

Romania borders the western end of the Black Sea, which is an inland body of water lying between Europe and Asia. The Black Sea contains calm waters that are free of tides and dangerous marine life. Called the "Hospitable Sea" by the ancient Greeks, the Black Sea is half as saline as the Mediterranean Sea and has gentle sandy slopes, making it ideal for swimming.

The floor of the Black Sea is composed of a shallow shelf that extends about 10 to 11 kilometers (6 to 7 miles) from the coast of Romania. On this shelf, the average sea depth is 100 to 110 meters (330 to 360 feet). This shelf then drops steeply to the sea floor,

EPD/Saxifraga/Adriaan Dijkse

Romania's coastal region near the Black Sea is flat and grassy.

which is unusually flat and reaches depths of 2,195 meters (7,200 feet). Romania claims the continental shelf off its coast to a depth of 200 meters (656 feet).

Sea Inlets and Straits

At the central part of the coastline, two large saltwater lagoons, Lake Razelm and Lake Sinoe, open onto the sea.

Coastal Features

The marshy delta of the Danube River makes up the northern third of the coast. To the south, steep cliffs extend to the sea, fringed by white sandy beaches whose popularity with tourists has given this area a reputation as the "Romanian Riviera."

6 ⊕ INLAND LAKES

Romania is said to have 2,500 lakes, but most of them are small and lakes occupy only about 1 percent of the country's total surface area. The largest lakes are along the Danube River and the Black Sea coast. Some of those, including the largest, the 390-square kilometer (150-square mile) Lake Razelm, are saltwater lakes, or lagoons that are open to the sea. These and a few of the freshwater lakes are commercially important for their fish. The many smaller ones scattered throughout the mountains are usually glacial in origin and add much to the beauty of the resort areas.

7 ⊕ RIVERS AND WATERFALLS

All of Romania's rivers and streams drain to the Black Sea. All of the rivers also join the Danube River, except for the minor streams that rise on the eastern slopes of the hills near the coast and flow directly into the sea. Those flowing southward and southeastward from the Transylvanian Alps drain to the Danube directly. Those flowing northward and eastward from Moldavia and Bukovina reach the Danube by way of the Prut River. Most of the Transylvanian streams draining to the north and west, including the Mureş and Someş Rivers, flow to the

Tisza River, which joins the Danube in Serbia and Montenegro, north of Belgrade.

The Danube rises in the southwestern part of Germany and follows a winding, generally eastern course through Austria, Hungary, Serbia and Montenegro, and Romania before finally emptying into the Black Sea, 2,850 kilometers (1,771 miles) from its source. It is the second-longest river in Europe and a vital commercial and transportation route.

As the Danube approaches its delta, it divides into a number of channels. It also forms several lakes, some of which are quite large. At the delta it divides into three major and several minor branches. The delta has an area of about 2,590 square kilometers (1,000 square miles) and grows steadily as the river deposits billions of cubic feet of sediment into the sea annually. Its main tributaries flowing through Romania include the Siret, Ialomiţa, Argeş, Olt, Jiu, and Timiş. The Argeş has an important tributary of its own: the Dîmboviţa River.

DID YOU KN🌐W?

The Balkan Peninsula, the southernmost peninsula of Europe, lies between the Adriatic and Ionian Seas to the west, the Black and Aegean Seas to the east, and the Mediterranean Sea to the south. The countries of this region are collectively called the Balkan States: Albania, Bulgaria, continental Greece, southeast Romania, European Turkey, Serbia and Montenegro, Slovenia, Croatia, Bosnia and Herzegovina, and Macedonia.

The Dobruja region provides Romania's access to the Black Sea and contains most of the Danube River delta. Much of the Danube River delta, as well as a belt of land up to 32 kilometers (20 miles) wide along most of the river's length, is marshland. The majority of this land is not easily exploited for agricultural purposes, although some of the reeds and natural vegetation have limited commercial value. The delta is a natural wildlife preserve, particularly for waterfowl, and is large enough so that many species can be protected. Willows flourish in parts of the delta and there are a few deciduous forests in the north-central section.

8 ⊕ DESERTS

There are no desert regions in Romania.

9 ⊕ FLAT AND ROLLING TERRAIN

Much of the original grassland vegetation of the steppe-like lowland area in the eastern and southern parts of the country has given way to human settlement and cultivation. Nearly all of the Walachian Plain and Danubian Plain to the south, except for the marshes along the Danube River and the seriously eroded foothills, is cultivated. Where the original vegetation remains, short grasses grow in the drier areas; taller grasses grow closer to the rivers.

Hills cover much of Romania, as parts of both the mountain and plateau regions as well as the transitional regions between the mountain ranges. The hills are mostly rolling plains with well-watered and fertile soil.

10 ⊕ MOUNTAINS AND VOLCANOES

The mountain ranges in the eastern part of the country are referred to as the Moldavian Carpathians. They have maximum elevations of about 2,286 meters (7,500 feet) and are the most extensively forested part of the country. Their highest peak, Mount Pietrosu (2,303 meters/7,556 feet), rises in the Rodna Mountains in the far north at the border with Ukraine. Two volcanic ranges, the Oas and Harghita Mountains, extend for about 400 kilometers (250 miles) along the western edge of the Moldavian Carpathians. They contain Romania's only crater lake, the St. Ana Lake, as well as roughly two thousand mineral water springs.

The slightly higher southern ranges, called the Transylvanian Alps, form the southern border of Transylvania and have the highest peaks and the steepest slopes in the country. Romania's highest point, Mount Moldoveanu, rises to a height of 2,544 meters (8,346 feet) about 161 kilometers (100 miles) northwest of Bucharest. Among the alpine features of the Transylvanian Range are glacial lakes, upland meadows and pastures, and bare rock along the higher ridges. Some of the mountains are predominantly limestone, with caves, waterfalls, and underground streams.

The ranges in the west are generally lower and, unlike those in the east and south, they are not an unbroken ridge of mountains. The northernmost group is the Bihor Mountains, originating south of the city of Oradea. The southernmost is the Banat Mountains, in the extreme southwestern corner of the country. In between these two ranges are the perpendicular ranges of the Poiana Ruscăi Mountains and the Apuseni Mountains. These four ranges are not as rugged as those found to the south and east, and average elevations run considerably lower. Only a few points in the Bihor Mountains approach 1,828 meters (6,000 feet), compared to maximum elevations of nearly 2,286 meters (7,500 feet) in the Moldavian Carpathians and over 2,438 meters (8,000 feet) in the Transylvanian Alps.

The various mountain groups of the western Carpathians are separated by a series of structural depressions, called "gates" because they provide gateways through the mountains. The best known is the Iron Gate on the Danube, in the southeastern corner of Romania.

On the outer fringes of the eastern and southern Carpathian Mountains is a band of lower, but still elevated, terrain called the Subcarpathians, which rises to elevations between 400 to 1,000 meters (1,300 and 3,300 feet).

11 ⊕ CANYONS AND CAVES

Romania has many mountain caves scattered throughout the country. Two of the most popular show caves (open to tourists) are Bear's Cave and Women's Cave. Bear's Cave (Peştera Urşilor), located in a northwest group of mountains, is best known for the large number of cave bear fossils found there. The particular species of bear (ursus spelaeus) that lived there fifteen thousand years ago is now extinct. Researchers believe that a rockslide closed the entrance to the cave thousands of years ago, trapping over one hundred bears inside. Research indicates that these bears, which were generally herbivores, ended up killing and eating one another until the last bear died, either from hunger or from the wounds of a fight.

Women's Cave (Peştera Muierii) is located in an area known as the Getic Depression of Oltenia, on the territory of Baia de Fier village, in Gorj county. The Galbenul River carved the four levels of the cave. Women's Cave was so named because it was an ancient hiding place for the women and children of the region during times of war and invasion. Today, visitors can walk through several large galleries and see wonderful stalactites. There is a cupola-like chamber in one gallery that is called Little Dome. This chamber houses a large colony of bats.

12 ⊕ PLATEAUS AND MONOLITHS

The Transylvanian Plateau, at elevations averaging 365 meters (1,200 feet), lies in the center of Romania, ringed by the three branches of the Carpathian Mountains.

Its terrain includes valleys and rounded hills, and it is bordered on the west by an area of the eroded limestone known as karst.

The Moldavian Plateau is marked by hills and narrow valleys and extends across the eastern region of Moldavia between the Subcarpathians and the Prut River, rising to between 488 and 610 meters (1,600 and 2,000 feet). Farther south, in the northern inland part of the Dobruja region, is a plateau that rises to a maximum height of 467 meters (1,532 feet).

13 ⊕ MAN-MADE FEATURES

Hydropower from the rivers flowing down the Carpathian Mountains provides an important energy source.

The two Iron Gate Dams on the Danube, located in the southeastern corner of Romania, were built not only to generate hydroelectric power, but also to supply irrigation waters and to serve as a reservoir site for farm fishing. The Vidraru Dam on the Argeş River provides hydroelectric power as well as water for irrigation and part of the drinking supply for the city of Bucharest. The Gura Apelor Dam on the Raul Mare River, near the town of Hateg, is specifically used for hydroelectric power.

14 ⊕ FURTHER READING

Books

Burford, Tim. *Hiking Guide to Romania*. Old Saybrook, CT: Globe Pequote Press, 1996.

DID YOU KN⊕W?

Bran Castle in the Transylvanian Alps is believed to have been the home of the fifteenth-century Romanian prince Vlad Tepes, who was born in the Transylvanian village of Sighisoara (central Romania, northwest of Bucharest) in 1431. He was known as "The Impaler" because of his cruelty in mass executions. He was also called "Dracula," which means "Son of a Dragon," because his father was a member of the Order of the Dragon, a group of knights established by the Holy Roman Emperor Sigismund to fight the Turks. British author Bram Stoker made Transylvania and Dracula famous when he chose the personality of Vlad Tepes as the basis for the vampire in his 1897 Gothic novel *Dracula*.

Dennis-Jones, Harold. *Where to Go in Romania*. London: Settle Press, 1994.

Richardson, Dan. *Romania: The Rough Guide*. New York: Penguin, 1995.

Williams, Nicola. *Romania and Moldova*. Hawthorn, Victoria: Lonely Planet, 1998.

Willis, Terrie. *Romania*. New York: Children's Press, 2000.

Russia

- **Official name:** Russian Federation
- **Area:** 17,075,200 square kilometers (6,592,771 square miles)
- **Highest point on mainland:** Mount El'brus (5,633 meters/18,481 feet)
- **Lowest point on land:** Caspian Sea (28 meters/92 feet below sea level)
- **Hemispheres:** Northern, Eastern, and Western
- **Time zones:** 3 P.M. Moscow = noon GMT; 12 A.M. Anadyr = noon GMT
- **Longest distances:** 4,000 kilometers (2,400 miles) from north to south; 10,000 kilometers (6,200 miles) from east to west
- **Coastline:** 37,653 kilometers (23,396 miles)

- **Land boundaries:** 19,961 kilometers (12,403 miles) total boundary length; Azerbaijan 284 kilometers (176 miles); Belarus 959 kilometers (596 miles); China 3,605 kilometers (2,265 miles); Estonia 294 kilometers (183 miles); Finland 1,313 kilometers (816 miles); Georgia 723 kilometers (449 miles); Kazakhstan 6,846 kilometers (4,254 miles); Latvia 217 kilometers (135 miles); Lithuania 227 kilometers (141 miles); Mongolia 3,485 kilometers (2,165 miles); North Korea 19 kilometers (12 miles); Norway 167 kilometers (104 miles); Poland 206 kilometers (128 miles); and Ukraine 1,576 kilometers (979 miles)
- **Territorial sea limits:** 22 kilometers (12 nautical miles)

1 ⊕ LOCATION AND SIZE

Russia is the largest country in the world, spreading from northeastern Europe across the entire northern width of the Asian continent. It shares borders with fourteen other countries and has coastlines on the Arctic and Pacific Oceans. With a total area of about 17,075,200 square kilometers (6,592,771 square miles), it is nearly twice the size of the United States. Russia is administratively divided into forty-nine oblasts, twenty-one republics, ten autonomous okrugs, six krays, two federal cities, and one autonomous oblast.

2 ⊕ TERRITORIES AND DEPENDENCIES

A small portion of Russia, the Kaliningrad Oblast, is located in Eastern Europe between Poland and Lithuania. There are no overseas dependencies of Russia.

3 ⊕ CLIMATE

It is said that Russia has only two seasons: summer and winter. Though this is a slight exaggeration, the statement accurately characterizes the country's harsh climate with its long, cold winters and short, cool summers. These conditions are owing to Russia's location in the high northerly latitudes. More than half the country lies above 60° north latitude, with only relatively small areas below 50° north. Furthermore, the high mountains that form Russia's southern border effectively block out warm air masses. The predominant movement of the country's weather systems from east to west essentially nullifies any moderating influence the warm waters of the Pacific Ocean might have on the climate. In winter, Siberia lies under a vast high-pressure cell centered in Mongolia, which keeps the region enveloped in frigid air. The magnitude of this cold is not easy to grasp. Soil in the far northern permafrost can be frozen several hundred meters deep. Even into southern Siberia, the land is covered by snow for more than six months. The annual average temperature for most of Siberia is below freezing. For the majority of European Russia, the average is only somewhat higher.

In summer, warm, moist air from the Atlantic Ocean is able to push east to central Siberia, under the influence of a prevailing low-pressure system. That area thus receives moisture-bearing air that delivers fairly high amounts of precipitation. Russia's short growing season relies heavily upon this rainfall to water its crops; unfortunately, distribution of the moisture in many areas is often irregular and unpredictable. Droughts are not uncommon, especially in early summer. On the other hand, heavy rains in middle and late summer may compromise harvesting. In the east, late-summer Pacific air can bring monsoon-like rainfall, with disastrous effects.

Overall, lack of sunshine characterizes the Russian climate. Overcast skies are the rule, especially in winter. In December, for example, Moscow typically experiences twenty-three days of cloud cover. Sunless winter days are the rule throughout the nation.

Russia's climate zones lie in easily distinguishable belts that run from east to west across the whole country. In the far north, Novaya Zemlya, Severnaya Zemlya, and numerous smaller Arctic islands experience a polar desert climate. Below this, a tundra climate predominates for at least 100 kilometers (60 miles) south, extending up into the steep mountain slopes far to the east. Next, a broad subarctic zone passes southward as far as St. Petersburg in the west, crosses the Urals, and takes in nearly all the rest of Siberia. Last is a wide belt of cold, dry steppe climate starting at the Black Sea, crossing the North Caucasian Plain, moving through the lower Volga Valley and the southern Urals into Siberia.

REGIONAL TEMPERATURE RANGES		
CITY	JANUARY TEMPERATURE AVERAGES	JULY TEMPERATURE AVERAGES
Moscow	-16°C to -9°C (3°F to 16°F)	13°C to 23°C (55°F to 73°F)
Vladivostok	-18°C to -11°C (0°F to 13°F)	16°C to 22°C (60°F to 71°F)
Verkhoyansk	-32°C (-26°F)	13°C to 37°C (56°F to 98°F)

Most of Russia experiences only modest precipitation, but the averages vary by region. On the Great European Plain, averages decrease from more than 80 centimeters (30 inches) in the west to less than 40 centimeters (16 inches) on the Caspian Sea shoreline. Siberia uniformly sees annual precipitation ranging from 50 to 80 centimeters (20 to 32 inches), although amounts are generally less than 30 centimeters (12 inches) in extreme northeastern Siberia. At high elevations, precipitation totals may reach 100 centimeters (40 inches) or more, but in the valleys they average less than 30 centimeters (12 inches).

4 ⊕ TOPOGRAPHIC REGIONS

Russia can be categorized into several large regions. From west to east, they are the Great European Plain; the Ural Mountains; the mountain systems and ranges along much of Russia's southern border; and Siberia, which includes the West Siberian Plain, the Central Siberian Plateau, and the mountain ranges of northeastern Siberia and the Kamchatka Peninsula.

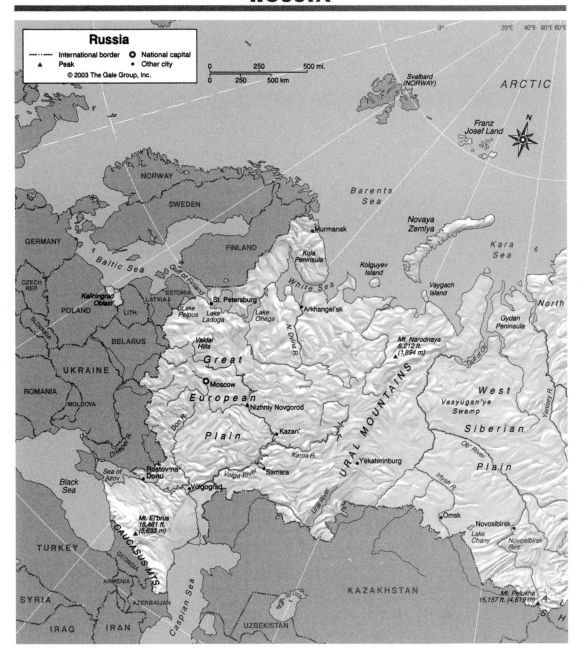

Most of Russia is located on the Eurasian Tectonic Plate, but eastern Russia is on the North American Plate. The exact boundary between the two plates is uncertain. The Pacific Plate is located off of Russia's eastern coastline.

The movement of these three plates against each other is a cause of significant earthquakes and volcanoes in this region, especially on Kamchatka. Seismic activity is also common in the Caucasus Mountains in the southwest.

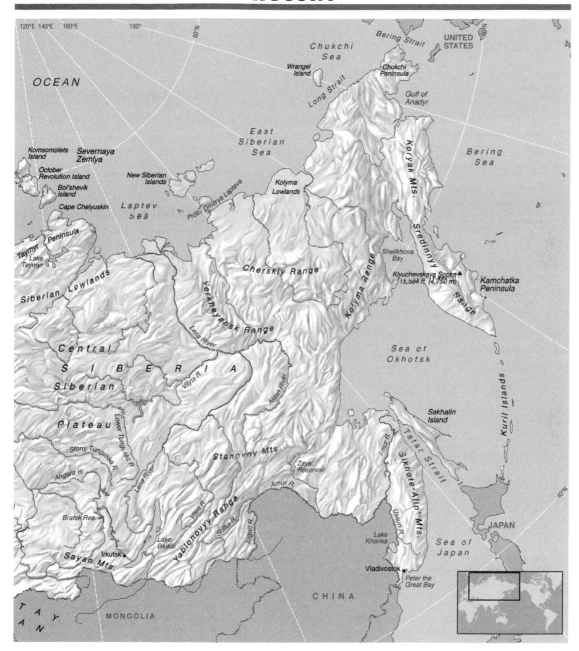

5 ⊕ OCEANS AND SEAS

Seacoast and Undersea Features

The majority of Russia's coastline is on the Arctic Ocean and its seas, including the White Sea, Barents Sea, Kara Sea, Laptev Sea, East Siberian Sea, and the Chukchi Sea. Located almost entirely north of the Arctic Circle, much of the water here remains frozen for the better part of the year. One exception is the area in

EPD/Saxifraga/Systske Dijksen

Animals graze in a valley lying in the mountains west of Lake Baikal.

the far west, where the Gulf Stream current warms the waters of the Barents Sea near the Kola Peninsula, allowing the port of Murmansk to function year-round. The eastern coastline of Russia lies on the Pacific Ocean and its seas, including the Bering Sea, the Sea of Okhotsk, and a portion of the Sea of Japan. Western Russia has short coastlines along the Baltic Sea (in northern Europe) and the Black Sea (an inland sea between southeastern Europe and Asia), both of which are seas of the Atlantic Ocean.

Sea Inlets and Straits

The Gulf of Ob' and the estuary of the Yenisey River are inlets of the coastline of the Kara Sea. A channel called the Proliv Dmitrya Lapteva connects the Laptev Sea to the East Siberian Sea. Long Strait near the northeast coast connects the East Siberian Sea to the Chukchi Sea and separates the

mainland from Wrangel Island. The Bering Strait separates Siberia and Alaska by a mere 86 kilometers (53 miles) and connects the Chukchi Sea to the Bering Sea. Shelikhova Bay is a deep inlet of the Sea of Okhotsk. The Gulf of Anadyr, near the northeastern tip of Russia, is an inlet of the Bering Sea. Russia's principal Pacific Ocean port, Vladivostok, is found on Peter the Great Bay, within the Sea of Japan. The Tatar Strait connects the Sea of Okhotsk to the Sea of Japan. The Gulf of Finland in the west is an inlet of the Baltic Sea. St. Petersburg is located at its apex. The Sea of Azov is an inlet of the Black Sea, located at the southwestern Russian border.

Islands and Archipelagos

Many islands lie within the Arctic and Pacific Oceans off the shores of Russia. Franz Josef Land is comprised of about one hundred small islands in the Arctic Ocean; it is the northern-

DID YOU KN⊕W?

Russia was even larger in the past than it is today. Russia controlled Finland, Alaska, and parts of modern-day Poland at various times in history. After World War I (1914–18), Russia technically ceased to be an independent country, instead becoming part of the Union of Soviet Socialist Republics (U.S.S.R., or the Soviet Union). Russia was by far the largest of the republics that made up the Soviet Union, however, and was considered to be the ruling power of that nation. The Soviet Union started to dissolve in 1991. Eventually, many nations within the Soviet Union became independent of Russia.

most part of Russia and is among the northernmost lands on Earth. Other large Arctic islands are Novaya Zemlya, Vaygach Island, Wrangel Island, and the Severnaya Zemlya and New Siberian Islands groups. Many small islands and island chains are scattered among these larger groups.

In the Pacific, the Kuril Islands curve southwest from the Kamchatka Peninsula to Japan. Although the Kuril Islands are under Russian administration, Japan and Russia dispute ownership of the four southernmost islands. Also lying in the Pacific is Sakhalin, a large island that separates the Seas of Okhotsk and Japan.

Coastal Features

No country in the world can surpass Russia's 37,653 kilometers (23,396 miles) of coastline. Yet most of this coastline is so far north that it is frozen for much of the year. Despite the fact that frozen harbors mean Russia has very few outlets to the ocean that remain open all year, Russian shipping and fishing thrives on all its seas.

The coastlines contain many peninsulas and capes. Gydan Peninsula lies between the Gulf of Ob' and the estuary of the Yenisey River. Continuing to the east, the Taymyr Peninsula extends north, reaching mainland Russia's northernmost point at Cape Chelyuskin.

The Chukchi Peninsula stretches out to become Russia's easternmost point, with the Chukchi Sea of the Arctic Ocean to the north and the Bering Sea of the Pacific Ocean to the south. Further south is the large Kamchatka Peninsula. Kamchatka encloses the Sea of Okhotsk to the west.

6 ⊕ INLAND LAKES

The Caspian Sea, on Russia's southern border between Europe and Asia, is not a true sea; it is actually a saltwater lake and the largest inland body of water in the world. The Caspian is held in a vast land depression with no outlet to any ocean. Although many rivers drain into it, water escapes only through evaporation. The Caspian's salinity results from accumulated salts. The sea extends approximately 1,210 kilometers (750 miles) from north to south and 210 to 436 kilometers (130 to 271 miles) from east to west. Its area is 371,000 square kilometers (143,000 square miles). Its mean depth is about 170 meters (550 feet), with the deepest areas in the south.

Most other Russian lakes were formed by glaciation. The largest such lakes in European Russia are Ladoga (17,703 square kilometers/6,835 square miles) and Onega (9,609 square kilometers/3,701 square miles), northeast of St. Petersburg. They are also the two largest lakes in all of Europe (since the Caspian Sea is generally not counted as a lake). Other large lakes in western Russia include Lake Peipus on the Estonian border and the reservoirs of the Volga River.

Lake Baikal in southern Siberia is the largest lake in Russia and the largest lake in Asia (excluding the Caspian Sea). It is 632 kilometers (392 miles) long and 59 kilometers (32 miles) wide, with a surface area of 30,510 square kilometers (11,870 square miles). It has a maximum depth of 1,742 meters (5,715 feet), making it the deepest body of freshwater on Earth. Due to its great depth, Lake Baikal also has the greatest volume of any freshwater lake. It is said to contain one-fifth of Earth's fresh surface water. Other large Siberian lakes include Lakes Taymyr, Chany, and Khanka and the Novosibirsk, Bratsk, and Zeya Reservoirs. There also are many smaller lakes.

7 ⊕ RIVERS AND WATERFALLS

Most of Russia's urban population lives along the banks of the nation's many rivers. The most important commercial river in Russia is the Volga, which is also the longest river in Europe. The Volga begins in the hills west of Moscow and flows southeastward for 3,689 kilometers (2,293 miles) to the Caspian Sea. Four of Russia's largest cities are located on its banks: Nizhniy Novgorod, Samara, Kazan', and Volgograd. The Kama River flows west out of the southern Urals and into the Volga. This also is a major waterway for both Russia and Europe.

Also located in European Russia are the Dnieper and the Don Rivers. Although the Dnieper flows mainly through Belarus and

EPD/Saxifraga/Sytske Dijksen

Aerial view of the Kolyma lowlands, a tundra region in eastern Russia.

Ukraine, it has headwaters in the hills west of Moscow. The Don flows from its origins in the Central Russian Upland south of Moscow for 1,860 kilometers (1,153 miles) before emptying into the Sea of Azov at Rostov-na-Donu.

Further east is the Ural River, which flows south from the Ural Mountains into Kazakhstan before reaching the Caspian Sea. The Ural River is traditionally considered part of the boundary between Europe and Asia.

A number of major rivers drain into the Pacific and Arctic Oceans from the Siberian plateau and mountain areas in the east. The

Irtysh-Ob' river system flows through the West Siberian Plain, emptying into the Arctic at the Gulf of Ob'. The Irtysh is the longer of the two rivers, but is a tributary to the Ob'. Together they have a length of 5,380 kilometers (3,335 miles), making them the longest river system in Russia.

On the far side of the Central Siberian Plateau is the Lena, the longest individual river in Russia at 4,400 kilometers (2,700 miles). It too empties into the Arctic, and it has many large tributaries including the Aldan, Vitim, and Vilyui. The third great Arctic river, the Yenisey (4,000 kilometers/2,480 miles), flows across the Central Siberian Plateau. Its largest tributary, the Lower Tunguska, is itself roughly 3,226 kilometers (2,000 miles) long. Other major tributaries include the Stony Tunguska and Angara.

The same river systems that account for such an enormous flow of water into the Arctic Ocean are also responsible for creating vast swamps in the West Siberian Plain. Snow and ice in the warmer regions, where the rivers have their sources, thaw well before the northern regions, causing great flooding to the north. The Vasyugan'ye Swamp in the center of the West Siberian Plain, for example, covers 48,000 square kilometers (18,500 square feet). The same effect can be observed with other Siberian river systems.

The Amur River (2,874 kilometers/1,768 miles) is the most important Siberian river flowing into the Pacific Ocean. Its major tributaries are the Argun, Ussuri, and Shilka. The Amur River, with its primary tributary the Ussuri River, comprises a significant section of the boundary between Russia and China.

8 ⊕ DESERTS

There are no desert regions in Russia.

9 ⊕ FLAT AND ROLLING TERRAIN

In all nearly 10 percent of Russian territory can be classified as swampland. Much of this

DID YOU KN⊕W?

The areas now known as Siberia and Alaska were once connected by a stretch of land that surfaced during the Ice Ages, an area that researchers have called the Bering Land Bridge or Beringia. Archaeologists believe that the first ancestors of the Native Americans crossed this bridge from Asia into North America more than thirteen thousand years ago. Over time, as the Bering and Chukchi Seas rose, they covered Beringia. Remnants of the region can still be seen at the Bering Land Bridge National Preserve on Seward Peninsula in Alaska.

is concentrated in the West Siberian Plain, which lies between the Ural Mountains and the Yenisey River. This plain is a vast area of lowlands, probably the largest expanse of flat land anywhere in the world. It stretches from the steppes of Central Asia in the south to the Arctic Ocean in the north, covering a region nearly 1,800 kilometers (1,100 miles) wide. Flat and poorly drained, these lowlands feature many swamps, marshes, and peat bogs, with significant oil and natural gas deposits in their central and northern regions.

The Ural Mountains separate two vast plains: the Great European Plain and the even larger West Siberian Plain. Both of these so-called plains contain a wide variety of terrain, including vast forests, swamps, and stretches

DID YOU KN⊕W?

The areas now known as Siberia and Alaska were once connected by a stretch of land that surfaced during the Ice Ages, an area that researchers have called the Bering Land Bridge or Beringia. Archaeologists believe that the first ancestors of the Native Americans crossed this bridge from Asia into North America more than thirteen thousand years ago. Over time, as the Bering and Chukchi Seas rose, they covered Beringia. Remnants of the region can still be seen at the Bering Land Bridge National Preserve on Seward Peninsula in Alaska.

of tundra. The plains also contain many areas of grassland and farmland, however, especially the Great European Plain.

The central portion of the Great European Plain between St. Petersburg and the Ukrainian border features a mixed forest of both conifers and deciduous trees. Oak, beech, maple, and hornbeam are the primary broad-leaf tree species. Moving south, the mixed forest passes through a narrow zone of forest steppe, which is 150 kilometers (95 miles) wide, on average, before giving way to a zone of true steppe.

The steppe is a broad band of nearly tree-less, grassy plains that extends across Hungary, Ukraine, southern Russia, and Kazakhstan before ending in Manchuria. Although historically presented as the typical Russian landscape, the steppe in Russia proper is in fact quite small, located mainly northwest of the Greater Caucasus Mountains and stretching across the southern Volga Valley, the southern Urals, and parts of western Siberia.

Isolated pockets of steppe can also be found in the mountain valleys of southeastern Siberia. Moderate temperatures and normally adequate levels of sunshine and moisture give the steppe zone relatively favorable conditions for agriculture, although precipitation here can be unpredictable, sometimes even catastrophically dry.

Tundra makes up about 10 percent of Russian land, a treeless and marshy plain that lies along Russia's northernmost zone. The tundra stretches from the Finnish border to the Bering Strait, then extends south along the Pacific coast to the Kamchatka Peninsula. The North Siberian and Kolyma lowlands are entirely made up of tundra. Only mosses, lichens, dwarf willows and shrubs can grow on the permafrost and survive the long, harsh, sunless winters. In summer, dusk comes at midnight and dawn follows within minutes. The powerful Siberian rivers that cut across the tundra toward the Arctic Ocean do a poor job of draining the region, due to partial and intermittent thawing. The most important physical process at work in the tundra is frost weathering, a vestige of the glaciation that shaped it during the last Ice Age.

There are many regions of hills and uplands in Russia. The Valdai Hills are the most noteworthy. Although not particularly tall (from 182 to 304 meters/600 to 1000 feet in elevation), they are among the highest summits located in the Great European Plain of western Russia. Many important rivers have their source there, including the Volga.

10 ⊕ MOUNTAINS AND VOLCANOES

With nine major mountain ranges, Russia can be considered among the most mountainous countries in the world. Eastern Russia is by far more mountainous than the west, while the center section of the country is primarily low plains.

The Urals are perhaps the best known of Russia's mountain ranges, as they define the boundary between Asia to the east and Europe to the west. A lengthy range, the Urals extend 2,100 kilometers (1,300 miles) from the northern border of Kazakhstan all the way to the Arctic Ocean. The highest peak, Mount Narodnaya, is only 1,894 meters (6,212 feet) in elevation, however. The Urals have never offered any significant barrier to travel.

Located between the Black and Caspian Seas, the Caucasus Mountains consist of two major chains separated by lowlands. The northern Greater Caucasus range forms most of the border between Russia, Azerbaijan, and Georgia, as well as marking the boundary between Asia to the south and Europe to the north. These mountain systems are made up of granite, other crystalline rocks, and some volcanic formations. Elevations in the Greater Caucasus reach a maximum of 5,633 meters (18,481 feet) at the extinct volcano Mount El'brus, the highest peak both in Russia and on the continent of Europe.

Russia's other mountains are far to the east. The Altay Shan and Sayan Mountains are found in the area north of Mongolia, west of Lake Baikal. Further east are the Yablonovyy Range and Stanovoy Mountains. They follow much of the southern border of central and eastern Siberia on toward the Pacific Ocean, where they join the other eastern ranges. The Altay Shan are the tallest of these; they include Mount Pelukha (4,619 meters/15,157 feet). The other ranges average less than 3,048 meters (10,000 feet) in height.

DID YOU KN⊕W?

In an area known as the Kursk Magnetic Anomaly, near Ukraine, vast iron-ore deposits affect Earth's magnetic field.

The topography east of the Lena River is predominantly mountainous, with the elevations becoming higher and more rugged farther to the east. Major ranges in this region are Verkhoyanskiy, Cherskiy, Kolyma, Koryak, and Sredinnyy. The easternmost ranges feature live volcanoes. As many as 120 volcanoes dot the Kamchatka Peninsula, and no fewer than 23 are active. Klyuchevskaya Sopka, the highest of these, reaches 4,750 meters (15,584 feet).

Moving offshore, these same mountains form the Kuril Islands, where thirty of one hundred volcanoes are active. Across the Sea of Okhotsk, in Russia's southeasternmost area, there are several low mountain ranges, including the Sikhote-Alin' Mountains and the mountains of Sakhalin Island.

11 ⊕ CANYONS AND CAVES

Though there are many caves throughout the country of Russia, geological information or maps concerning them are not easy to obtain. One of the most famous of the many caves is Kapova Cave, which is known for its Paleolithic paintings of mammoths, rhinos, horses, and bison. Excavations from the two-level cavern uncovered human remains as well as animal bones and charcoal, indicating that people once lived there.

Another famous site is the Kungur Ice Cave, located near the town of Kungur, southeast of Perm. It contains over 6,000 meters (19,685 feet) of passageways. The entire depth of the cavern, however, has not been completely explored. The cave features many large columns of stalagmites and huge icicle stalactites.

12 ⊕ PLATEAUS AND MONOLITHS

The Central Siberian Plateau is an enormous stretch of rolling land between the Yenisey and the Lena Rivers. Heights of this vast plateau range from 500 to 700 meters (1,600 to 2,300 feet) on average. Its surface is eroded by the many rivers, some forming deep canyons. Layers of sedimentary rock, subsequently intruded by volcanic lava, were deposited long ago on top of igneous and metamorphic rock. Within the layers of sedimentary rock are rich deposits of coal.

13 ⊕ MAN-MADE FEATURES

Several canals connect most of European Russia's rivers. These rivers provide a vital transportation system, carrying fully two-thirds of the nation's inland water traffic. Because of one series of canals, it is possible to travel from St. Petersburg to Moscow entirely by boat.

Russia's many rivers give the nation a great potential for hydroelectric power. In fact, Russia already has four of the ten largest hydroelectric plants in the world. The Sayano-Shushensk Dam on the Yenisey River is part of the fourth-largest plant and is also the twelfth-highest dam in the world, with a height of 242 meters (794 feet). The Krasnoyarsk Dam belongs to the fifth-largest hydroelectric plant in the world, while the Bratsk Dam and the Ust-Ilim Dam are eighth and tenth, respectively. The Saratov Dam on the Volga River is also listed as one of the world's largest dams.

14 ⊕ FURTHER READING

Books and Periodicals

Clark, Miles. "A Russian Voyage." *National Geographic*, June 1994, 114-138.

Edwards, Mike. "Siberia: In from the Cold." *National Geographic*, March 1990, 2-39.

Jacobsen, Karen. *The Russian Federation*. Chicago: Children's Press, 1994.

Lydolph, Paul E. *Geography of the U.S.S.R.* New York: John Wiley and Sons, 1964.

Torchinsky, Oleg. *Russia*. New York: Marshall Cavendish, 1994

Web Site

Russian National Tourism Office. http://www.russia-travel.com (accessed June 13, 2003).

Rwanda

- **Official name:** Republic of Rwanda
- **Area:** 26,338 square kilometers (10,169 square miles)
- **Highest point on mainland:** Mount Karisimbi (4,519 meters/14,826 feet)
- **Lowest point on land:** Rusizi River (950 meters/3,117 feet)
- **Hemispheres:** Southern and Eastern
- **Time zone:** 2 P.M. = noon GMT
- **Longest distances:** 248 kilometers (154 miles) from northeast to southwest; 166 kilometers (103 miles) from southeast to northwest

- **Land boundaries:** 893 kilometers (555 miles) total boundary length; Burundi 290 kilometers (180 miles); Democratic Republic of the Congo 217 kilometers (135 miles); Tanzania 217 kilometers (135 miles); Uganda 169 kilometers (105 miles)
- **Coastline:** None
- **Territorial sea limits:** None

1 ⊕ LOCATION AND SIZE

Rwanda is a small, landlocked country located south of the equator in east-central Africa. With an area of 26,338 square kilometers (10,169 square miles), it is almost as large as the state of Maryland.

2 ⊕ TERRITORIES AND DEPENDENCIES

Rwanda has no territories or dependencies.

3 ⊕ CLIMATE

High altitudes keep the climate moderate in much of Rwanda despite its proximity to the equator. In addition, trade winds from the Indian Ocean moderate the temperatures on the Central Plateau, where the annual average is 21°C (70°F). Temperatures in the mountains of the northwest are lower, especially at night, yet they average near 32°C (90°F) in parts of the eastern lowlands. Average annual rainfall can range from as little as 76 centimeters (30 inches) in the eastern lowlands to 179 centimeters (70 inches) in the mountains. The yearly average rainfall on the Central Plateau is about 114 centimeters (45 inches).

4 ⊕ TOPOGRAPHIC REGIONS

The divide between two of Africa's great watersheds, the Congo and Nile basins, extends from north to south through western Rwanda at an average elevation of almost 2,743 meters (9,000 feet). On the western slopes of this Congo-Nile ridgeline, the land slopes abruptly toward Lake Kivu in the Great Rift Valley on the western border of the country. The eastern slopes are more moderate, with rolling hills extending across the central uplands at gradually reducing altitudes to the plains, swamps, and lakes of the eastern border region.

Rwanda can be divided into five regions from west to east: 1) the narrow Great Rift Valley region along or near Lake Kivu,

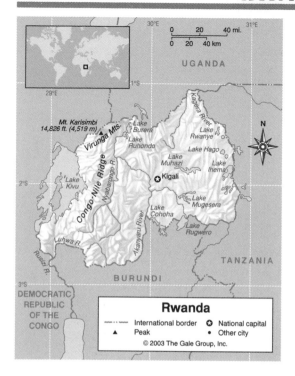

Rwanda

---·--- International border ⊕ National capital
▲ Peak · Other city

© 2003 The Gale Group, Inc.

meters (1,558 feet). Lake Cohoha and Lake Rugwero lie in Rwanda's southeast, partly extending into Burundi. There are also eight sizable lakes that lie entirely within Rwanda: Lakes Rwehikama, Ihema, Muhazi, Mugesera, Hago, and Rwanye in the east, and Lakes Ruhondo and Burera in the north.

7 ⊕ RIVERS AND WATERFALLS

Most of Rwanda's rivers are in the eastern part of the country. The Kagera River in the east forms the boundary with Tanzania and part of the boundary with Burundi. With a total length of 692 kilometers (430 miles), the Kagera is the longest river in Rwanda. The Nyabarongo River and its tributaries drain much of the Central Plateau. In the west, the Ruzizi flows southward from Lake Kivu along the border with the Democratic Republic of the Congo, into Burundi, and on to Lake Tanganyika. In the south, the Luhwa and Akanyaru Rivers form parts of the boundary with Burundi.

8 ⊕ DESERTS

There are no deserts in Rwanda.

9 ⊕ FLAT AND ROLLING TERRAIN

Much of the countryside is covered by grasslands and small farms extending over the rolling hills that cover much of the Central Plateau; this terrain has given Rwanda the nickname "Land of a Thousand Hills."

10 ⊕ MOUNTAINS AND VOLCANOES

Rising from high lava plains in the northwest corner of Rwanda are the Virunga Mountains, Rwanda's only mountain range. They consist of five volcanic peaks, two of which still emit smoke and steam. The highest of these is Mount Karisimbi, which rises to over 4,519 meters (14,826 feet).

2) the volcanic Virunga Mountains and high lava plains of northwestern Rwanda, 3) the Congo-Nile Ridge, 4) the rolling hills and valleys of the central plateaus, which slope eastward from the Congo-Nile Ridge, and 5) the savannahs and marshlands of the eastern and southeastern border areas, which are lower, warmer, and drier than the central upland plateaus.

5 ⊕ OCEANS AND SEAS

Rwanda is landlocked and therefore has no oceanic coast.

6 ⊕ INLAND LAKES

Rwanda has many lakes. The largest, Lake Kivu, is located in the midst of the volcanic peaks in the Virunga Mountains and forms part of the border with the Democratic Republic of the Congo. The lake has a surface area of 2,665 square kilometers (1,025 square miles) and reaches a maximum depth of 475

EPD/Cynthia Bassett

The Virunga Mountains are Rwanda's only mountain range.

11 ⊕ CANYONS AND CAVES

The system of caves in the Gisenyi region of northwestern Rwanda is infamous for the 1994 massacre of some eight thousand Hutus, an ethnic minority, by the rival Tutsi people.

12 ⊕ PLATEAUS AND MONOLITHS

The Central Plateau has an average altitude of 1,432 meters (4,700 feet); becoming progressively lower in elevation as it extends toward the eastern border.

13 ⊕ MAN-MADE FEATURES

There are no railways in Rwanda. The capital city of Kigali is connected with nearby towns in Burundi and Uganda by a well-traveled road.

14 ⊕ FURTHER READING

Books

Carr, Rosamond Halsey, and Ann Howard Halsey. *Land of a Thousand Hills: My Life in Rwanda.* Rockland, MA: Compass Press, 2000.

Harelimana, Froduald. *Rwanda: Society and Culture of a Nation in Transition.* Corvallis, OR: Harelimana, 1997.

Murphy, Dervla. *Visiting Rwanda.* Dublin, Ireland: Lilliput Press, 1998.

Web Sites

Rwanda Information Exchange. http://www.rwanda.net/ (accessed April 11, 2003).

Rwanda Page. http://www.sas.upenn.edu/African_Studies/Country_Specific/Rwanda.html (accessed April 4, 2003).

Saint Kitts and Nevis

■ **Official name:** Federation of Saint Kitts and Nevis

■ **Area:** 261 square kilometers (101 square miles)

■ **Highest point on mainland:** Mount Misery (1,156 meters/3,793 feet)

■ **Lowest point on land:** Sea level

■ **Hemispheres:** Northern and Western

■ **Time zone:** 8 A.M. = noon GMT

■ **Longest distances:** 37 kilometers (23 miles) from north to south; 8 kilometers (5 miles) from east to west

■ **Land boundaries:** None

■ **Coastline:** 135 kilometers (84 miles)

■ **Territorial sea limits:** 22 kilometers (12 nautical miles)

1 ⊕ LOCATION AND SIZE

Shaped like an exclamation mark, the popular tourist destinations of Saint Kitts and Nevis lie in the northern part of the Leeward Islands in the Eastern Caribbean, with Barbuda to the northeast and Antigua to the southwest. Covering an area of 261 square kilometers (101 square miles), Saint Kitts and Nevis is over one-and-one-half times the size of Washington, D.C.

2 ⊕ TERRITORIES AND DEPENDENCIES

Saint Kitts and Nevis has no territories or dependencies.

3 ⊕ CLIMATE

The temperatures recorded on Saint Kitts and Nevis change very little during the year, due to their close proximity to the equator. Year-round temperatures average 26°C (79°F) and rarely exceed 32°C (89°F).

Rainfall is greater and more frequent in higher elevations. Most rain falls between May and November, with an average annual rainfall of 109 centimeters (43 inches). The summer months are especially humid; hurricanes are possible in the late summer and early fall months.

4 ⊕ TOPOGRAPHIC REGIONS

Both Saint Kitts and Nevis are volcanic islands. The larger of the two, Saint Kitts, contains a dormant volcano, a salt lake, and tropical forests. The circular island of Nevis, also home to a dormant volcano, slopes to its highest peak, Nevis Peak, and is home to rich forests and sandy beaches. Both islands are known for their lush vegetation.

5 ⊕ OCEANS AND SEAS

Saint Kitts and Nevis are located in the Caribbean Sea.

Seacoast and Undersea Features

While there are coral reefs throughout the Caribbean, none of the reefs near the islands are of significant size. The highest concentration of these reefs is near Nag's Head and the southwestern coast of Saint Kitts. The coral reefs on Saint Kitts, notably those near Sandy Point Bay, are rich in marine life.

Sea Inlets and Straits

A two-mile-wide channel, known as the Narrows, separates Saint Kitts from Nevis.

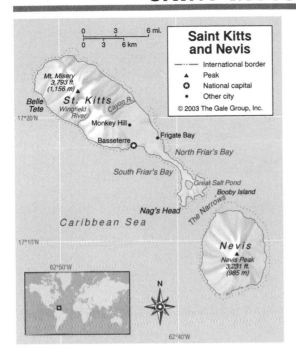

AP Photo/David Langford

Islands and Archipelagos

Located in the channel separating the islands of Saint Kitts and Nevis is the small Booby Island.

Coastal Features

The coastlines of the islands are rather jagged and indented, with many bay and beach areas. Located on the southern tip of Saint Kitts are Majors Bay, Banana Bay, and Cockleshell Bay. Other bays line the coastline, including Half Moon Bay, Sandy Bay, Frigate and North Frigate Bays, and North and South Friar's Bays. There are two capes of interest: Belle Tete, on the northwestern shore of Saint Kitts, and Nag's Head, at the end of the Frigate Bay Peninsula. The beaches on both islands range from smooth with white sand to coarse with black sand. The northern end of Saint Kitts has numerous black volcanic sand beaches.

6 ⊕ INLAND LAKES

The Great Salt Pond, located near the southeastern tip of Saint Kitts, is the only lake of significant size on the islands.

Mount Nevis, a dormant volcano, is often hidden by clouds. It is said that when Christopher Columbus sighted the island in 1493 he named it "Nuestro Senora de las Nieves" (Our Lady of the Snows) because of the white clouds around Mount Nevis.

7 ⊕ RIVERS AND WATERFALLS

Most of the rivers on Saint Kitts and Nevis no longer flow year-round. Those that remain are small and drain from the mountain ranges in the wet season, drying up partially or completely in the dry season. Two seasonal rivers of note are the Wingfield and Cayon Rivers, which during the wet seasons will flow almost to the Caribbean.

8 ⊕ DESERTS

There are no deserts on Saint Kitts and Nevis.

9 ⊕ FLAT AND ROLLING TERRAIN

Plots of sugarcane cover the foothills of the central mountain range on Saint Kitts. The island's southern peninsula consists of many low hills and expansive reaches of flat terrain, which include large swamps and marshes of all kinds.

10 ⊕ MOUNTAINS AND VOLCANOES

The major mountain range on the island of Saint Kitts runs through the middle of the island from northeast to southwest. Rainforests surround the higher slopes. Mount Misery (also called Mount Liamuiga) is the highest summit on the island at 1,156 meters (3,793 feet). The highest peak on Nevis, called Nevis Peak, has an elevation of 985 meters (3,232 feet); it is often capped in white clouds.

11 ⊕ CANYONS AND CAVES

Coral grottoes located some 12 meters (40 feet) beneath Nevis's western coast are a popular dive site, providing underwater access to the island's coral reefs.

12 ⊕ PLATEAUS AND MONOLITHS

There are no plateaus or significant monoliths on Saint Kitts and Nevis.

13 ⊕ MAN-MADE FEATURES

Once known as "the Gibraltar of the West Indies," Brimstone Hill on the island of Saint Kitts is home to an eighteenth-century fortress that was restored in the 1960s.

14 ⊕ FURTHER READING

Books

Gordon, Joyce. *Nevis: Queen of the Caribees.* London: Macmillan Caribbean, 1990.

Merrill, Gordon Clark. *The Historical Geography of St. Kitts and Nevis, the West Indies.* Mexico: Instituto Panamericano de Geografia e Historia, 1958.

Richardson, Bonham C. *Caribbean Migrants: Environment and Human Survival on Saint Kitts and Nevis.* Knoxville: University of Tennessee Press, 1983.

Web Sites

Lonely Planet: Destination St. Kitts and Nevis. http://www.lonelyplanet.com/destinations/caribbean/saint_kitts_and_nevis/attractions.htm (accessed March 13, 2003).

St. Kitts Tourism Authority. http://www.stkitts-tourism.com/index2.html (accessed March 13, 2003).

Saint Lucia

- **Official name:** Saint Lucia
- **Area:** 620 square kilometers (239 square miles)
- **Highest point on mainland:** Mount Gimie (950 meters/3,117 feet)
- **Lowest point on land:** Sea level
- **Hemispheres:** Northern and Western
- **Time zone:** 8 A.M. = noon GMT

- **Longest distances:** 43 kilometers (27 miles) from north to south; 23 kilometers (14 miles) from east to west
- **Land boundaries:** None
- **Coastline:** 158 kilometers (98 miles)
- **Territorial sea limits:** 22 kilometers (12 nautical miles)

1 ⊕ LOCATION AND SIZE

Saint Lucia, located in the eastern Caribbean Sea between Martinique and Saint Vincent, is the second-largest of the Windward Islands. With an area of 620 square kilometers (239 square miles), Saint Lucia is almost three-and-a-half times as large as Washington, D.C.

2 ⊕ TERRITORIES AND DEPENDENCIES

Saint Lucia has no territories or dependencies.

3 ⊕ CLIMATE

Saint Lucia's tropical climate is moderated by trade winds off the Atlantic Ocean. The mean temperature year-round is about 27°C (80°F). Hurricanes are a hazard in the late summer months of June, July, and August.

Average annual rainfall ranges from about 127 centimeters (50 inches) in the coastal areas to as much as 381 centimeters (150 inches) at higher elevations in the interior. The wet season lasts from June to September, and the dry season runs from February to May.

4 ⊕ TOPOGRAPHIC REGIONS

The volcanically formed island consists of mountains and hills in the interior, surrounded by a coastal strip.

5 ⊕ OCEANS AND SEAS

Saint Lucia is located between the Atlantic Ocean and the Caribbean Sea.

Seacoast and Undersea Features

The harbor waters at the port of Castries are 8 meters (27 feet) deep, but the underwater geography around the island varies drastically. There are extensive coral reefs, underwater cliffs, walls, and mountains in the waters surrounding Saint Lucia.

Sea Inlets and Straits

Saint Lucia is separated from Martinique to the north by the Saint Lucia Channel, and from Saint Vincent to the south by the Saint Vincent Passage.

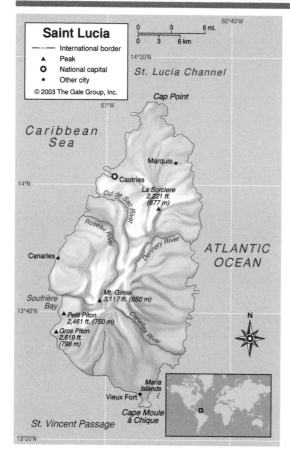

Islands and Archipelagos

Other than the main island, Saint Lucia also includes the Maria Islands, located off the southeast coast. The Maria Islands contain a nature reserve.

Coastal Features

Saint Lucia has two major ports: Castries and Vieux Fort. The eastern coast has many small indentations, while the western coast is mostly smoother, with major indentations at the port of Castries in the northwest and Soufrière Bay in the southwest, at which the mountain peaks of Gros Piton and Petit Piton are located. The island has two major capes, Cap Point at its northern tip and Cape Moule à Chique at its southern one. Saint Lucia is known for its many scenic beaches, some of which are covered with black volcanic sand.

6 ⊕ INLAND LAKES

Saint Lucia has no sizable lakes.

7 ⊕ RIVERS AND WATERFALLS

A number of small rivers flow outward from the central highlands to the coast. The principal ones are the Cul de Sac, Canelles, Dennery, Fond, Piaye, Doree, Canaries, Roseau, and Marquis Rivers.

8 ⊕ DESERTS

There are no deserts on Saint Lucia.

9 ⊕ FLAT AND ROLLING TERRAIN

A narrow strip of coastal plains fringe the exterior perimeter of Saint Lucia, giving way to foothills further inland. The northern half of the island is hillier, while the southern half is more mountainous.

10 ⊕ MOUNTAINS AND VOLCANOES

The cone-like twin summits of Gros Piton and Petit Piton are Saint Lucia's outstanding natural feature. Mountains occupy much of the country's interior, spanning the island from north to south. Although the highest elevation is in the south-central part of the island, where Mt. Gimie reaches a height of 950 meters (3,117 feet), the country's best-known peaks are Gros Piton and Petit Piton. These pyramids of volcanic rock rise out of the ocean at Soufrière Bay on the southwest coast, at elevations of 798 meters (2,619 feet) and 750 meters (2,461 feet), respectively.

11 ⊕ CANYONS AND CAVES

There are underwater caves carved out of Saint Lucia's coral reefs, which are a popular site for divers.

Susan D. Rock

Bubbling sulfur pools in Saint Lucia.

12 ⊕ PLATEAUS AND MONOLITHS

Saint Lucia has no plateaus and no significant monoliths.

13 ⊕ MAN-MADE FEATURES

The 91-meter- (300-foot-) deep Roseau Dam, completed in 1995, has a capacity of more than 2.6 billion liters (700 million gallons) of water. The Castries/Cul de Sac highway tunnel, completed early in 2000 and nicknamed the Millennium Highway, connects the city of Castries with the valley of the Cul de Sac River.

14 ⊕ FURTHER READING

Books

Eggleston, George Teeple. *Orchids on the Calabash Tree.* New York: Putnam, 1962.

Ellis, G. *Saint Lucia: Helen of the West Indies.* London: Macmillan, 1988.

Kingsolver, Barbara. *Homeland and Other Stories.* Rockland, MA: Wheeler Publishing, 1989.

Nieminen, Raija. *Voyage to the Island.* Washington, D.C.: Gallaudet University Press, 1990.

Philpott, Don. *Saint Lucia.* Lincolnwood, IL: Passport Books, 1996.

Web Sites

Lonely Planet: Destination St. Lucia. http://www.lonelyplanet.com/destinations/caribbean/saint_lucia/obt.htm (accessed May 5, 2003).

"Saint Lucia: Simply Beautiful." *Interknowledge Corporation.* http://www.st-lucia.com (accessed May 5, 2003).

Saint Vincent and the Grenadines

- **Official name:** Saint Vincent and the Grenadines

- **Area:** 389 square kilometers (150 square miles)

- **Highest point on mainland:** Soufrière (1,234 meters/4,049 feet)

- **Lowest point on land:** Sea level

- **Hemispheres:** Northern and Western

- **Time zone:** 8 A.M. = noon GMT

- **Longest distances:** Saint Vincent Island: 29 kilometers (18 miles) from north to south; 18 kilometers (11 miles) from east to west

- **Land boundaries:** None

- **Coastline:** 84 kilometers (52 miles)

- **Territorial sea limits:** 22 kilometers (12 nautical miles)

1 ⊕ LOCATION AND SIZE

Saint Vincent and the Grenadines (often simply called Saint Vincent) is part of the Windward Islands group of the Lesser Antilles in the Caribbean Sea, north of the island of Grenada. With an area of about 389 square kilometers (150 square miles), the country is twice the size of Washington, D.C. Saint Vincent is divided into six parishes. The island of Saint Vincent itself is by far the largest of these; with an area of 344 square kilometers (133 square miles), it accounts for almost 90 percent of the country's total area.

2 ⊕ TERRITORIES AND DEPENDENCIES

Saint Vincent and the Grenadines has no outside territories or dependencies.

3 ⊕ CLIMATE

Saint Vincent has a tropical climate with an average temperature of 26°C (79°F). September is the warmest month, with an average temperature of 27°C (81°F), and January is the coolest, with an average temperature of 25°C (77°F).

On Saint Vincent, yearly rainfall averages 231 centimeters (91 inches); in the mountainous regions, however, rainfall averages more than 380 centimeters (150 inches). The rainy season occurs from May or June through December. In most of the Grenadines, rainfall is the only source of fresh water.

4 ⊕ TOPOGRAPHIC REGIONS

Saint Vincent is a volcanic island that still has the active volcano, Soufrière, in its northern mountains. The remainder of the island contains rugged land, except for the lowlands and a valley in the interior, which are home, respectively, to tropical rainforests and Saint Vincent's best farmland. The Grenadines are generally rugged but low-lying.

5 ⊕ OCEANS AND SEAS

Seacoast and Undersea Features

Saint Vincent and the Grenadines is located between the Caribbean Sea to the west and the Atlantic Ocean to the east. Coral reefs

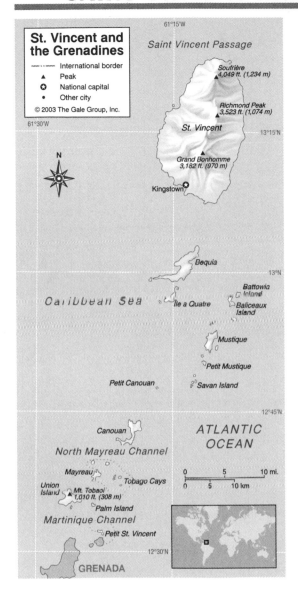

St. Vincent and the Grenadines

- - - - International border
▲ Peak
⊙ National capital
• Other city

© 2003 The Gale Group, Inc.

Saint Vincent Passage

Soufrière ▲ 4,049 ft. (1,234 m)

Richmond Peak ▲ 3,523 ft. (1,074 m)

St. Vincent

Grand Bonhomme ▲ 3,182 ft. (970 m)

Kingstown ⊙

Bequia

Battowia Island

Île a Quatre

Baliceaux Island

Caribbean Sea

Mustique

Petit Mustique

Petit Canouan

Savan Island

Canouan

ATLANTIC OCEAN

North Mayreau Channel

Mayreau

Tobago Cays

Union Island

Mt. Tobaoi ▲ 1,010 ft. (308 m)

Palm Island

Martinique Channel

Petit St. Vincent

GRENADA

0   5   10 mi.
0   5   10 km

lies between the Grenadine islands of Mayreau and Canouan.

Greathead Bay is located on the southern coast of Saint Vincent Island. The capital city of Kingstown is located on the shores of Kingstown Bay, also on the southern coaSaint

Islands and Archipelagos

The island of Saint Vincent itself is by far the largest in the country, with an area of 344 square kilometers (133 square miles). The Grenadines are a group of low-lying islands south of Saint Vincent, with wide beaches and coral reefs surrounding them. Union Island, Mayreau, Mustique, Canouan, Bequia, and many other uninhabited rocks, reefs, and cays are part of the Grenadines that belong to Saint Vincent. The remaining islands of the Grenadines belong to Grenada.

Coastal Features

Saint Vincent's eastern and western coasts are comprised of alternating rock cliffs and stretches of black sand beaches. The Grenadines have low-lying land, wide beaches, and shallow harbors and bays.

6 ⊕ INLAND LAKES

The Soufrière volcano on Saint Vincent contains a crater lake that is 1.6 kilometers (1 mile) wide.

7 ⊕ RIVERS AND WATERFALLS

Rivers in Saint Vincent tend to be short and straight. The longest river is the Colonarie. It lies slightly northeast of Kingstown and is the site of a hydroelectric power plant.

The Falls of Baleine, located on the northern end of Saint Vincent, can be reached only by boat. These freshwater cascades drop about 18 meters (60 feet) to a natural pool. The area is a designated wildlife reserve.

surround the Grenadines. An underwater depression called the Tobago Basin lies to the east of the islands.

Sea Inlets and Straits

The Saint Vincent Passage is found north of that island. The Martinique Channel is situated to the south and separates the country from Grenada. The North Mayreau Channel

EPD/Saxifraga

Bequia lies south of Saint Vincent. Its few inhabitants have built their homes on the rocky hillsides.

8 ⊕ DESERTS

There are no desert regions in Saint Vincent.

9 ⊕ FLAT AND ROLLING TERRAIN

The lowlands on Saint Vincent are covered with coconut and banana trees and arrowroot. Some of the island's most fertile farmland is housed in the Mesopotamia Valley, which is northeast of Kingstown. Forests and woodlands comprise 36 percent of Saint Vincent and the Grenadines, with most of Saint Vincent's interior containing tropical rainforest.

10 ⊕ MOUNTAINS AND VOLCANOES

Saint Vincent is dominated by a central volcanic range of mountains with four peaks: Soufrière, Richmond, Grand Bonhomme, and Saint Andrew. The Soufrière volcano is the country's highest peak. It is 1,234 meters (4,049 feet) high. A rugged landscape with steep slopes comprises most of the remaining areas of Saint Vincent. A volcanic ridge between Saint Vincent and Grenada that runs north to south forms the Grenadines. Mount Tobaoi (308 meters/1,010 feet), the highest point in the Grenadines, is found on Union Island.

11 ⊕ CANYONS AND CAVES

There are no significant caves or canyons in Saint Vincent.

12 ⊕ PLATEAUS AND MONOLITHS

There are no major plateau regions in Saint Vincent.

13 ⊕ MAN-MADE FEATURES

Black Point Tunnel is a passage of about 107 meters (350 feet) that links Grand Sable with Byrea Bay. British slaves constructed the tunnel to provide a transportation route for sugar exports.

DID YOU KN🌐W?

The Windward and Leeward Islands of the eastern Carribean are named for their relationship to the prevailing eastern blowing winds. "Windward" is the direction from which the wind blows, or the side that is most exposed to the wind. "Leeward" indicates the direction toward which the wind is blowing.

14 ⊕ FURTHER READING

Books

Philpott, Don. *Saint Vincent & Grenadines.* Lincolnwood, IL: Passport Books, 1996.

Potter, Robert B. *Saint Vincent and the Grenadines.* Santa Barbara, CA: Clio, 1992.

Walker, Cas. *Focus on the Carribean.* London: Evans Brothers, 1992.

Walton, Chelle Koster. *Caribbean Ways: A Cultural Guide.* Westwood, MA: Riverdale, 1993.

Web Site

Welcome to St. Vincent & The Grenadines. http://www.svgtourism.com (accessed June 13, 2003).

Samoa

- **Official name:** Independent State of Samoa

- **Area:** 2,860 square kilometers (1,104 square miles)

- **Highest point on mainland:** Mauga Silisili (1,857 meters/6,093 feet)

- **Lowest point on land:** Sea level

- **Hemispheres:** Southern and Western

- **Time zone:** 1 A.M. = noon GMT

- **Longest distances:** 150 kilometers (93 miles) from east-southeast to west-northwest; 39 kilometers (24 miles) from north-northeast to south-southwest

- **Land boundaries:** None

- **Coastline:** 403 kilometers (250 miles)

- **Territorial sea limits:** 22 kilometers (12 nautical miles)

1 ⊕ LOCATION AND SIZE

Samoa (formerly Western Samoa) is located almost centrally in the Polynesian region of the South Pacific. It consists of the two main islands of Upolu and Savai'i and seven small islets, of which only Manono and Apolima are inhabited. At 2,860 square kilometers (1,104 square miles), the total land area of Samoa is almost as large as the state of Rhode Island.

2 ⊕ TERRITORIES AND DEPENDENCIES

Samoa has no territories or dependencies.

3 ⊕ CLIMATE

Samoa has a tropical marine climate. The hottest month is December and the coldest is July. Due to the oceanic surroundings, the temperature ranges on the islands are not appreciable. The mean daily temperature is about 27°C (81°F) year-round. The dry season runs from May to October; the wet season extends from November to April. Rainfall averages 287 centimeters (113 inches) annually, and the average yearly relative humidity is 83 percent. Because the interior of the islands is mountainous, there is also a considerable difference between the rainfall on the coast and that of the inland jungle. Average annual rainfall varies from 500 to 700 centimeters (200 to 280 inches) on the southern windward side to 250 to 300 centimeters (100 to 120 inches) on the leeward side. Trade winds from the southeast are fairly constant throughout the dry season.

4 ⊕ TOPOGRAPHIC REGIONS

Samoa's islands are volcanic, with coral reefs surrounding most of them. They have narrow coastal plains with rocky volcanic mountains in the interior.

5 ⊕ OCEANS AND SEAS

Samoa lies in the central Pacific Ocean.

Seacoast and Undersea Features

Coral reefs nearly surround the Samoan island, broken in only a few places by constant wave action or by lava flow. The total reef area is 1,269 square kilometers (490 square miles). The southern coast of Savai'i island is known for its blow holes, places where ocean waves create geyser-like spouts as they crash through

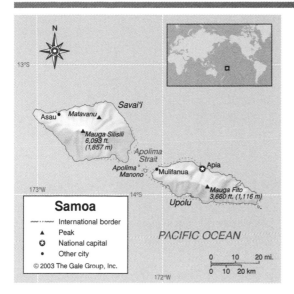

Samoa
- – – – – International border
- ▲ Peak
- ✪ National capital
- • Other city
- © 2003 The Gale Group, Inc.

EPD/Peter Langer

Falefa Falls on Upolu Island.

underground lava tubes (hollow tubes left by the flow of molten lava).

Sea Inlets and Straits

The Apolima Strait separates Upolu and Savai'i.

Coastal Features

The Fagaloa and Safata Bays are located on the north and south coasts of Upolu, respectively. There are ports and harbors at Apia and Mulifanua on Upolu, and at Asau and Salelologa on Savai'i. The southern shore of Upolu has a series of beaches. Toward the eastern end of the island are Aganoa Black Sand Beach and Salamuma Beach, both of which draw snorkelers to their coves and shallow waters. At the extreme eastern end of Upolu are spectacular turquoise reefs.

6 ⊕ INLAND LAKES

Crater lakes are fed by rainfall that averages 300 centimeters (118 inches) annually at Apia. On Upolu, there is a very deep lake, Lake Lanoto'o (Goldfish Lake), in the center of a volcanic crater. There is also a freshwater

pool at Piula that extends from a cave nearly all the way to the shore.

7 ⊕ RIVERS AND WATERFALLS

Both islands have numerous, swiftly flowing rivers with plenty of rapids and waterfalls. most of the rivers, however, flow only during the wet season. Sinaloa Falls on Savai'i is 183 meters (600 feet) high.

8 ⊕ DESERTS

There are no deserts in Samoa.

9 ⊕ FLAT AND ROLLING TERRAIN

Both Savai'i and Upolu have narrow coastal plains. Upolu's central volcanic range slopes down on both sides to hills and coastal plains. The island's south coast is particularly known for its scenic beaches, which have picturesque coves, rock pools, and palm trees.

EPD/Peter Langer

These palm trees thrive on a volcanic ridge near Apia.

10 ⊕ MOUNTAINS AND VOLCANOES

Rugged ranges are prevalent on both major islands, reaching 1,100 meters (3,608 feet) on Upolu and 1,857 meters (6,093 feet) on Savai'i. The significant peaks are Mauga Silisili—at 1,857 meters (6,093 feet) the highest point in Samoa—Mauga Loa (1,176 meters/3,857 feet), and Mauga Fito (Va'aifetu) (1,116 meters/ 3,660 feet). The islands are in an area of active volcanism that has recently progressed westward. Savai'i, geologically the youngest island, last experienced eruptions from Matavanu from 1905 through 1910 and Mauga Mu in 1902. Other volcanoes on Savai'i are Mauga Afi and Mauga Silisili. The volcanoes on Upolu are Mauga Ali'i and Mauga-o-Savai'i.

11 ⊕ CANYONS AND CAVES

The numerous caves on the Samoan islands are located within lava tubes, places where molten lava flowed under existing fields of solidified lava.

12 ⊕ PLATEAUS AND MONOLITHS

Savai'i's central volcanoes are surrounded by lava plateaus that descend to hills and coastal plains.

13 ⊕ MAN-MADE FEATURES

A unique star-shaped formation on Savai'i, called the Pulemelei Mound, is thought to be the oldest man-made structure in Polynesia. It consists of a central pyramid 12 meters (39 feet) high, surrounded by four smaller mounds.

DID YOU KN⊕W?

Vailima, a house built by Robert Louis Stevenson, author of the classic adventure tale *Treasure Island*, is located on Upolu at Apia. He named the place Vailima, meaning "five waters," for the small streams that ran across the property. Stevenson is buried on the island, and tourists often visit his gravesite.

14 ⊕ FURTHER READING

Books

Dahl, Arthur L. *Regional Ecosystems Survey of the South Pacific Area.* Noumea, New Caledonia: South Pacific Commission, 1980.

Tamua, Evotia. *Samoa.* Auckland, New Zealand: Pasifika Press, 2000.

Vaai, Saleimoa. *Samoa Faamatai and the Rule of Law.* Western Samoa: National University of Samoa, 1999.

Web Sites

Samoa Observer Online. http://www.samoaobserver.ws/index.htm (accessed April 24, 2003).

Samoan Sensation. http://www.samoa.co.uk/things-to-do.html (accessed April 24, 2003).

San Marino

- **Official name:** The Most Serene Republic of San Marino
- **Area:** 61 square kilometers (24 square miles)
- **Highest point on mainland:** Monte Titano (755 meters/2,477 feet)
- **Lowest point on land:** Sea level
- **Hemispheres:** Northern and Eastern
- **Time zone:** 1 P.M. = noon GMT

- **Longest distances:** 13 kilometers (8 miles) northeast to southwest; 9 kilometers (6 miles) southeast to northwest
- **Land boundaries:** 39 kilometers (24 miles) total boundary length, all with Italy
- **Coastline:** None
- **Territorial sea limits:** None

1 ⊕ LOCATION AND SIZE

San Marino is a tiny, landlocked country located entirely within Italy, about 24 kilometers (15 miles) southwest of the city of Rimini, in the Apennine Mountains between Italy's Marche and Romagna regions. It is Europe's third-smallest independent state (only Vatican City and Monaco are smaller) and the world's second-smallest republic (after Nauru). With an area of 61 square kilometers (24 square miles), San Marino is about one-third the size of Washington, D.C.

2 ⊕ TERRITORIES AND DEPENDENCIES

San Marino has no territories or dependencies.

3 ⊕ CLIMATE

San Marino has the mild, temperate climate typical of northeastern Italy. Summer highs rarely rise above 26°C (79°F), and winter lows rarely fall below 7°C (44°F). Annual rainfall averages between 56 centimeters (22 inches) and 80 centimeters (32 inches).

4 ⊕ TOPOGRAPHIC REGIONS

Mount Titano dominates the landscape of San Marino; most of the irregularly shaped country is situated on its slopes and crest. There is enough level land at the base of the mountain for agriculture, however.

5 ⊕ OCEANS AND SEAS

San Marino is landlocked.

6 ⊕ INLAND LAKES

There are no sizable lakes in San Marino.

7 ⊕ RIVERS AND WATERFALLS

San Marino lies largely within the basin of Italy's Marecchia River, into which the San Marino River drains, flowing northward and forming part of the republic's border with Italy. The Marano and Ausa Rivers drain into the Adriatic Sea.

8 ⊕ DESERTS

There are no deserts in San Marino.

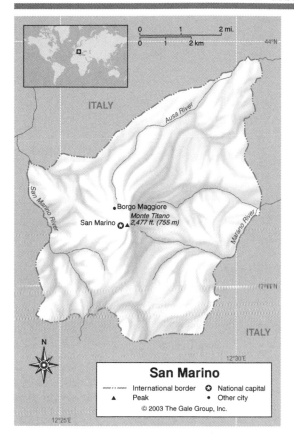

San Marino

- ·—·—· International border
- ▲ Peak
- ⊕ National capital
- • Other city

© 2003 The Gale Group, Inc.

11 ⊕ CANYONS AND CAVES

There are no well-known caves in San Marino. The famous Frasassi Caves, which are among the largest and most scenic in Europe, are located within 100 kilometers (62 miles) of the country, however, in the Apennines between Ancona and Assisi.

12 ⊕ PLATEAUS AND MONOLITHS

San Marino's mountains rise steeply from its lower elevations, with no plateaus among them.

13 ⊕ MAN-MADE FEATURES

San Marino's most famous man-made features are the three medieval fortresses that sit atop the three peaks of Mt. Titano, on steep cliffs overlooking both the Italian town of Rimini and the Adriatic Sea.

14 ⊕ FURTHER READING

Books and Periodicals

Carrick, Noel. *San Marino.* New York: Chelsea House, 1988

Catling, Christopher. *Umbria, The Marches, and San Marino.* London: Black, 1994.

"Now, After 1,600 Years, Time to Join the World (San Marino to Become Member of the United Nations)." *New York Times:* February 26, 1992.

Web Sites

Lonely Planet: Destination San Marino. http://www.lonelyplanet.com/destinations/europe/san_marino/printable.htm (accessed April 24, 2003).

U.S. Department of State: Background note: San Marino. http://www.state.gov/r/pa/ei/bgn/5387.htm (accessed April 24, 2003).

9 ⊕ FLAT AND ROLLING TERRAIN

Mt. Titano is bordered by hills to the southwest, and there is also some level land at its base that has been cultivated.

10 ⊕ MOUNTAINS AND VOLCANOES

The limestone peaks of Mt. Titano occupy the central part of the republic. There are three major peaks, each of which houses ruins of ancient fortifications. The summit of Mt. Titano (755 meters/2,477 feet) commands a panoramic view of the Adriatic Sea, which is only 19 kilometers (12 miles) away.

São Tomé and Príncipe

- **Official name:** Democratic Republic of São Tomé and Príncipe

- **Area:** 1,001 square kilometers (386 square miles)

- **Highest point on mainland:** São Tomé Peak (2,024 meters/6,640 feet)

- **Lowest point on land:** Sea level

- **Hemispheres:** Northern and Eastern

- **Time zone:** Noon = noon GMT

- **Coastline:** 209 kilometers (130 miles)

- **Longest distances:** São Tomé: 49 kilometers (30 miles) from north-northeast to south-southwest; 29 kilometers (18 miles) from east-southeast to west-northwest. Príncipe: 21 kilometers (13 miles) from south-southeast to north-northwest, 15 kilometers (9 miles) from east-northeast to west-southwest

- **Land boundaries:** None

- **Territorial sea limits:** 22 kilometers (12 nautical miles)

1 ⊕ LOCATION AND SIZE

São Tomé and Príncipe, the smallest country in Africa, is a group of islands located in the Gulf of Guinea off the coast of Gabon, just barely north of the equator. With a total area of about 1,001 square kilometers (386 square miles), the country is about five times the size of Washington, D.C. São Tomé and Príncipe is divided into two provinces.

2 ⊕ TERRITORIES AND DEPENDENCIES

São Tomé and Príncipe has no territories or dependencies.

3 ⊕ CLIMATE

Lying near the equator, the islands' climate is tropical and temperatures vary with the different altitudes. Temperatures in the coastal regions average 27°C (81°F), while the mountain areas average 20°C (68°F). Precipitation changes differentiate the seasons, rather than temperature fluctuations.

The northern regions of São Tomé and Príncipe receive approximately 100 to 150 centimeters (40 to 60 inches) of rain during the rainy season from October through May, while most of the southern regions receive between 380 and 510 centimeters (150 and 200 inches). The dry season occurs from early June through September.

4 ⊕ TOPOGRAPHIC REGIONS

São Tomé and Príncipe is part of a chain of extinct volcanoes. The two main islands are São Tomé (855 square kilometers/330 square miles) and Príncipe (109 square kilometers/42 square miles). The country also includes the tiny Ilhéu Bombom, Ilhéu Caroço, and Ilhéu das Rôlas.

São Tomé and Príncipe's landscape is mostly mountainous. Rainforest covers other large areas of land, most of which give way to cloud forests at higher elevations. Most of the coastline is comprised of white sand beaches.

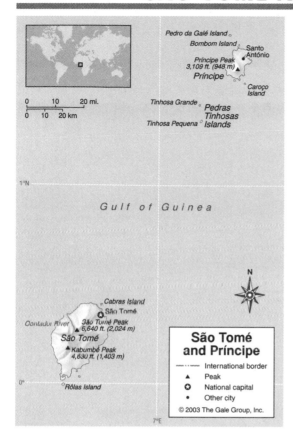

In the waters between the two main islands are Tinhosa Peqeuna, Pedras Tinhosas, and Tinhosa Grande. These islets are uninhabited.

Coastal Features

Untouched white sand beaches line most of the coasts and the country is attempting to develop a tourist industry around them. São Tomé on the island of the same name and Santo António on Príncipe are the main ports.

6 ⊕ INLAND LAKES

There are no significant lakes on São Tomé and Príncipe.

7 ⊕ RIVERS AND WATERFALLS

The Contador River is located in the northwest of São Tomé and its river valley is possibly the deepest in the country. Several streams run down from the volcanic highlands into the Gulf of Guinea.

8 ⊕ DESERTS

There are no deserts in São Tomé and Príncipe.

9 ⊕ FLAT AND ROLLING TERRAIN

In the northern region of São Tomé, there is a dry area where the climate resembles that of savannah grasslands. Forest covers most of the islands. Tropical rainforest changes to cloud forest above elevations of 1,370 meters (4,500 feet). Cloud forests are so named because they tend to be continually covered in clouds throughout the entire year.

10 ⊕ MOUNTAINS AND VOLCANOES

The islands of São Tomé and Príncipe were once part of a chain of ocean volcanoes that are now extinct. As a result, both São Tomé and Príncipe are mountainous. São Tomé's highest peaks are São Tomé Peak (Pico de São Tomé) at 2,024 meters (6,640 feet) and Kabumbé Peak (Pico Kabumbé) at 1,403 meters (4,630 feet). While there are ten peaks that rise over 1,067 meters (3,500 feet), many of the

Almost all of the population lives on the island of São Tomé.

The islands of São Tomé and Príncipe are located on the African Tectonic Plate.

5 ⊕ OCEANS AND SEAS

Seacoast and Undersea Features

São Tomé and Príncipe is surrounded by the Gulf of Guinea, an extension of the Atlantic Ocean that lies along the coast of West Africa.

Islands and Archipelagoes

São Tomé and Príncipe comprise an island nation. Small islets that lie around the two main islands include Ilhéu das Rôlas, straddling the equator off the southern tip of São Tomé; Ilhéu Caroço, off the southern tip of Príncipe; and Bombom, off the northern coast of Príncipe.

island's other peaks reach only a little more than half that height. Príncipe's highest elevation is Príncipe Peak (Pico de Príncipe) at 948 meters (3,109 feet).

11 ⊕ CANYONS AND CAVES

There are no major caves or canyons in São Tomé and Príncipe.

12 ⊕ PLATEAUS AND MONOLITHS

Príncipe features a large plateau that extends along the northwestern coast at elevations that reach 948 meters (3,109 feet). The terrain of São Tomé also features a plateau, although it is smaller.

13 ⊕ MAN-MADE FEATURES

There are no major man-made structures affecting the geography of the country.

14 ⊕ FURTHER READING

Books

Hodges, Tony. *São Tomé and Príncipe: From Plantation Colony to Microstate.* Boulder, CO: Westview Press, 1988.

Shaw, Caroline S. *São Tomé and Príncipe.* Santa Barbara, CA: Clio Press, 1994.

Web Sites

Iafrica.com. *São Tomé and Príncipe.* http://www.africa.iafrica.com/countryinfo/ saotome/geography (Accessed June 12, 2003).

Saudi Arabia

- **Official name:** Kingdom of Saudi Arabia

- **Area:** 1,960,582 square kilometers (756,984 square miles)

- **Highest point on mainland:** Jabal Sawdā' (3,133 meters/10,279 feet)

- **Lowest point on land:** Sea level

- **Hemispheres:** Northern and Eastern

- **Time zone:** 3 P.M. = noon GMT

- **Longest distances:** 2,295 kilometers (1,426 miles) from east-southeast to west-northwest; 1,423 kilometers (884 miles) from north-northeast to south-southwest

- **Land boundaries:** 4,415 kilometers (2,743 miles) total boundary length; Iraq 814 kilometers (506 miles); Jordan 728 kilometers (452 miles); Kuwait 222 kilometers (138 miles); Oman 676 kilometers (420 miles); Qatar 60 kilometers (37.3 miles); United Arab Emirates 457 kilometers (284 miles); Yemen 1,458 kilometers (906 miles)

- **Coastline:** 2,640 kilometers (1,640 miles)

- **Territorial sea limits:** 22 kilometers (12 nautical miles)

1 ⊕ LOCATION AND SIZE

The Kingdom of Saudi Arabia covers about four-fifths of the Arabian Peninsula and constitutes a land bridge connecting Africa with the Middle East. It is about three times as large as the state of Texas, and the third-largest country in Asia, after China and India. Because several of its borders are incompletely demarcated, however, its precise area is difficult to specify. Saudi Arabia has the largest oil reserves in the world, and the nation ranks as the largest petroleum exporter. Its extensive coastlines on the Persian Gulf and the Red Sea provide abundant shipping access through the Persian Gulf and the Suez Canal.

2 ⊕ TERRITORIES AND DEPENDENCIES

Saudi Arabia has no territories or dependencies.

3 ⊕ CLIMATE

Saudi Arabia's desert climate is generally very dry and very hot. In winter, however, there can be frost and freezing temperatures. Day and night temperatures vary greatly. Two main climate extremes are the coastal lands and the interior. Coastal regions along the Red Sea and the Persian Gulf encounter high humidity and high temperatures, hot mists during the day, and a warm fog at night. In the interior, daytime temperatures from May to September can reach 54°C (129°F) and are among the highest recorded anywhere in the world. The climate is more moderate from October through April, with evening temperatures between 16°C and 21°C (61°F and 70°F). The prevailing winds are from the north. A southerly wind brings an increase in temperature and humidity, along with a Gulf storm known as *kauf*. A strong northwesterly wind, the *shamal*, blows in late spring and early summer.

Average annual rainfall is only 9 centimeters (3.5 inches). A year's rainfall may consist of one or two torrential outbursts that flood the wadis and quickly disappear into the sand. Most rain falls from November to May.

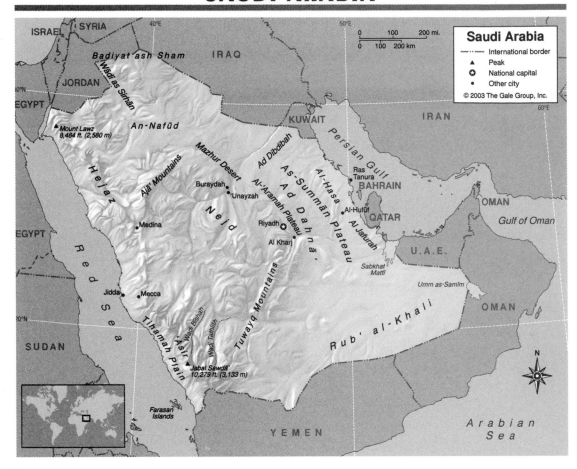

The eastern coast is noted for heavy fogs, and humidity there can reach 90 percent. Between 3 and 5 centimeters (10 and 20 inches) of rain falls in the mountainous 'Asir area, where there is a summer monsoon. Much of the Rub' al-Khali is considered "hyper-arid," often going without rainfall for more than twelve consecutive months.

4 ⊕ TOPOGRAPHIC REGIONS

The country can be divided into six geographical regions: the Red Sea escarpment, from Hejaz in the north to 'Asir in the south; the Tihamah, a coastal plain that rises gradually from the sea to the mountains in the southeast; Nejd, the central plateau, which extends to the

Tuwayq Mountains and further; and three sand deserts: the Ad Dahnā', the An-Nafūd, and, south of Nejd, the Rub' al-Khali Desert, one of the largest sand deserts in the world.

5 ⊕ OCEANS AND SEAS

Two bodies of water border Saudi Arabia: the Persian (Arabian) Gulf to the east, and the Red Sea to the west. The Red Sea is the warmest and saltiest sea in the world. The Persian Gulf is the marginal offshoot of the Indian Ocean that lies between the Arabian Peninsula and Iran, extending about 970 kilometers (600 miles) from the Shatt al Arab delta to the Strait of Hormuz. The gulf's width varies from a maximum of 338 kilometers (210 miles) to a

ARAMCO/Tor Eigeland

Bulldozers build a new road to Jabal Sawdā'.

minimum of 55 kilometers (34 miles) in the Strait of Hormuz, which links the Arabian Sea to the Gulf of Oman.

Seacoast and Undersea Features

The shallow gulf waters have very slow currents and a limited tidal range. There are practically no natural harbors along the Red Sea. The Red Sea eco-region is best known for the spectacular corals that live in the central and northern areas. Fewer coral species thrive in the Persian Gulf than in the Red Sea. Nevertheless, the entire Arabian Peninsula is fringed by some of the most beautiful coral reefs in the world

Sea Inlets and Straits

The southeastern portion of Saudi Arabia's coast borders the Gulf of Bahrain and the Dawhat Salwa, an inlet of this gulf. The sea border between Saudi Arabia and Qatar is an imaginary line drawn down the middle of the Dawhat Salwa.

Islands and Archipelagos

The Farasān Islands, in an archipelago in the Red Sea, are fringed by pristine coral reefs, seagrass beds, and mangroves. Of the more than 120 islands, the largest are Farasān al Kabir, at 395 square kilometers (152 square miles); Sajid, at 156 square kilometers (60 square miles); and Zufaf, at 33 square kilometers (13 square miles). All are uninhabited.

Tarut Island in the Persian Gulf near Ras Tanura has the oldest town on the Arabian peninsula.

ARAMCO/Tor Eigeland

Desert sands on Tarut Island near Ras Tanura in eastern Saudi Arabia.

Coastal Features

Saudi Arabia's coast has no significant bays or capes. The Persian Gulf coast is extremely irregular and the shoreline is unstable. The Tihamah Plain borders the Red Sea; Jidda, which is located on this plain, is the chief port of entry for Muslim pilgrims traveling to Mecca. A flat, lowland coastal plain borders the Persian Gulf.

6 ⊕ INLAND LAKES

Except for artesian wells in the eastern oases, Saudi Arabia has no perennially existing freshwater, either pooled in lakes or flowing in rivers. Medina is the site of the largest and most important oasis in the Hejaz region. In the southern 'Asir, fertile wadis such as Wadi Bīshah and Wadi Tathlīth support oasis ag-

riculture. Eastern Arabia is also known as Al Ahsa, or Al-Hasa, after the largest oasis in the country, which actually encompasses two neighboring oases and the town of Al-Hufūf.

7 ⊕ RIVERS AND WATERFALLS

In the northern Hejaz region, dry riverbeds (wadis) trace the courses of ancient rivers and contain water for a brief period following significant rainfall. The only consistent sources of inland water are oases, however. Oases are fertile areas of otherwise unfertile land.

8 ⊕ DESERTS

At least one-third of the total area of Saudi Arabia is sandy desert. The Rub' al-Khali (the Empty Quarter) in the south is the largest desert region in the country. It consists of sand overlying gravel or gypsum plains, with a surface elevation that varies from 800 meters (2,624 feet) in the far southwest to near sea level in the northeast. Types of dunes include longitudinal dunes more than 160 kilometers (100 miles) long, moving dunes, crescent-shaped dunes (barchan), and enormous mountainous dunes. The northern counterpart of the Rub' al-Khali, the An-Nafūd, covers an area of about 57,000 square kilometers (2,000 square miles) with an elevation of about 1,000 meters (3, 280 feet). Longitudinal dunes here can reach heights of 90 meters (300 feet). The dunes are separated by valleys up to 16 kilometers (10 miles) wide. Connecting the Rub' al-Khali and An-Nafūd deserts is the Ad Dahnä' Desert, also called "the river of sand." The Ad Dahnä' connects to the An-Nafūd Desert by way of the Mazhur Desert.

9 ⊕ FLAT AND ROLLING TERRAIN

The Tihamah Plain bordering the Red Sea is a salty tidal plain with an average width of only about 65 kilometers (40 miles). The flat, lowland coastal plain along the Persian Gulf is about 60 kilometers (37 miles) wide. The northern part is the Ad Dibdibah gravel plain;

the southern section is a sandy desert called Al Jafurah. The salt flats of the Rub' al-Khali can harbor quicksand.

10 ⊕ MOUNTAINS AND VOLCANOES

The Hejaz Mountains (with elevations from 910 to 2,740 meters/3,000 to 9,000 feet) rise sharply from the Red Sea and run parallel to the seacoast from north to south. Mount Lawz, at 2,580 meters (8,464 feet), rises in the far north of the Hejaz near the Red Sea and the neighboring country of Jordan. The northern range in the Hejaz seldom exceeds 2,100 meters (6,888 feet) and gradually decreases to about 600 meters (1,968 feet) around Mecca. Close to Mecca, the Hejaz coastal escarpment is separated by a gap. In the plateau region of Nejd, the Aja' Mountains are just south of the An-Nafûd desert. The highest mountains (over 2,740 meters/9,000 feet) are in 'Asir in the south. This region extends along the Red Sea for 370 kilometers (230 miles) and inland about 290 to 320 kilometers (180 to 200 miles). Saudi Arabia's highest peak, Jabal Sawdâ', is found here; this summit reaches 3,133 meters (10,276 feet).

11 ⊕ CANYONS AND CAVES

The Tuwayq escarpment—800 kilometers (496 miles) of spectacular limestone cliffs, plateaus, and canyons eroded by wind and sand—cuts across the Ad Dahnâ' Desert. Its steep west face rises anywhere from 100 to 250 meters (328 to 820 feet) above the Nejd Plateau.

12 ⊕ PLATEAUS AND MONOLITHS

East of Hejaz and 'Asir lie the central uplands of the Nejd, a large, mainly rocky plateau with widths ranging from about 1,520 meters (5,000 feet) in the west to about 610 meters (2,000 feet) in the east. The Nejd is scarred by extensive lava beds (*harrat*), which are evidence of fairly recent volcanic activity. Al-Hasa, a low plateau to the east, gives way to the low-lying gulf region. The area north of the An-Nafûd, Badiyat ash Sham, is an upland plateau that is geographically part of the Syrian Desert. The Wādī as Sirhān, a large basin that lies 984 feet (300 meters) below the surrounding plateau, is a vestige of an ancient inland sea. East of the Ad Dahnâ' lies the rocky, barren As-Summān Plateau, about 120 kilometers (74 miles) wide and descending in elevation from about 400 meters (1,312 feet) in the west to about 240 meters (787 feet) in the east. Separated from the As-Summān Plateau by the Ad Dahnâ' is the Al-'Aramah Plateau, which runs right up to Riyadh.

13 ⊕ MAN-MADE FEATURES

More than 40 percent of Saudi Arabia's Persian Gulf coastline consists of land reclaimed by dredging and sedimentation. The completion of the breakwater, or mole, at the port of Ras Tanura in 1945 allowed tankers to dock on the gulf coast. This site is still the largest oil port in the world. Over two hundred dams capture water from seasonal flooding for drinking and irrigation. Among the largest are those at the following wadis: Jizan, Fatima, Bisha, and Najran. In fact, the dam at Wadi Bisha is one of the largest in the Middle East.

14 ⊕ FURTHER READING

Books

Long, David E. *The Kingdom of Saudi Arabia.* Gainesville: University Press of Florida, 1997.

Nance, Paul J. *The Nance Museum: A Journey into Traditional Saudi Arabia.* St. Louis, MO: Nance Museum Publications, 1999.

Walker, Dale. *Fool's Paradise.* New York: Vintage Books, 1988.

Web Sites

Lonely Planet: Destination Saudi Arabia. http://www.lonelyplanet.com/destinations/middle_east/saudi_arabia/ (accessed April 14, 2003).

Saudi Arabian Information Resource. http://www.saudinf.com/main/a.htm (accessed April 14, 2003).

Senegal

- **Official name:** Republic of Senegal
- **Area:** 196,190 square kilometers (75,749 square miles)
- **Highest point on mainland:** Unnamed feature near Nepen Diakha (581 meters/ 1,906 feet)
- **Lowest point on land:** Sea level
- **Hemispheres:** Northern and Western
- **Time zone:** Noon = noon GMT
- **Longest distances:** 690 kilometers (429 miles) from southeast to northwest; 406 kilometers (252 miles) from northeast to southwest

- **Land boundaries:** 3,101 kilometers (1,927 miles) total boundary length; The Gambia 740 kilometers (460 miles); Guinea 330 kilometers (205 miles); Guinea-Bissau 338 kilometers (210 miles); Mali 419 kilometers (260 miles); Mauritania 813 kilometers (505 miles)
- **Coastline:** 531 kilometers (330 miles)
- **Territorial sea limits:** 22 kilometers (12 nautical miles)

1 ⊕ LOCATION AND SIZE

Senegal is located on the western bulge of Africa between the countries of Mauritania and Guinea-Bissau. It shares borders with a total of five countries, including The Gambia, which is entirely surrounded by Senegalese territory. With a total area of about 196,190 square kilometers (75,749 square miles), the country is slightly smaller than the state of South Dakota. Senegal is divided into ten regions.

2 ⊕ TERRITORIES AND DEPENDENCIES

Senegal has no outside territories or dependencies.

3 ⊕ CLIMATE

Senegal has a tropical climate. Temperatures are lowest along the coast. At Dakar they vary from 26°C (79°F) to 17°C (63°F) from December to April, and from 30°C (86°F) to 20°C (68°F) from May to November.

The rainy season generally lasts from June through October. The southern Casamance River region, however, has a longer rainy season than the area north of The Gambia. In the semi-arid extreme north, for example, Podor has an average rainfall of 34 centimeters (13 inches); while Ziguinchor, near the Guinea-Bissau border, receives an average of 155 centimeters (61 inches). Dakar averages 57 centimeters (22 inches) of rain each year.

4 ⊕ TOPOGRAPHIC REGIONS

Senegal is the westernmost part of a broad savannah extending across the Sahel. Most of the country lies upon a low sedimentary basin characterized by an expanse of flat and undulating plains with sparse grasses and woody shrubs. There are no significant natural landmarks or major changes in elevation. Broken terrain and steep slopes are found only in the extreme southeast.

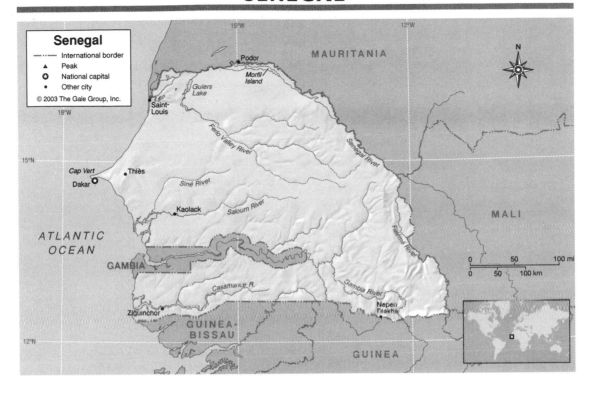

Extensive riverine areas have been converted to farmland, especially in the Siné and Saloum River basins; the lowlands between Thiès and Kaolack yield significant peanut and other food crops. Beyond these areas, most of the land has little potential except as pasturage. Volcanic action created the Cap Vert promontory, which is the westernmost point in Africa, and the nearby islets. Senegal lies on the African Tectonic Plate.

5 ⊕ OCEANS AND SEAS

Seacoast and Undersea Features

The western coast of Senegal faces the North Atlantic Ocean. The North Atlantic provides Senegal with a great deal of rich fishing ground, which is a major component of Senegal's economy. The goblin shark, an animal with a peculiarly shaped body of which little is known, is prevalent in the ocean waters near Senegal.

Sea Inlets and Straits

There are many ports and harbors along the Atlantic coast, the largest of which is the capital city of Dakar. Other harbors up and down the coast are Kaolack, Matam, Podor, Richard Toll, Saint-Louis, and Ziguinchor.

Islands and Archipelagos

Saint-Louis, the former capital of colonial French West Africa, is located on an island near the mouth of the Senegal River. Ile de Gorée, once a slave transshipment point, is situated between the Cap Vert peninsula and the Petite Côte of the mainland. In the Senegal River valley above Dagana is the Ile à Morfil, a narrow island several hundred miles long between the river's main channel and the Doué channel on the opposite side. Senegal's estuaries contain many flat islands dividing numerous river channels

Credit: EPD/Cory Langley

The waters of the North Atlantic provide rich fishing grounds.

Coastal Features

North of the Cap Vert promontory, the pounding of heavy surf, northeast trade winds, and the southwest-flowing Canary Current formed the coastal belt. It is covered by small swamps or pools separated by very old dunes as high as 30 meters (100 feet). The peninsula of Cap Vert itself is the westernmost point in Africa. South of Dakar, the coastal strip of sand beach narrows and is interrupted by a rocky promontory at Popenguine. Just above The Gambia, the coast is broken by the channels and islands of the Saloum River estuary. South of the Casamance River, silt and sand clog various creeks and estuaries in an area of salt flats.

6 ⊕ INLAND LAKES

The largest lake in Senegal is the artificially controlled Lac de Guiers (Guiers Lake). This shallow lake is fed by the Senegal River and extends for an average length of about 80 kilometers (50 miles), averaging about 12 kilometers (8 miles) in width. A dam, as well as a gate on what is known as the Taoué channel, control water flow into this lake. At the highest level, the lake waters reach another 64 to 80 kilometers (40 to 50 miles) southeastward into the Ferlo Valley.

To the north of the Cap Vert peninsula lies Lac Rose (Pink Lake), a shallow saltwater lake occupying a depression behind the coastal dunes. Organisms that live in the lake give it a pinkish color, and villagers extract its salt for commercial purposes.

7 ⊕ RIVERS AND WATERFALLS

Senegal's largest rivers—the Senegal, Siné, Saloum, Gambia, and Casamance—are sluggish, marsh-lined streams emptying into broad estuaries along the Atlantic Ocean. The Senegal River is the longest at 4,023 kilometers (2,500 miles). It rises in Guinea from the Bafing River, which is joined in eastern Mali by the Bakoye River. As it enters Senegal, the Falémé River joins it from the south. At high flood stage, water from the Senegal River spreads through a system of channels, sloughs, and adjacent lowlands until most of the valley is a sheet of water, from which the tops of trees appear as green patches and villages stand out as isolated islands. At the onset of the long dry season, ocean tides extend nearly 483 kilometers (300 miles) upstream. During the rainy season, however, the salty water is forced seaward and the system is refilled with fresh water.

The Gambia River, which rises in Guinea, receives the flow of a perennial river, the Koulountou, which also runs north from Guinea to join it near the Gambian border. Between The Gambia and Guinea-Bissau, the Casamance River drains a narrow basin less than 32 kilometers (20 miles) wide, becoming a broad estuary 104 kilometers (65 miles) from the sea, 10 kilometers (6 miles) wide at the mouth.

The Saloum River and its major tributary, the Siné River, feed into an extensive tidal swamp just north of The Gambia. Only the lower reaches carry water all year, and these are brackish, as the tides penetrate far up the various channels through the swamp.

8 ⊕ DESERTS

Senegal lies at the edge of the region known as the Sahel. Sahel is an Arabic word that means "shore." It refers to the 5,000-kilometer (3,125-mile) stretch of savannah that is the shore, or edge, of the Sahara desert. The Sahel spreads west to east from Mauritania and Senegal to Somalia.

9 ⊕ FLAT AND ROLLING TERRAIN

The terrain of Senegal is primarily low, rolling plains. Mangroves, thick forest, and oil palms characterize the coastal area of the Casamance River. This vegetation changes to wooded or open savannah in the central and eastern parts of the Casamance and throughout the Siné-Saloum River area. From Mauritania to The Gambia lies the Ferlo Valley, a featureless expanse of savannah in which dried tufts of grass, scrub, and thorn trees dominate over the long, dry season.

Except for the dunes in the coastal belt and several minor hills northwest of Thiès, the southeast is the only area with elevations of more than 91 meters (300 feet) above sea level; and even there, only a few ridges exceed 396 meters (1,300 feet). The country reaches its highest point, 581 meters (1,906 feet), at an unnamed point near Nepen Diakha.

10 ⊕ MOUNTAINS AND VOLCANOES

There are no mountain regions or volcanoes in Senegal.

11 ⊕ CANYONS AND CAVES

There are no significant caves or canyons in Senegal.

12 ⊕ PLATEAUS AND MONOLITHS

In the extreme southeast, the Fouta Djallon plateau extends into Senegal from Guinea.

13 ⊕ MAN-MADE FEATURES

The ebb and flow of the Senegal River is checked at some points by dikes; these are opened to admit the fresh water and are later closed to impound it for use during the dry season and to exclude advancing salt water.

DID YOU KN⊕W?

There are two sites in Senegal that have been designated as UNESCO World Heritage Sites. In the Senegal River delta, the Djoudj Sanctuary is a wetland that serves as home to over one million birds, including the white pelican, the purple heron, the African spoonbill, the great egret, and the cormorant.

Along the banks of the Gambia River, Niokolo-Koba National Park is a protected area that is home to the Derby eland (largest of the antelopes), chimpanzees, lions, leopards, and a large population of elephants, as well as many birds, reptiles, and amphibians.

14 ⊕ FURTHER READING

Books

Africa South of the Sahara 2002. *Senegal.* London: Europa Publishers, 2001.

Beaton, Margaret. *Senegal.* New York: Children's Press, 1997.

Clark, Andrew F., and Lucie C. Phillips. *Historical Dictionary of Senegal.* 2nd ed. Meutchen, NJ: Scarecrow Press, 1994.

Gellar, Sheldon. *Senegal: An African Nation between Islam and the West.* 2nd ed. Boulder, CO: Westview Press, 1995.

Web Sites

Senegal Online: Geography. http://www.senegal-online.com/senega06E.htm (accessed May 5, 2003).

Serbia and Montenegro

- **Official name:** Serbia and Montenegro

- **Area:** 102,350 square kilometers (39,518 square miles)

- **Highest point on mainland:** Mount Daravica (2,656 meters/8,714 feet)

- **Lowest point on land:** Sea level

- **Hemispheres:** Northern and Western

- **Time zone:** 1 P.M. = noon GMT

- **Longest distances:** 492 kilometers (306 miles) from north to south; 378 kilometers (235 miles) from east to west

- **Land boundaries:** 2,246 kilometers (1,396 miles) total boundary length; Albania 287 kilometers (178 miles), Bosnia and Herzegovina 527 kilometers (327 miles), Bulgaria 318 kilometers (198 miles), Croatia 266 kilometers (166 miles), Hungary 151 kilometers (94 miles), Macedonia 221 kilometers (137 miles), Romania 476 kilometers (296 miles)

- **Coastline:** 199 kilometers (124 miles)

- **Territorial sea limits:** Not available

1 ⊕ LOCATION AND SIZE

Serbia and Montenegro is located in southeastern Europe, sharing borders with Hungary, Romania, Bulgaria, Macedonia, Albania, Croatia, and Bosnia and Herzegovina. It has a southwest coastline on the Adriatic Sea. With a total area of about 102,350 square kilometers (39,518 square miles), the country is slightly smaller than the state of Kentucky. Serbia and Montenegro has two nominally autonomous provinces (Kosovo and Vojvodina).

2 ⊕ TERRITORIES AND DEPENDENCIES

Serbia and Montenegro has no outside territories or dependencies.

3 ⊕ CLIMATE

Serbia and Montenegro's climate varies greatly from one part of the country to another, due to the many mountain ranges. Most of Serbia's climate is continental, with cold, dry winters and warm, humid summers. The Pannonian Plains have cold winters with hot and dry summers. In Vojvodina, July temperatures average 21°C (70°F) while temperatures in January average about 0°C (32°F).

The Adriatic coast has a more temperate Mediterranean climate, but the Dinaric Mountains prevent the Mediterranean weather from penetrating to inland Montenegro. The average seaside July temperatures are between 23°C (74°F) and 25°C (78°F). Summers are usually long and dry while winters are short and mild. Intense summer heat penetrates the Bojana River Valley over the Lake Scutari basin and upstream along the Morača River. Podgorica, on the Morača River, is the warmest city in Serbia and Montenegro, with July temperatures averaging 26°C (80°F), with highs sometimes reaching 40°C (104°F). January temperatures average around 5°C (41°F), with lows reaching -10°C (14°F).

Annual precipitation in Serbia ranges from 56 to 190 centimeters (22 to 75 inches), depending on elevation and exposure. Heavy

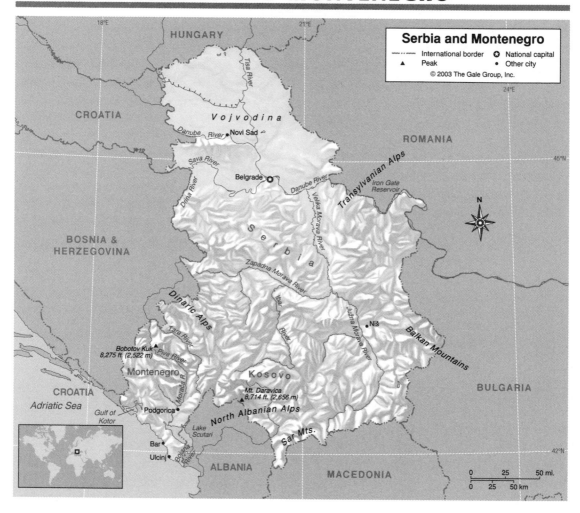

rains in spring and autumn frequently cause floods. Snow is rare along the Montenegrin coast and in the Lake Scutari basin. In the inland regions, however, near elevated limestone mountain ranges, the climate is typically sub-alpine, with cold, snowy winters and mild summers. In some of these areas, snow lingers into the summer months; the highest mountain peaks are covered with snow year-round.

4 ⊕ TOPOGRAPHIC REGIONS

Serbia and Montenegro covers the middle of the Balkan Peninsula and extends westward to meet the Adriatic Sea. The southern half, made up of Montenegro and Kosovo, is rugged and mountainous; the northern half, Serbia, contains the Danube River basin and the southern extent of the Pannonian Plain.

Serbia and Montenegro was known as Yugoslavia from 1992 to March 2003, when it became Serbia and Montenegro. It consists of two republics: Serbia, comprising the eastern 86 percent of the country; and coastal Montenegro, which occupies the southwestern 14 percent. Within Serbia are two nominally autonomous provinces: Kosovo (10,887 square kilometers/4,203 square miles), in the south;

and Vojvodina (21,506 square kilometers/ 8,303 square miles), in the north.

Located on the Eurasian Tectonic Plate, Serbia and Montenegro is seismically active. Two parallel fault lines extend from northwest to southeast Montenegro. Serbia has thrust fault lines on either side of the river basins surrounding the Velika Morava and Južna Morava Rivers. There is also a tectonic contact line along the eastern border with Romania. These structural seams in the earth's crust periodically shift, causing tremors and occasional destructive earthquakes.

5 ⊕ OCEANS AND SEAS

Seacoast and Undersea Features

Serbia and Montenegro has a short southwestern coastline on the Adriatic Sea, which is an extension of the Mediterranean Sea. The Adriatic Sea is at its widest between Serbia and Montenegro and southern Italy, with a width of about 200 kilometers (125 miles). This portion of the Adriatic is also the deepest, reaching some 1,330 meters (4,360 feet) at a point about 120 kilometers (75 miles) southwest of the Gulf of Kotor.

Sea Inlets and Straits

The coast is indented with numerous bays and coves. The largest and most impressive is the Gulf of Kotor, the world's southernmost fjord.

Coastal Features

The slopes of the Dinaric Alps rise very close to the water in most places. Only 52 kilometers (32 miles) of coast can be considered beach. Velika Plaza (Long Beach) at Ulcinj has the longest continuous stretch of sandy beach, at 13 kilometers (8 miles). Since the coastline is so rugged, access to the sea is limited. The port of Bar and the Gulf of Kotor are the main access points.

6 ⊕ INLAND LAKES

Lake Scutari (Skadar) is only 7 kilometers (4 miles) from the Adriatic coast in Montenegro. One of forty lakes in Montenegro, it is by far the largest lake in Serbia and Montenegro (as well as in the entire Balkan region). Covering approximately 400 square kilometers (150 square miles), about two-thirds of the lake lies within Serbia and Montenegro's borders, with the rest extending into Albania. Although its surface area is large, its average depth is only 5 meters (16 feet).

High mountains rise to the southwest of the lake, while to the northeast is a wide swamp. Although Lake Scutari is adjacent to the Adriatic Sea, there are about thirty spots, known as *oke* (singular: *oko*) where its bed is under sea level and groundwater springs forth from the bottom of the lake. The Morača River is the largest stream that flows into Lake Scutari.

7 ⊕ RIVERS AND WATERFALLS

Most of Serbia and Montenegro's rivers travel eastward towards the Black Sea basin. Serbia and Montenegro's most important river is the Danube, which forms part of the country's border with Croatia, then flows across northern Serbia and along the border with Romania. The Danube rises in the southwestern part of Germany and follows a winding, generally eastern course, traversing over 2,850 kilometers (1,771 miles) through Austria, Hungary, Serbia and Montenegro, and Romania before finally emptying into the Black Sea. Only 588 kilometers (365 miles) of the river's length is located in Serbia and Montenegro, however. As the second-longest river in Europe, the Danube serves as a vital commercial and transportation route.

Along Serbia and Montenegro's northeastern border with Romania, the Danube flows through the Iron Gate. This is a gorge with rapids where the Danube cuts through the Transylvanian Alps.

AP/Darko Vojinovic

Fishing at dusk in the Adriatic Sea south of Podgorica in Montenegro.

The Danube's main tributaries in Serbia and Montenegro are the Tisa, Sava, and Morava Rivers. The Tisa River is 966 kilometers (600 miles) long; 168 kilometers (103 miles) of the river's length flows through Serbia and Montenegro. It enters the country from Hungary and travels south across the Pannonian Plain to the Danube.

The Sava River is 945 kilometers (587 miles) long, entering the country from Bosnia and Herzegovina and flowing east for 206 kilometers (128 miles) before meeting the Danube at Belgrade (Beograd). The Drina is a major tributary of the Sava and makes up part of Serbia and Montenegro's border with Bosnia and Herzegovina.

The Zapadna Morava (308 kilometers/ 191 miles), flowing eastward, and the Južna Morava (295 kilometers/183 miles), flowing towards the north, merge to form the Velika Morava (185 kilometers/115 miles) near the center of the country. The Morava Rivers and their tributary, the Ibar, drain the mountainous areas of central and southern Serbia and flow northward to join the Danube east of Belgrade.

8 ⊕ DESERTS

There are no desert regions in Serbia and Montenegro.

9 ⊕ FLAT AND ROLLING TERRAIN

Occupying northern Serbia is the Pannonian Plain and the low-lying plains of Vojvodina, where the Danube River is joined by two of its major tributaries, the Sava and Tisa Rivers. The region is mostly flat, with some low hills, and it contains fertile soils used for farmland

and grazing. The Pannonian Plain is situated within an ancient dry seabed. It is filled with rich alluvial deposits, forming fertile farmland and rolling hills. Kosovo, at the southern end of the country, covers a montane basin with high plains.

10 ⊕ MOUNTAINS AND VOLCANOES

Mountains cover about half of Serbia. Serbia is ringed by the Dinaric Alps on the west, the Sar Mountains and the North Albanian Alps (or Prokletije) on the south, and the Balkan Mountains and the Transylvanian Alps on the east. Many peaks exceed 1,800 meters (6,000 feet) above sea level, including thirteen summits that top 2,400 meters (7,870 feet).

Nearly all of Montenegro is mountainous. The name Montenegro (which means Black Mountain) is believed to come from the thick "black" forests that once covered the area. The high Dinaric Alps of Montenegro rise steeply from the Adriatic coastline, framing a narrow ribbon of coastal plain only 2 to 10 kilometers (1 to 6 miles) wide.

The four highest peaks in Serbia and Montenegro are all in Serbia: Daravica, at 2,656 meters (8,714 feet); Crni Vrh, at 2,585 meters (8,481 feet); Gusan, at 2,539 meters (8,330 feet); and Bogdaš, at 2,533 meters (8,311 feet). Bobotov Kuk, which at an elevation of 2,522 meters (8,275 feet) is the fifth-highest mountain in the country, lies in Montenegro. This is the highest point in the Dinaric Alps.

11 ⊕ CANYONS AND CAVES

Tara Canyon follows the Tara River along Montenegro's northwestern border with Bosnia and Herzegovina. At a maximum depth of 1,300 meters (4,265 feet), Tara Canyon is Europe's deepest canyon. The Piva and Morača River Basins of Montenegro contain canyons that are about 1,200 meters (3,940 feet) deep.

The Zlotske Caves in eastern Serbia consist of two separate cave systems: the Vernjikica and the Lazareva. The Vernjikica has eleven large chambers. The largest in floor area is Vilingrad (about 29,950 square meters/322,379 square miles), which features a large number of stalagmites shaped like humans and animals. The Gothic Cathedral Hall chamber, also in the Vernjikica, has fine, lace-like carvings in its rock formations. The Coliseum Hall, the largest cavern in the Vernjikica, is so named for its circular shape and column-like formations. The Lazareva has an underground river flowing through the lower of its two levels.

12 ⊕ PLATEAUS AND MONOLITHS

There are no major plateau regions in Serbia and Montenegro.

13 ⊕ MAN-MADE FEATURES

In 1972, the joint Yugoslav-Romanian Iron Gate Dam, with its two hydroelectric plants, was completed at the gorge of the same name. Because of this dam and other engineering feats, the Danube River is now navigable throughout Serbia and Montenegro. The large reservoir also serves to supply irrigation waters and as a site for farm fishing.

14 ⊕ FURTHER READING

Books and Periodicals

Brân, Zoë. *After Yugoslavia*. Oakland, CA: Lonely Planet, 2001.

Malcolm, Noel. *Kosovo: A Short History*. New York: HarperPerennial, 1999.

Radovanovic, Ivana. *The Iron Gates Mesolithic*. Ann Arbor, MI: International Monographs in Prehistory, 1996.

Web Site

The Government of Serbia, Office of Communications, Serbia Info: Online Encyclopedia of Serbia. http://www.serbia.sr.gov.yu/enc/ (accessed May 12, 2003).

Seychelles

- **Official name:** Republic of Seychelles
- **Area:** 455 square kilometers (176 square miles)
- **Highest point on mainland:** Mount Seychelles (Morne Seychellois) (912 meters/2,992 feet)
- **Lowest point on land:** Sea level
- **Hemispheres:** Southern and Eastern
- **Time zone:** 4 P.M. = noon GMT

- **Longest distances:** 27 kilometers (17 miles) from north to south; 11 kilometers (7 miles) from east to west; stretching 1,200 kilometers (100 miles) from northeast to southwest
- **Land boundaries:** None
- **Coastline:** 491 kilometers (305 miles)
- **Territorial sea limits:** 22 kilometers (12 nautical miles)

1 ⊕ LOCATION AND SIZE

Seychelles is an archipelago in the Indian Ocean, off the eastern coast of Africa and northeast of Madagascar. With an area of about 455 square kilometers (176 square miles), the country is about two-and-one-half times the size of Washington, D.C. Seychelles is divided into twenty-three districts.

2 ⊕ TERRITORIES AND DEPENDENCIES

Seychelles has no outside territories or dependencies.

3 ⊕ CLIMATE

Despite lying close to the equator, trade winds keep the country's climate temperate. Coastal temperatures remain fairly constant at 27°C (81°F) throughout the year. Temperatures are generally lower at the higher altitudes, especially at night. Humidity tends to be high, particularly in the coastal regions.

Average annual rainfall varies markedly across the islands of the Seychelles. The coastal regions on Mahé experience an annual rainfall of 236 centimeters (93 inches), while the areas at higher elevations receive about 356 centimeters (140 inches). The coral islands of the southwest, such as Aldabra and Assumption, experience much less rainfall, averaging about 50 centimeters (20 inches) annually.

Generally, the period from May through October is slightly drier, although southeasterly winds bring brief rains every two to three days even during these months of the year. The northeasterly winds prevail from December through March, bringing heavier and more frequent rains.

4 ⊕ TOPOGRAPHIC REGIONS

There are more than one hundred islands that make up the country of Seychelles. Generally they fall into two categories: the core group of high-rising granite islands, and a group of low coralline atolls in the southwest part of the country. Seychelles is located on the African Tectonic Plate.

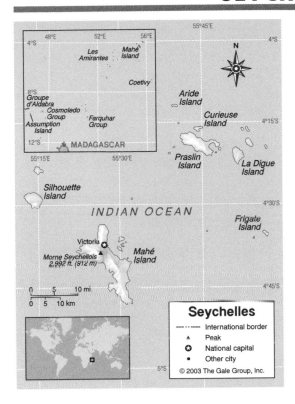

ninety islands are coralline. The total land area of the granitic group is about 259 square kilometers (100 square miles).

The largest granitic island is Mahé (144 square kilometers/56 square miles). It is surrounded by coral reefs and ringed by beaches featuring fine white sand. Praslin, the second-largest island, is located northeast of Mahé. The United Nations' Educational, Scientific, and Cultural Organization (UNESCO) has designated Vallée de Mai near the center of the island as a World Heritage Site. It is the only place in the world where the coco-de-mer palm tree is found. It is also home to three of the world's rarest birds: the Seychelles bulbul, the fruit pigeon, and the black parrot.

Other inhabited (or tourist destination) islands include La Digue (east of Praslin); Frigate (directly east of Mahé and south of La Digue); and Silhouette (northwest of Mahé). The most northerly of the granitic islands is Aride, home to a bird sanctuary.

The Cosmoledo Group makes up the most southwesterly of the Seychelles. The coralline Aldabra, part of the Aldabra Group (Groupe d'Aldabra), is the world's largest atoll. The group includes a ring of four islands with a central lagoon that fills and empties twice each day through four channels. The diversity of wildlife, including giant tortoises and the Aldabran Rail (a species of flightless bird), have also earned the island a designation as a UNESCO World Heritage Site.

Coastal Features

White, sandy beaches surround the granitic islands with flats of corals and shells behind them. Tar balls have washed up on the beaches for decades, indicating the possibility of undersea oil reserves.

5 ⊕ OCEANS AND SEAS

Seacoast and Undersea Features

The Seychelles archipelago is spread over approximately 388,498 square kilometers (150,000 square miles) of the Indian Ocean east of Africa. Surrounding the islands are coral reefs.

Sea Inlets and Straits

Baie Ternay and Port Launay, both on Mahé Island, are adjacent marine parks edged in stunning coral reefs.

Islands and Archipelagos

The total number of islands varies depending upon what is considered an island. Some are merely sand cays and shoals barely above the high tide mark. There are thirty-two granitic Seychelles islands; the remaining seventy to

Susan D. Rock

Reefs and islets lie along the shores of Seychelles.

6 ⊕ INLAND LAKES

There are no major lakes in Seychelles, but there are small ponds and marshes on some of the islands.

7 ⊕ RIVERS AND WATERFALLS

There are no major rivers in Seychelles. There are, however, many small streams that drain the mountain slopes.

8 ⊕ DESERTS

There are no desert regions in Seychelles.

9 ⊕ FLAT AND ROLLING TERRAIN

Seychelles has no permanent pastures and only 13 percent of its land is used for crops. Only 11 percent of Seychelles is considered forest land. Primary forests exist only on Praslin and Curieuse Islands, both of which lie north of Mahé. These native forests of the coco-de-mer palm tree are now protected in small reserves. Coconut plantations have virtually replaced all broadleaf evergreen rain forests. Other native tree species on Seychelles have adapted to the local conditions. Many forests are planted with fruit and spice plants, making good use of scarce land resources.

10 ⊕ MOUNTAINS AND VOLCANOES

The Mascarene Ridge, a granite ridge that runs from north to south mostly underwater in the Indian Ocean, formed most of the islands of the Seychelles. On Mahé, Mount Seychelles (Morne Seychellois) reaches the highest point in the nation at 912 meters (2,992 feet). The mountainous characteristics of the granitic islands are among the notable characteristics that appeal to tourists.

Susan D. Rock

A tea plantation on Mahé Island, Seychelles.

11 ⊕ CANYONS AND CAVES

There are no major land caves in Seychelles. Several underwater caves surround the coastlines of the islands, however; these provide homes to a variety of marine life.

12 ⊕ PLATEAUS AND MONOLITHS

There are no major plateau regions in Seychelles.

13 ⊕ MAN-MADE FEATURES

There are no major man-made structures affecting the geography of Seychelles.

14 ⊕ FURTHER READING

Books

Carpin, Sarah. *Seychelles*. Chicago: Passport Books, 1997.

Journey through Seychelles. Edison, NJ: Hunter Publishing Co, 1994.

Ozanne, J.A.F. *Coconuts and Créoles*. London: P. Allan & Co., 1936.

Travis, William. *Beyond the Reefs*. New York: Dutton, 1959.

Vine, Peter. *Seychelles*. London: Immel Publishing, 1992.

Web Sites

Seychelles: Islands and Parks. http://www.sey.net/isl_mahe (accessed April 15, 2003).

Seychelles Nation. http://www.seychelles-online.com.sc/geography.html (accessed April 15, 2003).

Sierra Leone

- **Official name:** Republic of Sierra Leone
- **Area:** 71,740 square kilometers (27,699 square miles)
- **Highest point on mainland:** Loma Mansa (1,948 meters/6,391 feet)
- **Lowest point on land:** Sea level
- **Hemispheres:** Northern and Western
- **Time zone:** Noon = noon GMT
- **Longest distances:** 338 kilometers (210 miles) from north to south; 304 kilometers (189 miles) from east to west

- **Land boundaries:** 958 kilometers (595 miles) total boundary length; Guinea 652 kilometers (405 miles); Liberia 306 kilometers (190 miles)
- **Coastline:** 402 kilometers (250 miles)
- **Territorial sea limits:** 370 kilometers (200 nautical miles)

1 ⊕ LOCATION AND SIZE

Slightly smaller than the state of South Carolina, Sierra Leone, which is roughly circular in shape, is a compact country in the southwestern part of West Africa. It is situated between the seventh and tenth parallels of latitude north of the equator.

2 ⊕ TERRITORIES AND DEPENDENCIES

Sierra Leone has no territories or dependencies.

3 ⊕ CLIMATE

Because it is so close to the equator, Sierra Leone has a tropical climate; temperatures stay fairly constant throughout the year. The mean temperature is about 27°C (81°F) on the coast and almost as high on the eastern plateau. The dry season lasts from November to April, with a wet season occurring during the rest of the year. The prevailing winds from the southwest monsoon characterize the rainy season. Rainfall is greatest along the coast, especially in the mountains, which receive more than 580 centimeters (230 inches) of rainfall annually, compared to an average of approximately 315 centimeters (125 inches) in the rest of the country. During the dry season, *harmattan* winds blow from the Sahara Desert, bringing sandstorms but little rain.

4 ⊕ TOPOGRAPHIC REGIONS

Sierra Leone's varied terrain includes the striking, mountainous Sierra Leone Peninsula; a zone of low-lying coastal marshland along the Atlantic Ocean; and a wide plains area extending inland to about the middle of the country. East of the plains, the land rises to a broad, moderately elevated plateau interspersed with occasional hills and mountains.

5 ⊕ OCEANS AND SEAS

Sierra Leone is bounded on the southwest and west by the Atlantic Ocean; the country is located northwest of that part of the Atlantic Coast known as the Grain Coast, which borders Liberia.

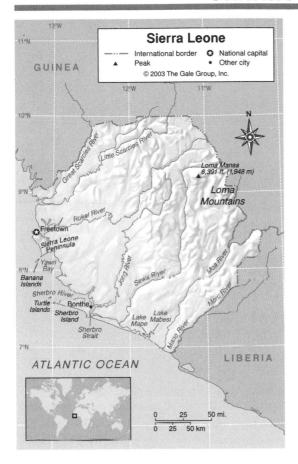

Sierra Leone

- – – – – International border
- ▲ Peak
- ⊙ National capital
- • Other city

© 2003 The Gale Group, Inc.

GUINEA

Great Scarcies River

Little Scarcies River

Loma Mansa
6,391 ft. (1,948 m) ▲

Loma Mountains

Rokel River

⊙ Freetown
Sierra Leone Peninsula

Yawri Bay

Banana Islands

Jong River

Sewa River

Moa River

Moro River

Sherbro River

Turtle Islands

Bonthe •

Sherbro Island

Lake Mape

Lake Mabesi

Mano River

Sherbro Strait

ATLANTIC OCEAN

LIBERIA

0   25   50 mi.

0   25   50 km

Seacoast and Undersea Features

There are oil and gas reserves under the ocean floor off the coast of Sierra Leone.

Sea Inlets and Straits

Sherbro Island is separated from the mainland by Sherbro River on the north and Sherbro Strait on the east.

Islands and Archipelagos

There are three major island groups off the coast of Sierra Leone: the Banana Islands, the Turtle Islands, and Sherbro Island. Sherbro Island is by far the largest. The city of Bonthe is located on this island.

Coastal Features

The coast is very irregular, forming many bays, inlets, and peninsulas. The most significant features are the Sierra Leone Peninsula, where Freetown is located, and Yawri Bay, which is located in the center of the coast just south of the peninsula. The coastal plain has numerous estuaries whose river channels, like that of the Sierra Leone River, continue to flow under the sea. Mangrove swamps line much of the coast, and behind the trees, marine and freshwater swamps occupy large areas.

6 ⊕ INLAND LAKES

Most of the small lakes in Sierra Leone are located in the south. The three largest and most important are Lake Sonfon, Lake Mabesi, and Lake Mape.

7 ⊕ RIVERS AND WATERFALLS

Most of the rivers of Sierra Leone drain into the Atlantic Ocean; a few, however, terminate at inland lakes. Of the numerous rivers, the most important ones are the Great and Little Scarcies in the north and the Rokel in the central region. The Great Scarcies forms part of the northern border with Guinea. The Rokel River originates in the Loma Mountains and flows west to the Atlantic Ocean near Freetown. At 440 kilometers (270 miles), the Rokel is the longest river in the country. Also important are the Mano and Moro Rivers, which form the southern border with Liberia. Other major rivers include the Jong, Sewa, Soa, and Moa.

8 ⊕ DESERTS

There are no deserts in Sierra Leone.

9 ⊕ FLAT AND ROLLING TERRAIN

The coastal plain covers a zone varying in width from about 8 to 40 kilometers (5 to 25 miles). In the southern section of the plateau region, erosion has formed a large area

AP Photo/Peter Macdiarmid/POOL

A British soldier helps the Sierra Leone government patrol the coastal area near Freetown.
Over 17,000 peacekeeping troops make up the United Nations Mission in Sierra Leone (UNAMSIL).

of rolling terrain, which is 64 kilometers (40 miles) wide at certain points and reaches elevations between 152 and 304 meters (500 and 1,000 feet).

10 ⊕ MOUNTAINS AND VOLCANOES

The mountainous Sierra Leone Peninsula, on which Freetown is located, is 40 kilometers (25 miles) long and about 16 kilometers (10 miles) wide. The highest point in Sierra Leone, Mount Loma Mansa (Bintimani), rises to a height of 1,948 meters (6,391 feet) in the Loma Mountains, which span the northeastern part of the country.

11 ⊕ CANYONS AND CAVES

There are no well-known named caves or canyons in Sierra Leone.

12 ⊕ PLATEAUS AND MONOLITHS

The plateau region, which encompasses roughly the eastern half of the country, has elevations ranging from roughly 304 meters (1,000 feet) to about 608 meters (2,000 feet).

13 ⊕ MAN-MADE FEATURES

The most significant dam in Sierra Leone is the Guma Valley Dam, which is 68 meters (223 feet) high and supplies water to an area that includes the capital city of Freetown.

14 ⊕ FURTHER READING

Books

Ferme, Mariane. *The Underneath of Things: Violence, History, and the Everyday in Sierra Leone.* Berkeley: University of California Press, 2001.

Hirsh, John. *Sierra Leone: Diamonds and the Struggle for Democracy. (*International Peace Academy Occasional Paper Series*).* Boulder, CO: Lynne Rienner Publishers, 2000.

Richards, Paul. *Fighting for the Rain Forest: War, Youth, and Resources in Sierra Leone* (African Issues Series). Portsmouth, NH: Heinemann, 1996.

Web Sites

Global Geografia.com. http://www.globalgeografia.com/africa_eng/sierra_leone.htm (accessed April 10, 2003).

Sierra Leone Web. http://www.sierra-leone.org/index.html (accessed April 10, 2003).

Singapore

- **Official name:** Republic of Singapore
- **Area:** 648 square kilometers (250 square miles)
- **Highest point on mainland:** Bukit Timah (166 meters/545 feet)
- **Lowest point on land:** Sea level
- **Hemispheres:** Northern and Eastern
- **Time zone:** 8 P.M. = noon GMT

- **Longest distances:** 42 kilometers (26 miles) from east-northeast to west-southwest; 23 kilometers (14 miles) from south-southeast to north-northwest
- **Land boundaries:** None
- **Coastline:** 193 kilometers (120 miles)
- **Territorial sea limits:** 5.6 kilometers (3 nautical miles)

1 ⊕ LOCATION AND SIZE

The Republic of Singapore consists of a main island and sixty-three islets just south of the tip of the Malay Peninsula in Southeast Asia. Singapore, the second smallest country in Asia, is often described as a city-state. The diamond-shaped main island, which accounts for all but about 38 square kilometers (15 square miles) of the republic's area, is almost entirely urban. With a total area of 648 square kilometers (250 square miles), Singapore is nearly 3.5 times the size of Washington, D.C.

2 ⊕ TERRITORIES AND DEPENDENCIES

Singapore has no territories or dependencies.

3 ⊕ CLIMATE

Singapore has a humid, rainy, tropical climate, with temperatures moderated by the seas surrounding the islands. Temperatures are nearly uniform throughout the year, averaging 25°C (77°F) in January and 27°C (81°F) in June. Although the island lies between 1 and 2 degrees north of the equator, the maritime influences moderate the heat of the region. The highest temperature ever recorded in Singapore is only 36°C (97°F).

Singapore is very humid, with heavy rainfall all year. Annual rainfall averages 237 centimeters (93 inches). The northeast monsoon that occurs between November and March brings the heaviest rainfall of the year.

4 ⊕ TOPOGRAPHIC REGIONS

The main island has three major geographic divisions: an elevated, hilly area in the center; a section of lower, rolling land to the west; and flatlands to the east. Singapore's smaller islands are low-lying with coastal beaches.

5 ⊕ OCEANS AND SEAS

Singapore is located between the Indian Ocean and the South China Sea.

Seacoast and Undersea Features

The coastal waters surrounding Singapore are generally less than 30 meters (100 feet) deep.

Sea Inlets and Straits

Singapore is bordered on the north by the Johore Strait, which separates it from the Malay Peninsula, on the southeast by the Singapore Strait, and on the southwest by the Strait of Malacca.

Islands and Archipelagos

After Singapore Island, the next-largest island in the country is Pulau Tekong Besar to the northeast, with an area of only 18 square kilometers (7 square miles).

Coastal Features

The easternmost part of the coastline is smooth, but the rest has many indentations; the most important of these is the deep natural harbor at the mouth of the Singapore River on the southern coast.

6 ⊕ INLAND LAKES

Singapore has no significant natural lakes, but it has fourteen artificial bodies of water that were created by the construction of reservoirs.

7 ⊕ RIVERS AND WATERFALLS

Singapore's rivers are all short, including its main river, which has the same name as the island itself. The Singapore River flows into the wide harbor on the island's southeastern coast. Other rivers include the Seletar (at 14 kilometers/9 miles, the longest on the island), Jurong, Kalang, Kranji, and Serangoon.

8 ⊕ DESERTS

There are no deserts in Singapore.

9 ⊕ FLAT AND ROLLING TERRAIN

Aside from Bukit Timah Hill, the main island's highest point, Singapore's central hills include Mandai and Panjang. Lower ridges extend northwest-to-southeast in the western and southern parts of the island.

10 ⊕ MOUNTAINS AND VOLCANOES

The highest land on Singapore is a ridge of rugged hills in the center of the island. The highest is Bukit Timah Hill, at 165 meters (545 feet).

11 ⊕ CANYONS AND CAVES

Singapore has no significant caves or canyons.

12 ⊕ PLATEAUS AND MONOLITHS

The eastern part of the main island is a low, eroded plateau.

13 ⊕ MAN-MADE FEATURES

The Johore Causeway, built in the 1920s, is fewer than 3 kilometers (1 mile) long. It bridges the Johore Strait, connecting Singapore to the Malaysian state of Johore. A second causeway opened in 1999. Land reclamation has added almost 15 square kilometers (6 square miles) to Singapore's total territory since 1966, mostly along the southeast coast, including reclamation on nearby islands.

Fourteen reservoirs have been built on Singapore's rivers for flood control as well as for private and industrial water use. Almost all the reservoirs are located in the center of the island or at the mouths of rivers on the northeastern or western coasts. Among the largest are Seretar and Upper Pierce, both of which are situated in the center of the island.

UNESCO/Dominique Roger

High rise buildings fill much of Singapore's land area.

14 ⊕ FURTHER READING

Books

Fuller, Barbara. *Berlitz: Discover Singapore.* Oxford, England: Berlitz Publishing, 1993.

Rowthorn, Chris, et al. *Malaysia, Singapore and Brunei.* Oakland, CA: Lonely Planet, 1999.

Singapore and Malaysia. Knopf Guides. New York: Knopf, 1996.

Warren, William. *Singapore, City of Gardens.* Hong Kong: Periplus Editions, 2000.

Web Sites

Lonely Planet: Destination Singapore. http://www.lonelyplanet.com/destinations/south_east_asia/singapore (accessed April 15, 2003).

Singapore Tourism Board: North America site. http://www.tourismsingapore.com/ (accessed April 15, 2003).

Slovakia

- **Official name:** Slovak Republic
- **Area:** 48,845 square kilometers (18,859 square miles)
- **Highest point on mainland:** Gerlachovsky Peak (2,655 meters/8,711 feet)
- **Lowest point on land:** Bodrok River (94 meters/308 feet)
- **Hemispheres:** Northern and Eastern
- **Time zone:** 1 P.M. = noon GMT

- **Longest distances:** Not available
- **Land boundaries:** 1,355 kilometers (842 miles) total boundary length; Austria 91 kilometers (57 miles); Czech Republic 215 kilometers (134 miles); Hungary 515 kilometers (320 miles); Poland 444 kilometers (276 miles); Ukraine 90 kilometers (56 miles)
- **Coastline:** None
- **Territorial sea limits:** None

1 ⊕ LOCATION AND SIZE

Slovakia (or Slovak Republic) occupies an area of Central Europe that constituted the eastern part of Czechoslovakia from 1918 to 1993. With an area of 48,845 square kilometers (18,859 square miles), it is about two times as large as the state of New Hampshire.

2 ⊕ TERRITORIES AND DEPENDENCIES

Slovakia has no territories or dependencies.

3 ⊕ CLIMATE

Slovakia has a continental climate with sharp seasonal contrasts. Mean temperatures are -1°C (30°F) in January and 21°C (70°F) in July. Weather can vary considerably with elevation, however. The January average can be as low as -5°C (23°F) in the mountains, where temperatures are colder than in the lowlands.

Rainfall also varies with elevation. The annual average precipitation in the lowlands is about 64 centimeters (25 inches); in the High Tatras, however, it can be more than twice as high.

4 ⊕ TOPOGRAPHIC REGIONS

The western Carpathian Mountains, which extend over Slovakia's northern and central regions, dominate the landscape. To the south are subsidiary mountain ranges, with distinct lowland areas in the southwest and east. The capital city of Bratislava is located on the Danube River, which flows through the country for a short distance in the west and along part of its southern border.

5 ⊕ OCEANS AND SEAS

Slovakia is landlocked.

6 ⊕ INLAND LAKES

Clear lakes dot the mountains of Slovakia. Many of them, such as Lake Orava and Lake Popradské, are associated with rivers of the same names. In addition to the natural lakes, there are several artificial ones. Slovakia is known for its thermal springs and mineral waters; its spas are a major attraction for visitors.

7 ⊕ RIVERS AND WATERFALLS

Most of Slovakia's rivers flow south into the Danube, which, together with the Morava,

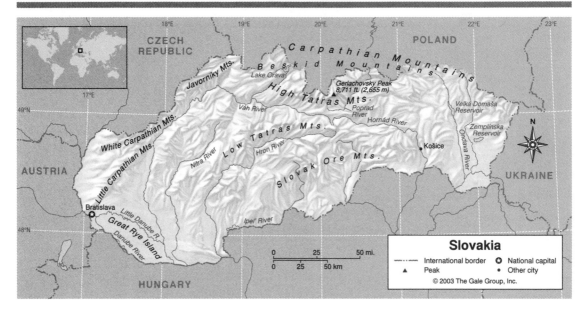

forms the country's southwestern border. From a point a few kilometers south of the Slovakian capital of Bratislava, the main channel of the Danube River demarcates the border between Slovakia and Hungary for about 175 kilometers (108 miles). As it leaves Bratislava, the Danube divides into two channels. The main channel, the Danube proper, continues southward along the border with Hungary. The smaller channel, called the Little Danube, branches eastward and then southeast to meet the Váh River. The Váh continues south and converges with the Nitra and with the main branch of the Danube at Komárno. The Hron and Ipel' Rivers also flow south and enter the Danube before the latter turns south into Hungary. Slovakia's eastern rivers also tend to flow to the south, eventually entering the Danube. Among them are the Hornád and the Ondava. The Poprad, also in the east, is the only sizable river that flows northward, into Poland.

8 ⊕ DESERTS

There are no deserts in Slovakia.

9 ⊕ FLAT AND ROLLING TERRAIN

The corner of southeastern Slovakia between the Little Danube and the Danube, known as the Great Rye Island (Velky Litny Ostrov), is a marshland that supports some agriculture. The lowlands in southwestern Slovakia belong to the Danube Basin, while the lowlands in the east are part of the Carpathian Depression. The mountains of central Slovakia give way to hills in the south-central part of the country.

10 ⊕ MOUNTAINS AND VOLCANOES

The portion of the Carpathian mountain system within Slovakia consists of a number of different ranges separated by valleys and river basins. The highest range is the High Tatras (or Vysoké Tatry); these mountains extend in a narrow ridge along the border with Poland and have traditionally been a popular summer resort area. They include Slovakia's highest peak, Gerlachovsky (2,655 meters/8,711 feet). Snow persists at the higher elevations well into the summer months and all year long in some sheltered pockets. To the south, across the Váh River, the Low Tatras (Nízke Tatry)

EPD/Saxifraga/Mihaly Végh

The High Tatras are the highest mountains in Slovakia.

rise to elevations of 1,981 meters (6,500 feet). Still farther south, across the Hron River, are the Slovak Ore (Slovenské Rudohrie) Mountains. In addition to the three major ranges in the center of the country, there are several smaller ones. In the west, the Little Carpathian (Małe Karpaty) range rises near Bratislava. Several ranges, including the Bíelé Karpaty, Javorníky, and Beskid Mountains, extend into the western part of the Czech Republic and southern Poland.

11 ⊕ CANYONS AND CAVES

There are a dozen caves open to the public in Slovakia. The Belian Cave in Tatra National Park is 5,778 feet (1,752 meters) long.

12 ⊕ PLATEAUS AND MONOLITHS

Slovakia's southwestern lowland includes some original steppe grassland.

13 ⊕ MAN-MADE FEATURES

Dikes and artificial drainage have made it possible to cultivate grain in the former marshlands of the Great Rye Island (Velky Litny Ostrov) in the southeast. Slovakia's largest artificial lake is the Orava Reservoir. Others include the Zemplínska, Velká Domaša, and Liptovská Reservoirs. The country's largest hydroelectric plant is located on the Danube River at Gabcikovo.

DID YOU KN⊕W?

The Belian Cave in Tatra National Park is home to a natural auditorium where musical performances are staged; the cave also provides a habitat for eight distinct bat species.

14 ⊕ FURTHER READING

Books

Brewer, Ted. *The Czech and Slovak Republics Guide*. New York: Open Road Publishing, 1997.

Humphreys, Rob, and Tim Nollen. *Czech and Slovak Republics: The Rough Guide*. New York: Penguin, 1998.

Husovská, 'Ludmilá. *Slovakia: Walking Through Centuries of Cities and Towns*. Bratislava, Slovakia: Priroda, 1997.

Web Sites

Israeli Chamber of Commerce in Slovakia. www.ilcham.sk (accessed April 21, 2003).

Slovakia, Heart of Europe. http://www.heartofeurope.co.uk/ (accessed April 21, 2003).

A ⊕ CONTINENTS BY AREA, FROM LARGEST TO SMALLEST			
RANK	CONTINENT	AREA (SQ MI)	AREA (SQ KM)
1	Asia	17,139,445	44,391,162
2	Africa	11,677,239	30,244,049
3	North America	9,361,791	24,247,039
4	South America	6,880,706	17,821,029
5	Antarctica	5,500,000	14,245,000
6	Europe	3,997,929	10,345,636
7	Australia	2,967,909	7,686,884

B ⊕ COUNTRIES OF THE WORLD BY LAND AREA, FROM LARGEST TO SMALLEST				
RANK	COUNTRY	AREA (SQ MI)	AREA (SQ KM)	PERCENT OF WORLD LAND AREA
1	Russia	6,592,735	17,075,200	11.0
2	Antarctica	5,405,000	14,000,000	9.4
3	Canada	3,851,788	9,976,140	6.7
4	United States of America	3,717,792	9,629,091	6.4
5	China	3,705,386	9,596,960	6.4
6	Brazil	3,286,470	8,511,965	5.7
7	Australia	2,967,893	7,686,850	5.1
8	India	1,269,338	3,287,590	2.3
9	Argentina	1,072,157	2,776,890	1.9
10	Kazakhstan	1,049,150	2,717,300	1.8
11	Sudan	967,493	2,505,810	1.7
12	Algeria	919,590	2,381,740	1.6
13	Congo, Democratic Republic of the	905,563	2,345,410	1.6
15	Mexico	761,606	1,972,550	1.3
16	Saudi Arabia	756,984	1,960,582	1.3
17	Indonesia	741,096	1,919,440	1.3
18	Libya	679,358	1,759,540	1.2
19	Iran	636,293	1,648,000	1.1
20	Mongolia	604,247	1,565,000	1.0
21	Peru	496,223	1,285,220	0.9
22	Chad	495,755	1,284,000	0.9
23	Niger	489,189	1,267,000	0.8
24	Angola	481,350	1,246,700	0.8
25	Mali	478,764	1,240,000	0.8

B ⊕ COUNTRIES OF THE WORLD BY LAND AREA, FROM LARGEST TO SMALLEST *(continued)*

RANK	COUNTRY	AREA (SQ MI)	AREA (SQ KM)	PERCENT OF WORLD LAND AREA
26	South Africa	471,008	1,219,912	0.8
27	Colombia	439,733	1,138,910	0.8
28	Ethiopia	435,184	1,127,127	0.8
29	Bolivia	424,162	1,098,580	0.7
30	Mauritania	397,953	1,030,700	0.7
31	Egypt	386,660	1,001,450	0.7
32	Tanzania	364,879	945,037	0.6
33	Nigeria	356,667	923,768	0.6
34	Venezuela	352,143	912,050	0.6
35	Namibia	318,694	825,418	0.6
36	Pakistan	310,401	803,940	0.5
37	Mozambique	309,494	801,590	0.5
38	Turkey	301,382	780,580	0.5
39	Chile	292,258	756,950	0.5
40	Zambia	290,584	752,614	0.5
41	Myanmar	261,969	678,500	0.5
42	Afghanistan	250,000	647,500	0.4
43	Somalia	246,199	637,657	0.4
44	Central African Republic	240,534	622,984	0.4
45	Ukraine	233,089	603,700	0.4
46	Botswana	231,803	600,370	0.4
47	Madagascar	226,656	587,040	0.4
48	Kenya	224,961	582,650	0.4
49	France	211,208	547,030	0.4
50	Yemen	203,849	527,970	0.4
51	Thailand	198,455	514,000	0.3
52	Spain	194,896	504,782	0.3
53	Turkmenistan	188,455	488,100	0.3
54	Cameroon	183,567	475,440	0.3
55	Papua New Guinea	178,703	462,840	0.3
56	Sweden	173,731	449,964	0.3
57	Uzbekistan	172,741	447,400	0.3
58	Morocco	172,413	446,550	0.3
59	Iraq	168,753	437,072	0.3

	B ⊕ COUNTRIES OF THE WORLD BY LAND AREA, FROM LARGEST TO SMALLEST (continued)			
RANK	COUNTRY	AREA (SQ MI)	AREA (SQ KM)	PERCENT OF WORLD LAND AREA
60	Paraguay	157,046	406,750	0.3
61	Zimbabwe	150,803	390,580	0.3
62	Japan	145,882	377,835	0.3
63	Germany	137,846	357,021	0.2
64	Congo, Republic of	132,047	342,000	0.2
65	Finland	130,127	337,030	0.2
66	Malaysia	127,316	329,750	0.2
67	Vietnam	127,243	329,560	0.2
68	Norway	125,181	324,220	0.2
69	Côte d'Ivoire	124,502	322,460	0.2
70	Poland	120,728	312,685	0.2
71	Italy	116,305	301,230	0.2
72	Philippines	115,830	300,000	0.2
73	Ecuador	109,483	283,560	0.2
74	Burkina Faso	105,869	274,200	0.2
75	New Zealand	103,737	268,680	0.2
76	Gabon	103,347	267,667	0.2
77	Guinea	94,926	245,857	0.2
78	United Kingdom	94,525	244,820	0.2
79	Ghana	92,100	238,540	0.2
80	Romania	91,699	237,500	0.2
81	Laos	91,428	236,800	0.2
82	Uganda	91,135	236,040	0.2
83	Guyana	83,000	214,970	0.1
84	Oman	82,031	212,460	0.1
85	Belarus	80,154	207,600	0.1
86	Kyrgyzstan	76,640	198,500	0.1
87	Senegal	75,749	196,190	0.1
88	Syria	71,498	185,180	0.1
89	Cambodia	69,900	181,040	0.1
90	Uruguay	68,039	176,220	0.1
91	Tunisia	63,170	163,610	0.1
92	Suriname	63,039	163,270	0.1
93	Bangladesh	55,598	144,000	0.1

	B ⊕ COUNTRIES OF THE WORLD BY LAND AREA, FROM LARGEST TO SMALLEST (continued)			
RANK	COUNTRY	AREA (SQ MI)	AREA (SQ KM)	PERCENT OF WORLD LAND AREA
94	Tajikistan	55,251	143,100	0.1
95	Nepal	54,363	140,800	0.1
96	Greece	50,942	131,940	0.1
97	Nicaragua	49,998	129,494	0.1
98	Eritrea	46,842	121,320	0.1
99	Korea, North (Democratic People's Republic of)	46,540	120,540	0.1
100	Malawi	45,745	118,480	0.1
101	Benin	43,483	112,620	0.1
102	Honduras	43,278	112,090	0.1
103	Liberia	43,000	111,370	0.1
104	Bulgaria	42,822	110,910	0.1
105	Cuba	42,803	110,860	0.1
106	Guatemala	42,042	108,890	0.1
107	Iceland	39,769	103,000	0.1
108	Serbia and Montenegro	39,517	102,350	0.1
109	Korea, South (Republic of)	38,023	98,480	0.1
110	Hungary	35,919	93,030	0.1
111	Portugal	35,672	92,391	0.1
112	Jordan	35,637	92,300	0.1
114	Azerbaijan	33,436	86,600	0.1
115	Austria	32,378	83,858	0.1
116	United Arab Emirates	32,000	82,880	0.1
117	Czech Republic	30,450	78,866	0.1
118	Panama	30,193	78,200	0.1
119	Sierra Leone	27,699	71,740	0.05
120	Ireland	27,135	70,280	0.05
121	Georgia	26,911	69,700	0.05
122	Sri Lanka	25,332	65,610	0.04
123	Lithuania	25,174	65,200	0.04
124	Latvia	24,938	64,589	0.04
125	Togo	21,925	56,785	0.04
126	Croatia	21,831	56,542	0.04
127	Bosnia and Herzegovina	19,741	51,129	0.03

	B ⊕ COUNTRIES OF THE WORLD BY LAND AREA, FROM LARGEST TO SMALLEST (continued)			
RANK	COUNTRY	AREA (SQ MI)	AREA (SQ KM)	PERCENT OF WORLD LAND AREA
128	Costa Rica	19,730	51,100	0.03
129	Slovakia	18,859	48,845	0.03
130	Dominican Republic	18,815	48,730	0.03
131	Bhutan	18,147	47,000	0.03
132	Estonia	17,462	45,226	0.03
133	Denmark	16,638	43,094	0.03
134	Netherlands	16,033	41,526	0.03
135	Switzerland	15,942	41,290	0.03
136	Guinea-Bissau	13,946	36,120	0.02
137	Moldova	13,067	33,843	0.02
137	Taiwan	13,892	35,980	0.02
138	Belgium	11,780	30,510	0.02
139	Lesotho	11,720	30,355	0.02
140	Armenia	11,506	29,800	0.02
141	Albania	11,100	28,748	0.02
142	Solomon Islands	10,985	28,450	0.02
143	Equatorial Guinea	10,831	28,051	0.02
144	Burundi	10,745	27,830	0.02
145	Haiti	10,714	27,750	0.02
146	Rwanda	10,169	26,338	0.02
147	Macedonia	9,781	25,333	0.02
148	Belize	8,867	22,966	0.02
149	Djibouti	8,494	22,000	0.01
150	El Salvador	8,124	21,040	0.01
151	Israel	8,019	20,770	0.01
152	Slovenia	7,820	20,253	0.01
153	Fiji	7,054	18,270	0.01
154	Kuwait	6,880	17,820	0.01
155	Swaziland	6,704	17,363	0.01
156	East Timor	5,640	14,609	0.01
157	Bahamas	5,382	13,940	0.01
158	Vanuatu	4,710	12,200	0.01
159	Qatar	4,416	11,437	0.01
160	Gambia, The	4,363	11,300	0.01

	B ⊕ COUNTRIES OF THE WORLD BY LAND AREA, FROM LARGEST TO SMALLEST *(continued)*			
RANK	COUNTRY	AREA (SQ MI)	AREA (SQ KM)	PERCENT OF WORLD LAND AREA
161	Jamaica	4,243	10,990	0.01
162	Lebanon	4,015	10,400	0.01
163	Cyprus	3,571	9,250	0.01
164	Brunei	2,228	5,770	0.004
164	Puerto Rico	3,515	9,104	0.01
165	Trinidad and Tobago	1,980	5,128	0.003
166	Cape Verde	1,557	4,033	0.003
167	Samoa	1,104	2,860	0.002
168	Luxembourg	998	2,586	0.002
169	Comoros	838	2,170	0.001
170	Mauritius	718	1,860	0.001
171	São Tomé and Príncipe	386	1,001	0.0007
172	Dominica	291	754	0.0005
173	Tonga	289	748	0.0005
174	Kiribati	277	717	0.0005
175	Micronesia	271	702	0.0005
176	Palau	177	458	0.0003
177	Bahrain	239	620	0.0004
178	Saint Lucia	239	620	0.0004
179	Andorra	181	468	0.0003
181	Singapore	250	647.5	0.0004
181	Seychelles	176	455	0.0003
182	Antigua and Barbuda	171	442	0.0003
183	Barbados	166	430	0.0003
184	Saint Vincent and the Grenadines	150	389	0.0003
185	Malta	122	316	0.0002
186	Maldives	115	300	0.0002
187	Saint Kitts and Nevis	101	261	0.0002
188	Marshall Islands	70	181.3	0.0001
189	Liechtenstein	62	160	0.0001
190	San Marino	24	61.2	--
191	Tuvalu	10	26	--
192	Nauru	8.1	21	--
193	Monaco	0.7	1.95	--
194	Vatican City	0.17	0.44	--

C ⊕ COUNTRIES OF THE WORLD, BY POPULATION			
RANK	**COUNTRY**	**CONTINENT**	**POPULATION (JULY 2002)**
1	China	Asia	1,284,303,705
2	India	Asia	1,045,845,226
3	United States of America	North America	280,562,489
4	Indonesia	Asia	231,328,092
5	Brazil	South America	176,029,560
6	Pakistan	Asia	147,663,429
7	Russia	Europe	144,978,573
8	Bangladesh	Asia	133,376,684
9	Nigeria	Africa	129,934,911
10	Japan	Asia	126,974,628
11	Mexico	North America	103,400,165
12	Philippines	Asia	84,525,639
13	Germany	Europe	83,251,851
14	Vietnam	Asia	81,098,416
15	Egypt	Africa	70,712,345
16	Ethiopia	Africa	67,673,031
17	Turkey	Asia	67,308,928
18	Iran	Asia	66,622,704
19	Thailand	Asia	62,354,402
20	United Kingdom	Europe	59,778,002
21	France	Europe	59,765,983
22	Italy	Europe	57,715,625
23	Congo, Democratic Republic of the	Africa	55,225,478
24	Ukraine	Europe	48,396,470
25	Korea, South (Republic of)	Asia	48,324,000
26	South Africa	Africa	43,647,658
27	Myanmar	Asia	42,238,224
28	Colombia	South America	41,008,227
29	Spain	Europe	40,077,100
30	Poland	Europe	38,625,478
31	Argentina	South America	37,812,817
32	Tanzania	Africa	37,187,939
33	Sudan	Africa	37,090,298

RANK	COUNTRY	CONTINENT	POPULATION (JULY 2002)
34	Algeria	Africa	32,277,942
35	Canada	North America	31,902,268
36	Morocco	Africa	31,167,783
37	Kenya	Africa	31,138,735
38	Peru	South America	27,949,639
39	Afghanistan	Asia	27,755,775
40	Nepal	Asia	25,873,917
41	Uzbekistan	Asia	25,563,441
42	Uganda	Africa	24,699,073
43	Venezuela	South America	24,287,670
44	Iraq	Asia	24,001,816
45	Saudi Arabia	Asia	23,513,330
46	Malaysia	Asia	22,662,365
47	Taiwan	Asia	22,548,009
48	Romania	Europe	22,317,730
49	Korea, North (Democratic People's Republic of)	Asia	22,224,195
50	Ghana	Africa	20,244,154
51	Mozambique	Africa	19,607,519
52	Sri Lanka	Asia	19,576,783
53	Australia	Australia	19,546,792
54	Yemen	Asia	18,701,257
55	Syria	Asia	17,155,814
56	Côte d'Ivoire	Africa	16,804,784
57	Kazakhstan	Asia	16,741,519
58	Madagascar	Africa	16,473,477
59	Cameroon	Africa	16,184,748
60	Netherlands	Europe	16,067,754
61	Chile	South America	15,498,930
62	Ecuador	South America	13,447,494
63	Guatemala	North America	13,314,079
64	Cambodia	Asia	12,775,324
65	Burkina Faso	Africa	12,603,185

C ⊕ COUNTRIES OF THE WORLD, BY POPULATION (continued)

RANK	COUNTRY	CONTINENT	POPULATION (JULY 2002)
\multicolumn{4}{c}{C ⊕ COUNTRIES OF THE WORLD, BY POPULATION (continued)}

RANK	COUNTRY	CONTINENT	POPULATION (JULY 2002)
66	Zimbabwe	Africa	11,376,676
67	Mali	Africa	11,340,480
68	Cuba	North America	11,224,321
69	Malawi	Africa	10,701,824
70	Serbia and Montenegro	Europe	10,656,929
71	Greece	Europe	10,645,343
72	Niger	Africa	10,639,744
73	Angola	Africa	10,593,171
74	Senegal	Africa	10,589,571
75	Belarus	Europe	10,335,382
76	Belgium	Europe	10,274,595
77	Czech Republic	Europe	10,256,760
78	Portugal	Europe	10,084,245
79	Hungary	Europe	10,075,034
80	Zambia	Africa	9,959,037
81	Tunisia	Africa	9,815,644
82	Chad	Africa	8,997,237
83	Sweden	Europe	8,876,744
84	Dominican Republic	North America	8,721,594
85	Bolivia	South America	8,445,134
86	Austria	Europe	8,169,929
87	Azerbaijan	Asia	7,798,497
88	Guinea	Africa	7,775,065
89	Somalia	Africa	7,753,310
90	Bulgaria	Europe	7,621,337
91	Rwanda	Africa	7,398,074
92	Switzerland	Europe	7,301,994
93	Haiti	North America	7,063,722
94	Benin	Africa	6,787,625
95	Tajikistan	Asia	6,719,567
96	Honduras	North America	6,560,608
97	El Salvador	North America	6,353,681
98	Burundi	Africa	6,373,002

RANK	COUNTRY	CONTINENT	POPULATION (JULY 2002)
\multicolumn{4}{c}{**C ⊕ COUNTRIES OF THE WORLD, BY POPULATION** *(continued)*}

RANK	COUNTRY	CONTINENT	POPULATION (JULY 2002)
99	Israel	Asia	6,029,529
100	Paraguay	South America	5,884,491
101	Laos	Asia	5,777,180
102	Sierra Leone	Africa	5,614,743
103	Slovakia	Europe	5,422,366
104	Denmark	Europe	5,368,854
105	Libya	Africa	5,368,585
106	Jordan	Asia	5,307,470
107	Togo	Africa	5,285,501
108	Finland	Europe	5,183,545
109	Papua New Guinea	Asia	5,172,033
110	Nicaragua	North America	5,023,818
111	Georgia	Asia	4,960,951
112	Kyrgyzstan	Asia	4,822,166
113	Turkmenistan	Asia	4,688,963
114	Norway	Europe	4,525,116
115	Eritrea	Africa	4,465,651
116	Singapore	Asia	4,452,732
117	Moldova	Europe	4,434,547
118	Croatia	Europe	4,390,751
119	Bosnia and Herzegovina	Europe	3,964,388
120	Puerto Rico	North America	3,957,988
121	New Zealand	Asia	3,908,037
122	Ireland	Europe	3,883,159
123	Costa Rica	North America	3,834,934
124	Lebanon	Asia	3,677,780
125	Central African Republic	Africa	3,642,739
126	Lithuania	Europe	3,601,138
127	Albania	Europe	3,544,841
128	Uruguay	South America	3,386,575
129	Armenia	Europe	3,330,099
130	Liberia	Africa	3,288,198
131	Congo, Republic of the	Africa	2,958,448

C ⊕ COUNTRIES OF THE WORLD, BY POPULATION (continued)

Rank	Country	Continent	Population (July 2002)
132	Panama	North America	2,882,329
133	Mauritania	Africa	2,828,858
134	Mongolia	Asia	2,694,432
135	Jamaica	North America	2,680,029
136	Oman	Asia	2,713,462
137	United Arab Emirates	Asia	2,445,989
138	Latvia	Europe	2,366,515
139	Kuwait	Asia	2,111,561
140	Lesotho	Africa	2,207,954
141	Bhutan	Asia	2,094,176
142	Macedonia, The Former Yugoslav Republic of	Europe	2,054,800
143	Slovenia	Europe	1,932,917
144	Namibia	Africa	1,820,916
145	Botswana	Africa	1,591,232
146	Estonia	Europe	1,415,681
147	Gambia, The	Africa	1,455,842
148	Guinea-Bissau	Africa	1,345,479
149	Gabon	Africa	1,233,353
150	Mauritius	Africa	1,200,206
151	Trinidad and Tobago	South America	1,163,724
152	Swaziland	Africa	1,123,605
153	East Timor	Asia	952,618
154	Fiji	Asia	856,346
155	Qatar	Asia	793,341
156	Cyprus	Asia	767,314
157	Guyana	South America	698,209
158	Bahrain	Asia	656,397
159	Comoros	Africa	614,382
160	Equatorial Guinea	Africa	498,144
161	Solomon Islands	Asia	494,786
162	Djibouti	Africa	472,810
163	Luxembourg	Europe	448,569
164	Suriname	South America	436,494

C ⊕ COUNTRIES OF THE WORLD, BY POPULATION *(continued)*

RANK	COUNTRY	CONTINENT	POPULATION (JULY 2002)
165	Cape Verde	Africa	408,760
166	Malta	Europe	397,499
167	Brunei Darussalam	Asia	350,898
168	Maldives	Asia	320,165
169	Bahamas, The	North America	300,529
170	Iceland	Europe	279,384
171	Barbados	North America	276,607
172	Belize	North America	262,999
173	Vanuatu	Asia	196,178
174	Samoa	Asia	178,631
175	São Tomé and Príncipe	Africa	170,372
176	Saint Lucia	North America	160,145
177	Micronesia, Federated States of	Asia	135,869
178	Saint Vincent and the Grenadines	North America	116,394
179	Tonga	Asia	106,137
180	Kiribati	Asia	96,335
181	Grenada	North America	89,211
182	Seychelles	Africa	80,098
183	Marshall Islands	Asia	73,630
184	Dominica	North America	70,158
185	Andorra	Europe	68,403
186	Antigua and Barbuda	North America	67,448
187	Saint Kitts and Nevis	North America	38,736
188	Liechtenstein	Europe	32,842
189	Monaco	Europe	31,987
190	San Marino	Europe	27,730
191	Palau	Asia	19,409
192	Nauru	Asia	12,329
193	Tuvalu	Asia	11,146
194	Holy See	Europe	900
195	Antarctica	Antarctica	No permanent population

D ⊕ OCEANS AND SEAS OF THE WORLD, BY AREA

All measurements are approximate and are rounded to the nearest thousand.

RANK	NAME	AREA (SQ MI)	AREA (SQ KM)
1	Pacific Ocean	60,060,000	155,557,000
2	Atlantic Ocean	29,638,000	76,762,000
3	Indian Ocean	26,469,000	68,556,000
4	Southern Ocean	7,848,000	20,327,000
5	Arctic Ocean	5,427,000	14,056,000
6	Coral Sea	1,850,000	4,791,000
7	Arabian Sea	1,492,000	3,864,000
8	South China Sea (Nan Hai)	1,423,000	3,685,000
9	Weddell Sea	1,080,000	2,796,000
10	Caribbean Sea	1,063,000	2,753,000
11	Mediterranean Sea	971,000	2,515,000
12	Tasman Sea	900,000	2,331,000
13	Bering Sea	890,000	2,305,000
14	Bay of Bengal	839,000	2,173,000
15	Sea of Okhotsk	614,000	1,590,000
16	Gulf of Mexico	596,000	1,544,000
17	Gulf of Guinea	592,000	1,533,000
18	Barents Sea	542,000	1,405,000
19	Norwegian Sea	534,000	1,383,000
20	Gulf of Alaska	512,000	1,327,000
21	Hudson Bay	476,000	1,233,000
22	Greenland Sea	465,000	1,205,000
23	Bellinghausen Sea	430,000	1,110,000
24	Amundsen Sea	400,000	1,036,000
25	Arafura Sea	400,000	1,036,000
26	Philippine Sea	400,000	1,036,000
27	Sea of Japan	378,000	979,000
28	Mozambique Channel	376,000	975,000
29	Ross Sea	370,000	958,000
30	East Siberian Sea	361,000	936,000
31	Scotia Sea	347,000	900,000

RANK	NAME	AREA (SQ MI)	AREA (SQ KM)
	D ⊕ OCEANS AND SEAS OF THE WORLD, BY AREA *(continued)*		
	All measurements are rounded to the nearest thousand.		
32	Kara Sea	341,000	883,000
33	Labrador Sea	309,000	800,000
34	East China Sea (Dong Hai / Tung Hai)	290,000	752,000
35	Solomon Sea	278,000	720,000
36	Laptev Sea	270,000	700,000
37	Baffin Bay	268,000	695,000
38	Banda Sea	268,000	695,000
39	Drake Passage	240,000	620,000
40	Timor Sea	237,000	615,000
41	Andaman Sea	232,000	601,000
42	North Sea	232,000	601,000
43	Davis Strait	230,000	596,000
44	Chukchi Sea	225,000	582,000
45	Great Australian Bight	187,000	484,000
46	Beaufort Sea	184,000	476,000
47	Celebes Sea	182,000	472,000
48	Black Sea	178,000	461,000
49	Red Sea	175,000	453,000
50	Java Sea	167,000	433,000
51	Sulu Sea	162,000	420,000
52	Yellow Sea (Huang Hai)	161,000	417,000
53	Baltic Sea	147,000	382,000
54	Gulf of Carpentaria	120,000	310,000
55	Molucca Sea	119,000	307,000
56	Persian Gulf	93,000	241,000
57	Gulf of Thailand	92,000	239,000
58	Gulf of St. Lawrence	92,000	239,000
59	Bismarck Sea	87,000	225,000
60	Gulf of Aden	85,000	220,000
61	Makassar Strait	75,000	194,000
62	Ceram Sea	72,000	187,000

E ⊕ OCEAN DEPTH

All measurements are approximate.

RANK	NAME	OCEAN	DEPTH (FT)	DEPTH (M)
1	Mariana Trench	Pacific	38,635	11,784
2	Philippine Trench	Pacific	37,720	11,505
3	Tonga Trench	Pacific	37,166	11,336
4	Izu Trench	Pacific	36,850	11,239
5	Kermadec Trench	Pacific	34,728	10,592
6	Kuril Trench	Pacific	34,678	10,577
7	New Britain Trench	Pacific	31,657	9,655
8	Puerto Rico Trench	Atlantic	31,037	9,466
9	Bonin Trench	Pacific	29,816	9,094
10	Japan Trench	Pacific	29,157	8,893
11	South Sandwich Trench	Atlantic	28,406	8,664
12	Palau Trench	Pacific	27,972	8,531
13	Peru-Chile Trench	Pacific	27,687	8,445
14	Yap Trench	Pacific	27,552	8,403
15	Aleutian Trench	Pacific	26,775	8,166
16	Roanche Gap	Atlantic	26,542	8,095
17	Cayman Trench	Atlantic	26,519	8,088
18	New Hebrides Trench	Pacific	25,971	7,921
19	Ryukyu Trench	Pacific	25,597	7,807
20	Java Trench	Indian	24,744	7,547
21	Diamantina Trench	Indian	24,249	7,396
22	Mid America Trench	Pacific	22,297	6,801
23	Brazil Basin	Atlantic	22,274	6,794
24	Ob Trench	Indian	21,785	6,644
25	Vema Trench	Indian	19,482	5,942
26	Agulhas Basin	Indian	19,380	5,911
27	Ionian Basin	Mediterranean Sea	17,306	5,278
28	Eurasia Basin	Arctic	16,122	4,917

F ⊕ MAJOR ISLANDS OF THE WORLD, BY AREA

All measurements are approximate.

Rank	Island	Continent	Body of Water	Area (sq mi)	Area (sq km)
1	Greenland	North America	Atlantic Ocean	840,000	2,175,600
2	New Guinea	Oceania	Pacific Ocean	305,000	790,000
3	Borneo	Asia	South China Sea	285,000	737,000
4	Madagascar	Africa	Indian Ocean	226,657	587,040
5	Baffin	North America	Baffin Bay	196,000	507,000
6	Sumatra	Asia	Andaman Sea	164,000	425,000
7	Honshu	Asia	Pacific Ocean	88,000	228,000
8	Great Britain	Europe	North Sea	84,400	219,000
9	Victoria	North America	Viscount Melville Sound	83,900	217,000
10	Ellesmere	North America	Arctic Ocean	75,800	196,000
11	Sulawesi (Celebes)	Asia	Celebes Sea	67,400	174,000
12	South Island (New Zealand)	Oceania	Pacific Ocean	58,200	151,000
13	Java	Asia	Indian Ocean	50,000	129,000
14	North Island (New Zealand)	Oceania	Pacific Ocean	44,200	114,000
15	Newfoundland	North America	Atlantic Ocean	42,000	109,000
16	Cuba	North America	Caribbean Sea	40,500	105,000
17	Luzon	Asia	Pacific Ocean	40,400	105,000
18	Iceland	Europe	Atlantic Ocean	39,769	103,000
19	Mindanao	Asia	Pacific Ocean	36,500	94,600
20	Ireland	Europe	Atlantic Ocean	32,500	84,100
21	Hokkaido	Asia	Pacific Ocean	30,100	78,000
22	Sakhalin	Asia	Sea of Okhotsk	29,500	76,400
23	Hispaniola	North America	Atlantic Ocean	29,200	75,600
24	Banks	North America	Arctic Ocean	27,000	70,000
25	Sri Lanka	Asia	Indian Ocean	25,332	65,610
26	Tasmania	Australia	Indian Ocean	24,900	64,400
27	Devon	North America	Baffin Bay	21,300	55,200
28	Novaya Zemlya	Europe	North Kara Sea	18,900	48,900
29	Grande de Tierra del Fuego	South America	Atlantic Ocean	18,700	48,400
30	Marajo	South America	Atlantic Ocean	18,500	48,000
31	Alexander	Antarctica	Bellingshausen Sea	16,700	43,200
32	Axel Heiberg	North America	Arctic Ocean	16,700	43,200
33	Melville	North America	Viscount Melville Sound	16,300	42,100

F ⊕ MAJOR ISLANDS OF THE WORLD, BY AREA (continued)					
All measurements are approximate.					
RANK	ISLAND	CONTINENT	BODY OF WATER	AREA (SQ MI)	AREA (SQ KM)
34	Southampton	North America	Husdon Bay	15,900	41,200
35	West Spitsbergen	Europe	Arctic Ocean	15,300	39,500
36	New Britain	Oceania	Bismarck Sea	14,600	37,800
37	Taiwan	Asia	Pacific Ocean	13,892	35,980
38	Kyushu	Asia	Pacific Ocean	13,800	35,700
39	Hainan	Asia	South China Sea	13,100	34,000
40	Prince of Wales	North America	Viscount Melville Sound	12,900	33,300
41	Novaya Zemlya	Europe	Barents Sea	12,800	33,300
42	Vancouver	North America	Pacific Ocean	12,100	31,300
43	Timor	Asia	Timor Sea	10,200	26,300
44	Sicily	Europe	Mediterranean	9,810	25,400
45	Somerset	North America	Lancaster Sound	9,570	24,800
46	Sardinia	Europe	Mediterranean	9,190	23,800
47	Bananal	South America	Araguaia River	7,720	20,000
48	Halmahera	Asia	Molucca Sea	6,950	18,000
49	Shikoku	Asia	Pacific Ocean	6,860	17,800
50	Ceram	Asia	Banda Sea	6,620	17,200
51	New Caledonia	Oceania	Coral Sea	6,470	16,700
52	Bathurst	North America	Viscount Melville Sound	6,190	16,000
53	Prince Patrick	North America	Arctic Ocean	6,120	15,800
54	North East Land	Europe	Barents Sea	5,790	15,000
55	Flores	Asia	Flores Sea	5,520	14,300
56	Oktyabrskoy Revolyutsii	Asia	Arctic Ocean	5,470	14,170
57	Sumbawa	Asia	Indian Ocean	5,160	13,400
58	King William	North America	Queen Maud Gulf	5,060	13,100
59	Samar	Asia	Pacific Ocean	5,050	13,100
60	Negros	Asia	Sulu Sea	4,900	12,700
61	Palawan	Asia	South China Sea	4,550	11,800
62	Kotelnyy	Asia	Arctic Ocean	4,500	11,700
63	Panay	Asia	Sulu Sea	4,450	11,500
64	Bangka	Asia	Java Sea	4,370	11,320
65	Ellef Ringnes	North America	Arctic Ocean	4,360	11,300
66	Bolshevik	Asia	Arctic Ocean	4,350	11,270
67	Sumba	Asia	Indian Ocean	4,310	11,200

F ⊕ MAJOR ISLANDS OF THE WORLD, BY AREA (continued)

All measurements are approximate.

RANK	ISLAND	CONTINENT	BODY OF WATER	AREA (SQ MI)	AREA (SQ KM)
68	Bylot	North America	Baffin Bay	4,270	11,100
69	Jamaica	North America	Caribbean Sea	4,243	10,990
70	Dolak	Asia	Arafura Sea	4,160	10,800
71	Hawaii	Oceania	Pacific Ocean	4,040	10,500
72	Viti Levu	Oceania	Pacific Ocean	4,010	10,400
73	Cape Breton	North America	Atlantic Ocean	3,980	10,300
74	Bougainville	Oceania	Pacific Ocean	3,880	10,000
75	Mindoro	Asia	South China Sea	3,760	9,730
76	Prince Charles	North America	Foxe Basin	3,680	9,520
77	Kodiak	North America	Pacific Ocean	3,670	9,510
78	Cyprus	Asia	Mediterranean	3,571	9,250
79	Komsomolets	Asia	Arctic Ocean	3,480	9,010
80	Buru	Asia	Banda Sea	3,470	9,000
81	Corsica	Europe	Mediterranean	3,370	8,720
82	Puerto Rico	North America	Atlantic Ocean	3,350	8,680
83	New Ireland	Oceania	Pacific Ocean	3,340	8,650
84	Disco	North America	Davis Strait	3,310	8,580
85	Chiloe	South America	Pacific Ocean	3,240	8,390
86	Crete	Europe	Mediterranean	3,190	8,260
87	Anticosti	North America	Gulf of St. Lawrence	3,070	7,940
88	Wrangel	Asia	Chukchi Sea	2,820	7,300
89	Leyte	Asia	Visayan Sea	2,780	7,210
90	Zealand	Europe	Baltic Sea	2,710	7,020
91	Cornwallis	North America	Barrow Strait	2,700	7,000
92	Wellington	South America	Trinidad Gulf	2,610	6,750
93	Iturup (Etorofu)	Asia	Pacific Ocean	2,600	6,720
94	Prince of Wales	North America	Pacific Ocean	2,590	6,700
95	Graham	North America	Pacific Ocean	2,460	6,360
96	East Falkland	South America	Atlantic Ocean	2,440	6,310
97	Melville	Asia	Timor Sea	2,400	6,220
98	Novaya Sibir	Asia	East Siberian Sea	2,390	6,200
99	Kerguelen	Antarctica	Indian Ocean	2,320	6,000
100	Andros	North America	Grand Bahama Bank	2,300	5,960

G ⊕ DESERTS OF THE WORLD, BY AREA

All measurements are approximate.

Rank	Name	Continent	Country	Area (sq mi)	Area (sq km)
1	Sahara	Africa	Algeria, Chad, Egypt, Libya, Mali, Mauritania, Morocco, Niger, Sudan, and Tunisia	3,475,000	9,000,000
2	Arabian*	Asia	Saudi Arabia, Kuwait, Qatar, the United Arab Emirates, Oman, Yemen, Jordan, Syria, Iraq	900,000	2,330,000
3	Gobi	Asia	China, Mongolia	500,000	1,300,000
4	Kalahari	Africa	Botswana, Namibia, South Africa	360,000	930,000
5	Great Victoria	Australia	Australia	134,652	348,750
6	Taklimakan (Takla Makan)	Asia	China	125,000	320,000
7	Sonoran	North America	United States of America, Mexico	120,000	310,000
8	Kara-Kum	Asia	Kazakhstan, Turkmenistan	115,830	300,000
9	Kyzyl Kum	Asia	Kazakhstan, Uzbekistan	115,000	297,850
10	Namib	Africa	Namibia, South Africa	110,000	285,000
11	Great Sandy	Australia	Australia	103,185	267,250
12	Somali	Africa	Somalia	100,000	260,000
13	Thar	Asia	India, Pakistan	90,000	233,000
14	Tanami	Australia	Australia	71,235	184,500
15	Atacama	South America	Chile, Peru	70,000	180,000
16	Simpson	Australia	Australia	68,150	176,500
17	Gibson	Australia	Australia	60,230	156,000
18	Little Sandy	Australia	Australia	43,050	111,500

* Two deserts are commonly referred to by this name. This entry refers to the deserts of the Arabian Peninsula and not the Arabian Desert of Egypt, which is part of the Sahara.

H ⊕ HIGHEST MOUNTAIN PEAKS, BY CONTINENT

All measurements are approximate.
Note that many mountains have multiple peaks, which will appear separately in the table.

AFRICA				
RANK	**NAME**	**COUNTRY**	**ELEVATION (FT)**	**ELEVATION (M)**
1	Kibo (Mt. Kilimanjaro)	Tanzania	19,341	5,895
2	Mawensi (Mt. Kilimanjaro)	Tanzania	17,100	5,210
3	Batian (Mt. Kenya)	Kenya	17,058	5,203
4	Nelion (Mt. Kenya)	Kenya	17,020	5,190
5	Margherita Peak (Mt. Stanley)	Dem. Rep. of the Congo, Uganda	16,756	5,110
6	Alexandra Peak (Mt. Stanley)	Dem. Rep. of the Congo, Uganda	16,700	5,094
7	Albert Peak (Mt. Stanley)	Dem. Rep. of the Congo	16,690	5,090
8	Savoia Peak (Mt. Stanley)	Uganda	16,330	4,981
9	Elena Peak (Mt. Stanley)	Uganda	16,300	4,972
10	Elizabeth Peak (Mt. Stanley)	Uganda	16,170	4,932
11	Phillip Peak (Mt. Stanley)	Uganda	16,140	4,923
12	Moebius Peak (Mt. Stanley)	Uganda	16,130	4,920
13	Vittorio Emanuele (Mt. Speke)	Uganda	16,040	4,892
14	Ensonga (Mt. Speke)	Uganda	15,960	4,868
15	Johnston (Mt. Speke)	Uganda	15,860	4,834
16	Edward (Mt. Baker)	Uganda	15,890	4,846
17	Umberto (Mt. Emin)	Dem. Rep. of the Congo	15,740	4,798
18	Semper (Mt. Baker)	Uganda	15,730	4,795
19	Kraepelin (Mt. Emin)	Dem. Rep. of the Congo	15,720	4,791
20	Iolanda (Mt. Gessi)	Dem. Rep. of the Congo	15,470	4,751
21	Bottego (Mt. Gesi)	Dem. Rep. of the Congo	15,418	4,699
22	Sella (Mt. Luigi)	Dem. Rep. of the Congo	15,178	4,626
23	Ras Deshen	Ethiopia	15,157	4,620
24	Weismann (Mt. Luigi)	Dem. Rep. of the Congo	15,157	4,620
25	Okusoma (Mt. Luigi)	Dem. Rep. of the Congo	15,020	4,578
ANTARCTICA				
RANK	**NAME**	**COUNTRY**	**ELEVATION (FT)**	**ELEVATION (M)**
1	Vinson	Antarctica	16,860	5,142
2	Tyree	Antarctica	16,290	4,968
3	Shinn	Antarctica	15,750	4,800
4	Gardner	Antarctica	15,370	4,690
5	Epperly	Antarctica	15,100	4,600

H ⊕ HIGHEST MOUNTAIN PEAKS, BY CONTINENT (continued)

ASIA

Rank	Name	Country	Elevation (ft)	Elevation (m)
1	Everest (Zhumulangma Feng)	Nepal, China	29,030	8,850
2	K2	China, Pakistan	28,251	8,611
3	Kanchenjunga	India, Nepal	28,169	8,586
4	Lhotse	China, Nepal	27,890	8,500
5	Makalu	China, Nepal	27,824	8,481
6	Kanchenjunga, south peak	India, Nepal	27,800	8,479
7	Kanchenjunga, west peak	India, Nepal	27,620	8,424
8	Lhotse Shar	China, Nepal	27,500	8,388
9	Dhaulagiri	Nepal	26,813	8,172
10	Man slu	Nepal	26,775	8,155
11	Cho Oyu	China, Nepal	26,750	8,150
12	Nanga Parbat I	Pakistan	26,660	8,130
13	Masherbrum I	Pakistan	26,610	7,810
14	Annapurna I	Nepal	26,500	8,080
15	Gasherbrum I	Pakistan	26,470	8,070
16	Broad, highest peak	Pakistan	26,400	8,050
17	Gasherbrum II	Pakistan	26,360	8,030
18	Gosainthan	China	26,290	8,010
19	Broad, middle peak	Pakistan	26,250	8,000
20	Gasherbrum III	Pakistan	26,090	7,950
21	Annapurna II	Nepal	26,040	7,940
22	Gasherbrum IV	Pakistan	26,000	7,930
23	Gyachung Kang	China, Nepal	25,990	7,927
24	Nanga Parbat II	Pakistan	25,950	7,910
25	Kangbachen	India, Nepal	25,930	7,909
26	Man slu, east pinnacle	Nepal	25,900	7,900
27	Distaghil Sar	Pakistan	25,870	7,890
28	Nuptse	Nepal	25,850	7,880
29	Himachuh	Nepal	25,800	7,860
30	Khiangyang Kish	Pakistan	25,760	7,850

H ⊕ HIGHEST MOUNTAIN PEAKS, BY CONTINENT (continued)

ASIA (continued)

Rank	Name	Country	Elevation (ft)	Elevation (m)
31	Ngojumba Ri	China, Nepal	25,720	7,847
32	Dakura	Nepal	25,710	7,842
33	Masherbrum II	Pakistan	25,660	7,826
34	Nanda Devi, west peak	India	25,650	7,823
35	Nanga Parbat III	Pakistan	25,650	7,823
36	Rakaposhi	Pakistan	25,550	7,793
37	Batura Mustagh I	Pakistan	25,540	7,790
38	GasherbrumV	Pakistan	25,500	7,770
39	Kamet	China, India	25,440	7,760

EUROPE

Rank	Name	Country	Elevation (ft)	Elevation (m)
1	El'brus (Elborus), west peak	Russia	18,481	5,633
2	El'brus (Elborus), east peak	Russia	18,360	5,590
3	Shkhara	Georgia, Russia	17,064	5,205
4	Dykh, west peak	Russia	17,050	5,200
5	Dykh, east peak	Russia	16,900	5,150
6	Koshtan	Russia	16,880	5,148
7	Pushkina	Russia	16,730	5,100
8	Kazbek, east peak	Georgia	16,526	5,040
9	Dzhangi	Georgia	16,520	5,039
10	Katyn	Georgia, Russia	16,310	4,975
11	Shota Rustaveli	Georgia, Russia	16,270	4,962
12	Mizhirgi, west peak	Russia	16,170	4,932
13	Mizhirgi, east peak	Russia	16,140	4,923
14	Kundyum-Mizhirgi	Russia	16,010	4,880
15	Gestola	Georgia, Russia	15,930	4,860
16	Tetnuld	Georgia, Russia	15,920	4,850
17	Mont Blanc, main peak	France, Italy	15,772	4,810
18	Dzhimariy	Georgia	15,680	4,780
19	Adish	Georgia, Russia	15,570	4,749
20	Courmayer (Mont Blanc)	France, Italy	15,577	4,748
21	Ushba	Georgia	15,450	4,710

H ⊕ HIGHEST MOUNTAIN PEAKS, BY CONTINENT *(continued)*				
NORTH AMERICA				
Rank	**Name**	**Country**	**Elevation (ft)**	**Elevation (m)**
1	McKinley (Denali), south peak	U.S.A.	20,323	6,194
2	Logan, central peak	Canada	19,550	5,959
3	Logan, west peak	Canada	19,470	5,930
4	McKinley (Denali), north peak	U.S.A.	19,470	5,930
5	Logan, east peak	Canada	19,420	5,920
6	Pico de Orizaba	Mexico	18,701	5,700
7	Logan, north peak	Canada	18,270	5,570
8	Saint Elias	U.S.A., Canada	18,010	5,490
9	Popocatepetl	Mexico	17,887	5,452
10	Foraker	U.S.A.	17,400	5,300
11	Ixtacihuatl	Mexico	17,342	5,286
12	Queen	Canada	17,300	5,270
13	Lucania	Canada	17,150	5,230
14	King	Canada	16,970	5,170
15	Steele	Canada	16,640	5,070
16	Bona	U.S.A.	16,500	5,033
17	Blackburn, highest peak	U.S.A.	16,390	5,000
18	Blackburn, southeast peak	U.S.A.	16,290	4,968
19	Sanford	U.S.A.	16,240	4,950
20	Wood	Canada	15,880	4,840
OCEANIA				
Rank	**Name**	**Country**	**Elevation (ft)**	**Elevation (m)**
1	Puncak Jaya	Indonesia	16,503	5,033
2	Daam	Indonesia	16,150	4,926
3	Pilimsit	Indonesia	15,750	4,800
4	Trikora	Indonesia	15,580	4,752
5	Mandala	Indonesia	15,420	4,700

H ⊕ HIGHEST MOUNTAIN PEAKS, BY CONTINENT *(continued)*				
OCEANIA *(continued)*				
RANK	**NAME**	**COUNTRY**	**ELEVATION (FT)**	**ELEVATION (M)**
6	Wisnumurti	Indonesia	15,080	4,590
7	Yamin	Indonesia	14,860	4,530
8	Wilhelm	Papua New Guinea	14,793	4,509
9	Kubor	Papua New Guinea	14,300	4,360
10	Herbert	Papua New Guinea	14,000	4,270
SOUTH AMERICA				
RANK	**NAME**	**COUNTRY**	**ELEVATION (FT)**	**ELEVATION (M)**
1	Aconcagua	Argentina	22,835	6,960
2	Ojos del Salado, southeast peak	Argentina, Chile	22,573	6,880
3	Bonete	Argentina	22,550	6,870
4	Tupungato	Argentina, Chile	22,310	6,800
5	Pissis	Argentina	22,240	6,780
6	Mercedario	Argentina	22,210	6,770
7	Huascarán, south peak	Peru	22,204	6,768
8	Llullaillaco	Argentina, Chile	22,100	6,730
9	Libertador	Argentina	22,050	6,720
10	Ojos del Salado, northwest peak	Argentina, Chile	22,050	6,720
11	Gonzalez, highest peak	Argentina, Chile	21,850	6,664
12	Huascarán, north peak	Peru	21,840	6,661
13	Muerto	Argentina, Chile	21,820	6,655
14	Yerupaja, north peak	Peru	21,760	6,630
15	Incahuasi	Argentina, Chile	21,700	6,610
16	Galan	Argentina	21,650	6,600
17	Tres Cruces	Argentina, Chile	21,540	6,560
18	Gonzalez, north peak	Argentina, Chile	21,490	6,550
19	Sajama	Bolivia	21,463	6,542
20	Yerupaja, south peak	Peru	21,380	6,510
21	Chimborazo	Ecuador	20,681	6,267

I ⊕ HIGHEST VOLCANOES OF THE WORLD, BY HEIGHT

All measurements are approximate.

Rank	Name	Continent	Country	Elevation (ft)	Elevation (m)
1	Tupungato	South America	Chile	22,310	6,800
2	Tipas	South America	Argentina	21,845	6,660
3	Cerro el Condor	South America	Argentina	21,425	6,532
4	Antofallo	South America	Argentina	20,008	6,100
5	Guallatiri	South America	Chile	19,882	6,060
6	Lascar	South America	Chile	19,652	5,990
7	Cotopaxi	South America	Ecuador	19,344	5,896
8	Kilimanjaro	Africa	Tanzania	19,341	5,895
9	El Misti	South America	Peru	19,031	5,801
10	Pico de Orizaba	North America	Mexico	18,701	5,700
11	Tolima	South America	Colombia	18,425	5,616
12	Popocatépetl	North America	Mexico	17,887	5,452
13	Yucamani	South America	Peru	17,860	5,444
14	Sangay	South America	Ecuador	17,159	5,230
15	Tungurahua	South America	Ecuador	16,684	5,085
16	Cotacachi	South America	Ecuador	16,250	4,939
17	Purace	South America	Colombia	15,604	4,756
18	Klyuchevskaya	Asia	Russia	15,584	4,750
19	Kronotskaya	Asia	Russia	15,580	4,749
20	Shiveluch	Asia	Russia	15,580	4,749
21	Pichincha	South America	Ecuador	15,173	4,625
22	Karasimbi	Africa	Dem. Rep. of the Congo	14,873	4,507
23	Rainier	North America	USA	14,410	4,395
24	Wrangell	North America	USA (Alaska)	14,163	4,317
25	Colima	North America	Mexico	13,993	4,265
26	Tajumulco	North America	Guatemala	13,845	4,220
27	Mauna Kea	North America	USA (Hawaii)	13,796	4,205
28	Mauna Loa	North America	USA (Hawaii)	13,680	4,170
29	Cameroon	Africa	Cameroon	13,353	4,070
30	Tacana	North America	Guatemala	13,300	4,053
31	Kerintji	Asia	Indonesia	12,483	3,805
32	Erebus	Antarctica	Antarctica	12,448	3,794
33	Fuji	Asia	Japan	12,388	3,776
34	Fuego	North America	Guatemala	12,346	3,763

I ⊕ HIGHEST VOLCANOES OF THE WORLD, BY HEIGHT (continued)

All measurements are approximate.

RANK	NAME	CONTINENT	COUNTRY	ELEVATION (FT)	ELEVATION (M)
35	Agua	North America	Guatemala	12,307	3,751
36	Rindjani	Asia	Indonesia	12,224	3,726
37	Pico de Teide	Africa	Spain (Canary Is.)	12,198	3,718
38	Tolbachik	Asia	Russia	12,077	3,682
39	Semeru	Asia	Indonesia	12,060	3,676
40	Ichinskaya	Asia	Russia	11,800	3,621
41	Atitlan	North America	Guatemala	11,650	3,551
42	Torbert	North America	USA (Alaska)	11,450	3,480
43	Nyirangongo	Africa	Dem. Rep. of the Congo	11,365	3,465
44	Kroyakskaya	Asia	Russia	11,336	3,456
45	Irazu	South America	Costa Rica	11,260	3,432
46	Slamet	Asia	Indonesia	11,247	3,428
47	Spurr	North America	USA (Alaska)	11,137	3,385
48	Lautaro	South America	Chile	11,120	3,380
49	Sumbing	Asia	Indonesia	11,060	3,371
50	Raung	Asia	Indonesia	10,932	3,332
51	Etna	Europe	Italy	10,902	3,323
52	Baker	North America	USA	10,778	3,285
53	Lassen	North America	USA	10,492	3,187
54	Dempo	Asia	Indonesia	10,390	3,158
55	Sundoro	Asia	Indonesia	10,367	3,151
56	Agung	Asia	Indonesia	10,337	3,142
57	Prahu	Asia	Indonesia	10,285	3,137
58	Llaima	South America	Chile	10,245	3,125
59	Redoubt	North America	USA (Alaska)	10,197	3,108
60	Tjiremai	Asia	Indonesia	10,098	3,078
61	One-Take	Asia	Japan	10,056	3,067
62	Nyamulagira	Africa	Dem. Rep. of the Congo	10,026	3,056
63	Iliamna	North America	USA (Alaska)	10,016	3,053
64	Ardjuno-Welirang	Asia	Indonesia	9,968	3,038
65	San Pedro	North America	Guatemala	9,902	3,020
66	Gede	Asia	Indonesia	9,705	2,958
67	Zhupanovsky	Asia	Russia	9,705	2,958
68	Apo	Asia	Philippines	9,692	2,954

I ⊕ HIGHEST VOLCANOES OF THE WORLD, BY HEIGHT (continued)

All measurements are approximate.

Rank	Name	Continent	Country	Elevation (ft)	Elevation (m)
69	Merapi	Asia	Indonesia	9,551	2,911
70	Marapi	Asia	Indonesia	9,479	2,891
71	Geureudong	Asia	Indonesia	9,459	2,885
72	Bezymianny	Asia	Russia	9,449	2,882
73	Shishaldin	North America	USA (Alaska)	9,372	2,856
74	Tambora	Asia	Indonesia	9,350	2,850
75	Villarrica	South America	Chile	9,318	2,840
76	Fogo	Africa	Cape Verde	9,281	2,829
77	Ruapehu	Oceania	New Zealand	9,175	2,796
78	Peuetsagoe	Asia	Indonesia	9,115	2,780
79	Paricutin	North America	Mexico	9,100	2,775
80	Big Ben	Antarctica	Heard Island (dependency of Australia)	9,006	2,745
81	Balbi	Oceania	Papua New Guinea	8,999	2,743
82	Avachinskaya	Asia	Russia	8,987	2,741
83	Melbourne	Antarctica	Antarctica	8,957	2,732
84	Poas	North America	Costa Rica	8,872	2,704
85	Papandajan	Asia	Indonesia	8,744	2,665
86	Piton de la Faournaise	Africa	Reunion (dependency of France)	8,626	2,631
87	Pacaya	North America	Guatemala	8,367	2,552
88	Mt. St. Helens	North America	USA	8,366	2,550
89	Asama	Asia	Japan	8,300	2,530
90	Pavlof	North America	USA (Alaska)	8,261	2,518
91	Veniaminof	North America	USA (Alaska)	8,220	2,507
92	Mayon	Asia	Philippines	8,077	2,462
93	Sinabung	Asia	Indonesia	8,066	2,460
94	Yake Dake	Asia	Japan	8,049	2,455
95	Tandikat	Asia	Indonesia	7,993	2,438
96	Canalaon	Asia	Philippines	7,984	2,435
97	Shoshuenco	South America	Chile	7,941	2,422
98	Idjen	Asia	Indonesia	7,823	2,386
99	Izalco	North America	El Salvador	7,828	2,386
100	Karthala	Africa	Comoros	7,746	2,361

J ⊕ RIVERS OF THE WORLD 1,000 MILES (1,600 KILOMETERS) OR LONGER

All measurements are approximate.

RANK	NAME	CONTINENT	COUNTRY	LENGTH (MI)	LENGTH (KM)
1	Nile	Africa	Egypt, Sudan, Uganda	4,160	6,693
2	Amazon	South America	Brazil, Colombia, Peru, Venezuela	3,900	6,280
3	Mississippi-Missouri	North America	U.S.A.	3,860	6,211
4	Chang Jiang (Yangtze or Yangtse)	Asia	China	3,434	5,525
5	Ob'-Irtysh	Asia	Kazakhstan, Russia	3,335	5,380
6	Paraná	South America	Argentina, Brazil, Paraguay	3,030	4,870
7	Huang He (Huang-ho or Yellow)	Asia	China	2,903	4,671
8	Irtysh	Asia	Kazakhstan, Russia	2,760	4,441
9	Lena	Asia	Russia	2,734	4,400
10	Amur	Asia	China, Russia	2,719	4,350
11	Congo (Zaire)	Africa	Angola, Dem. Rep. of the Congo, Rep. of the Congo	2,700	4,344
12	Mackenzie	North America	Canada	2,635	4,290
13	Mekong River (Lan ts'ang chiang or Lancang Jiang)	Asia	Cambodia, China, Laos, Myanmar, Thailand, Vietnam	2,600	4,200
14	Niger	Africa	Benin, Guinea, Mali, Niger, Nigeria	2,594	4,184
15	Yenisey	Asia	Russia	2,566	4,129
16	Missouri	North America	U.S.A.	2,466	3,968
17	Mississippi	North America	U.S.A.	2,348	3,787
18	Volga	Europe	Russia	2,293	3,689
19	Ob'	Asia	Russia	2,270	3,650
20	Euphrates	Asia	Iraq, Syria, Turkey	2,235	3,596
21	Purus	South America	Brazil, Peru	2,100	3,380
22	Madeira	South America	Brazil	2,013	3,241
23	Lower Tunguska	Asia	Russia	2,000	3,220
24	Indus	Asia	Pakistan	1,988	3,200
25	São Francisco	South America	Brazil	1,988	3,199
26	Yukon	North America	Canada, U.S.A.	1,980	3,180
27	Rio Grande	North America	Mexico, U.S.A.	1,885	3,034

J ⊕ RIVERS OF THE WORLD 1,000 MILES (1,600 KILOMETERS) OR LONGER *(continued)*					
All measurements are approximate.					
RANK	NAME	CONTINENT	COUNTRY	LENGTH (MI)	LENGTH (KM)
28	Brahmaputra (Jamuna)	Asia	Bangladesh, China, India	1,800	2,900
29	Danube	Europe	Austria, Bulgaria, Croatia, Germany, Hungary, Romania, Ukraine, Slovakia, Serbia-Montenegro	1,775	2,857
30	Salween	Asia	China, Myanmar	1,770	2,849
31	Darling	Australia	Australia	1,702	2,739
32	Tocantins	South America	Brazil	1,677	2,698
33	Nelson	North America	Canada	1,660	2,671
34	Vilyuy	Asia	Russia	1,650	2,650
35	Zambezi	Africa	Angola, Mozambique, Namibia, Zambia, Zimbabwe	1,650	2,650
36	Murray	Australia	Australia	1,609	2,589
37	Paraguay	South America	Argentina, Brazil, Paraguay	1,584	2,549
38	Amu Dar'ya	Asia	Afghanistan, Tajikistan, Turkmenistan, Uzbekistan	1,580	2,540
39	Kolyma	Asia	Russia	1,562	2,513
40	Ganges	Asia	Bangladesh, India	1,560	2,510
41	Ishim	Asia	Kazakhstan, Russia	1,520	2,450
42	Ural	Asia	Kazakhstan, Russia	1,510	2,430
43	Japurá	South America	Brazil, Colombia	1,500	2,414
44	Arkansas	North America	U.S.A.	1,460	2,350
45	Colorado	North America	U.S.A.	1,450	2,330
46	Dnieper	Europe	Belarus, Russia, Ukraine	1,420	2,290
47	Negro	South America	Brazil, Colombia, Venezuela	1,400	2,250
48	Ubangi	Africa	Central African Rep., Dem. Rep. of the Congo, Rep. of the Congo	1,400	2,253
49	Aldan	Asia	Russia	1,390	2,240
50	Columbia-Snake	North America	Canada, U.S.A.	1,390	2,240
51	Syr Dar'ya	Asia	Kazakhstan, Kyrgyzstan, Uzbekistan	1,370	2,200

J ⊕ RIVERS OF THE WORLD 1,000 MILES (1,600 KILOMETERS) OR LONGER (continued)

All measurements are approximate.

Rank	Name	Continent	Country	Length (mi)	Length (km)
52	Araguaia	South America	Brazil	1,366	2,198
53	Olenek	Asia	Russia	1,350	2,170
54	Irrawaddy	Asia	Myanmar	1,350	2,170
55	Kasai	Africa	Angola, Dem. Rep of the Congo	1,338	2,153
56	Ohio-Allegheny	North America	U.S.A.	1,310	2,109
57	Tarim	Asia	China	1,300	2,090
58	Orange	Africa	Lesotho, Namibia, South Africa	1,300	2,090
59	Orinoco	South America	Venezuela	1,281	2,061
60	Shabeelle	Africa	Ethiopia, Somalia	1,250	2,011
61	Xingu	South America	Brazil	1,230	1,979
62	Columbia	North America	Canada, U.S.A.	1,214	1,953
63	Mamoré	South America	Bolivia	1,200	1,931
64	Tigris	Asia	Iraq, Turkey	1,180	1,900
65	Northern Dvina	Europe	Russia	1,160	1,870
66	Don	Europe	Russia	1,153	1,860
67	Angara	Asia	Russia	1,151	1,852
68	Kama	Europe	Russia	1,120	1,800
69	Indigirka	Asia	Russia	1,112	1,789
70	Pechora	Europe	Russia	1,112	1,789
71	Limpopo	Africa	Botswana, South Africa, Mozambique	1,100	1,770
72	Sénégal	Africa	Guinea, Mali, Mauritania, Senegal	1,015	1,663
73	Salado	South America	Argentina	1,110	1,770
74	Guaporé	South America	Bolivia, Brazil	1,087	1,749
75	Tobol	Asia	Kazakhstan, Russia	1,042	1,677
76	Snake	North America	U.S.A.	1,038	1,670
77	Red	North America	U.S.A.	1,018	1,638
78	Churchill	North America	Canada	1,000	1,613
79	Jubba	Africa	Ethiopia, Somalia	1,000	1,613
80	Okavango	Africa	Angola, Botswana	1,000	1,613
81	Pilcomayo	South America	Argentina, Bolivia, Paraguay	1,000	1,613
82	Uruguay	South America	Uruguay	1,000	1,613

RANK	NAME	CONTINENT	COUNTRY	HEIGHT (FT)	HEIGHT (M)
	K ⊕ WATERFALLS OF THE WORLD, BY HEIGHT				
	All measurements are approximate. If a waterfall has multiple cascades they are listed separately.				
1	Angel (upper falls)	South America	Venezuela	2,648	807
2	Utigord	Europe	Norway	2,625	800
3	Monge	Europe	Norway	2,539	774
4	Mtarazi (Mutarazi)	Africa	Mozambique, Zimbabwe	2,500	760
5	Itatinga	South America	Brazil	2,060	628
6	Cuquenán (Kukenaam)	South America	Guyana, Venezuela	2,000	610
7	Kahiwa	North America	U.S.A. (Hawaii)	1,750	533
8	Tysse (Tusse)	Europe	Norway	1,749	533
9	Maradalsfos	Europe	Norway	1,696	517
10	Ribbon	North America	U.S.A.	1,612	491
11	Roraima	South America	Guyana	1,500	457
12	Della	North America	Canada	1,445	440
13	Yosemite, Upper	North America	U.S.A.	1,430	436
14	Gavarnie	Europe	France	1,385	422
15	Tugela (highest falls in chain)	Africa	South Africa	1,350	411
16	Krimml	Europe	Austria	1,250	380
17	Silver Strand	North America	U.S.A.	1,170	357
18	Basaseachic	North America	Mexico	1,020	311
19	Staubbach	Europe	Switzerland	980	299
20	Vettis	Europe	Norway	902	275
21	King George VI	South America	Guyana	850	260
22	Wallaman	Oceania	Australia	850	260
23	Takakkaw	North America	Canada	838	254
24	Hunlen	North America	Canada	830	253
25	Jog (Gersoppa)	Asia	India	830	253

	K ⊕ WATERFALLS OF THE WORLD, BY HEIGHT *(continued)*				
All measurements are approximate. If a waterfall has multiple cascades they are listed separately.					
RANK	**NAME**	**CONTINENT**	**COUNTRY**	**HEIGHT (FT)**	**HEIGHT (M)**
26	Skykje	Europe	Norway	820	250
27	Sutherland, Upper	Oceania	New Zealand	815	248
28	Sutherland, Middle	Oceania	New Zealand	751	229
29	Kaieteur	South America	Guyana	741	226
30	Wollomombi	Oceania	Australia	726	220
31	Kalambo	Africa	Tanzania, Zambia	704	215
32	Fairy	North America	U.S.A.	700	213
33	Feather	North America	U.S.A.	640	195
34	Maletsunyane	Africa	Lesotho	630	192
35	Bridalveil	North America	U.S.A.	620	189
36	Multnomah	North America	U.S.A.	620	189
37	Panther	North America	Canada	600	183
38	Voringfoss	Europe	Norway	597	182
39	Nevada	North America	U.S.A.	594	181
40	Angel, Lower	South America	Venezuela	564	172
41	Augrabies (Aughrabies)	Africa	South Africa	480	146
42	Tully	Oceania	Australia	450	137
43	Helmcken	North America	Canada	450	137
44	Nachi	Asia	Japan	430	131
45	Tequendama	South America	Colombia	427	130
46	Bridal Veil	North America	U.S.A.	400	122
47	Illilouette	North America	U.S.A.	370	113
48	Yosemite, Lower	North America	U.S.A.	320	98
49	Twin	North America	Canada	260	80

RANK	NAME	CONTINENT	COUNTRY	AREA (SQ MI)	AREA (SQ KM)
1	Caspian Sea	Asia	Azerbaijan, Iran, Kazakhstan, Russia, Turkmenistan	143,000	371,000
2	Superior	North America	Canada, U.S.A.	31,820	82,732
3	Victoria	Africa	Uganda, Tanzania, Kenya	26,828	69,484
4	Aral Sea	Asia	Kazakhstan, Uzbekistan	24,900	64,500
5	Huron	North America	Canada, U.S.A.	23,000	59,570
6	Michigan	North America	U.S.A.	22,400	58,020
7	Tanganyika	Africa	Burundi, Dem. Republic of the Congo, Tanzania, Zambia	12,700	32,020
8	Baikal	Asia	Russia	12,160	31,500
9	Great Bear	North America	Canada	12,095	31,328
10	Great Slave	North America	Canada	11,030	28,570
11	Erie	North America	Canada, U.S.A.	9,920	25,690
12	Winnipeg	North America	Canada	9,420	24,390
13	Malawi	Africa	Malawi, Mozambique, Tanzania,	8,680	22,490
14	Ontario	North America	Canada, U.S.A.	7,440	19,240
15	Balkhash	Asia	Kazakhstan	7,030	18,200
16	Ladoga	Russia	Russia	7,000	18,130
17	Maracaibo	South America	Venezuela	5,020	13,010
18	Chad	Africa	Cameroon, Chad, Niger, Nigeria	4,000–10,000	10,360–25,900
19	Embalse del Río Negro	South America	Uruguay	4,000	10,360
20	Patos	South America	Brazil	3,920	10,153
21	Onega	Europe	Russia	3,750	9,720
22	Eyre	Australia	Australia	3,668	9,500
23	Volta	Africa	Ghana	3,276	8,485
24	Titicaca	South America	Bolivia, Peru	3,200	8,288
25	Nicaragua	South America	Nicaragua	3,150	8,160
26	Athabasca	North America	Canada	3,060	7,940
27	Reindeer	North America	Canada	2,570	6,650

L ⊕ LAKES OF THE WORLD, BY AREA

All measurements are approximate.

L ⊕ LAKES OF THE WORLD, BY AREA (continued)

All measurements are approximate.

RANK	NAME	CONTINENT	COUNTRY	AREA (SQ MI)	AREA (SQ KM)
28	Smallwood Reservoir	North America	Canada	2,500	6,460
29	Turkana (Rudolf)	Africa	Ethiopia, Kenya	2,473	6,405
30	Issyk Kul	Asia	Kyrgyzstan	2,360	6,100
31	Torrens	Australia	Australia	2,230	5,780
32	Albert	Africa	Dem. Republic of the Congo, Uganda	2,160	5,590
33	Vanern	Europe	Sweden	2,160	5,580
34	Netilling	North America	Canada	2,140	5,540
35	Winnipegosis	North America	Canada	2,070	5,370
36	Nasser	Africa	Egypt, Sudan	2,026	5,248
37	Bangweulu	Africa	Zambia	1,930	5,000
38	Chott el Djerid	Africa	Tunisia	1,930	5,000
39	Urmia	Asia	Iran	1,879	4,868
40	Nipigon	North America	Canada	1,870	4,850
41	Gairdner	Australia	Australia	1,840	4,770
42	Manitoba	North America	Canada	1,800	4,660
43	Kyoga	Africa	Uganda	1,710	4,430
44	Khanka	Asia	China, Russia	1,700	4,400
45	Saimaa	Europe	Finland	1,700	4,403
46	Mweru	Africa	Dem. Republic of the Congo	1,680	4,350
47	Great Salt	North America	U.S.A.	1,680	4,350
48	Qinghai (Koko)	Asia	China	1,625	4,209
49	Woods	North America	Canada	1,580	4,100
50	Taymyr	Asia	Russia	1,540	3,990
51	Nasser	Africa	Egypt	1,522	3,942
52	Orumiyeh	Asia	Iran	1,500	3,880
53	Dubawnt	North America	Canada	1,480	3,830
54	Van	Asia	Turkey	1,430	3,710
55	Tana	Africa	Ethiopia	1,390	3,600
56	Peipus	Europe	Estonia, Russia	1,386	3,555
57	Uvs	Asia	Mongolia	1,300	3,366

RANK	LAKE	CONTINENT	COUNTRY	DEPTH (FT)	DEPTH (M)
1	Baikal	Asia	Russia	5,315	1,621
2	Tanganyika	Africa	Burundi, Tanzania, Dem. Congo (ROC), Zambia	4,825	1,471
3	Caspian Sea	Asia	Azerbaijan, Iran, Kazakhstan, Russia, Turkmenistan	3,363	1,025
4	Malawi	Africa	Malawi, Tanzania, Mozambique	2,316	706
5	Issyk Kul	Asia	Kyrgyzstan	2,303	702
6	Great Slave	North America	Canada	2,015	614
7	Matana	Asia	Indonesia	1,936	590
8	Crater	North America	U.S.A.	1,932	589
9	Toba	Asia	Indonesia	1,736	529
10	Hornindals	Europe	Norway	1,686	514
11	Sarez	Asia	Tajikistan	1,657	505
12	Tahoe	North America	U.S.A.	1,645	501
13	Chelan	North America	U.S.A.	1,605	489
14	Kivu	Africa	Rwanda, Congo (DROC)	1,575	480
15	Quesnel	North America	Canada	1,560	475
16	Sals	Europe	Norway	1,522	464
17	Adams	North America	Canada	1,500	457
18	Mjøsa	Europe	Norway	1,473	449
19	Manapuri	Oceania	New Zealand	1,453	443
20	Poso	Asia	Indonesia	1,444	440
21	Nahuel Huapi	South America	Argentina	1,437	438
22	Dead Sea	Asia	Israel, Jordan	1,421	433
23	Tazawa	Asia	Japan	1,394	425
24	Great Bear	North America	Canada	1,356	413
25	Como	Europe	Italy	1,352	412
26	Superior	North America	Canada, U.S.A.	1,333	406
27	Hawea	Asia	New Zealand	1,286	392
28	Wakatipu	Asia	New Zealand	1,240	378

M ⊕ LAKES OF THE WORLD, BY DEPTH

All measurements are approximate.

	M ⊕ LAKES OF THE WORLD, BY DEPTH *(continued)*				
All measurements are approximate.					
RANK	LAKE	CONTINENT	COUNTRY	DEPTH (FT)	DEPTH (M)
29	Suldals	Europe	Norway	1,234	376
30	Maggiore	Europe	Italy, Switzerland	1,221	372
31	Fyres	Europe	Norway	1,211	369
32	Chilko	North America	Canada	1,200	366
33	Pend Oreille	North America	U.S.A.	1,200	366
34	Shikotsu	Asia	Japan	1,191	363
35	Powell	North America	Canada	1,174	358
36	Llanquihue	South America	Chile	1,148	350
37	Garda	Europe	Italy	1,135	346
38	Towada	Asia	Japan	1,096	334
39	Wanaka	Asia	New Zealand	1,086	325
40	Bandak	Europe	Norway	1,066	325
41	Telestskoya	Asia	Russia	1,066	325
42	Eutsuk	North America	Canada	1,060	323
43	Atitlan	North America	Guatemala	1,050	320
44	Lunde	Europe	Norway	1,030	314
45	Geneva	Europe	France, Switzerland	1,017	310
46	Morar	Europe	Scotland	1,017	310
47	Kurile	Asia	Russia	1,004	306
48	Walker	North America	U.S.A.	1,000	305
49	Titicaca	South America	Bolivia, Peru	997	304
50	Argentino	South America	Argentina	984	300
51	Iliamna	North America	U.S.A.	980	299
52	Tyrifjorden	Europe	Norway	968	295
53	Lugano	Europe	Italy, Switzerland	945	288
54	Takla	North America	Canada	941	287
55	Ohrid	Europe	Albania, Serbia-Montenegro	938	286
56	Atlin	North America	Canada	930	283
57	Nuyakuk	North America	U.S.A.	930	283
58	Michigan	North America	U.S.A.	923	285
59	Harrison	North America	Canada	916	279
60	Te Anau	Oceania	New Zealand	906	276

Seven Wonders of the Ancient World

1 ⊕ The pyramids of Egypt

Constructed between 2700 and 2500 B.C., the pyramids are the last surviving structures of the Seven Wonders of the Ancient World. The largest of the pyramids, which rises over 137 meters (450 feet), was built as a tomb to house the body of Pharaoh Khufu. Historians believe that it must have taken over twenty years to build with over 100,000 slave laborers.

2 ⊕ The gardens of Semiramis at Babylon

The existence of these gardens is reputed, but according to fable they existed around 600 B.C. They are said to have been outside on a brick terrace 23 meters (75 feet) above the ground, encompassing an area of 37 square meters (400 square feet).

3 ⊕ The statue of Zeus at Olympia

Constructed around 450 B.C. by the sculptor Phidias, this 12-meter (40-foot) high statue is of an ivory Zeus wearing a robe of gold, seated atop a throne. In his right hand was Nike, his messenger and a symbol of victory, in his left hand was the scepter signifying his rule over the gods and humankind, and atop his head was a wreathed crown.

4 ⊕ The temple of Artemis at Ephesus

Built around 550 B.C. to celebrate the goddess of the hunt, this temple was one of the largest in ancient times. Beneath its tile-covered roof were rows of columns believed to be more than 12 meters (40 feet) high, leading to a marble sanctuary. The original temple was destroyed by fire in 356 B.C., but another temple was built on the same foundation. This temple was also burned, but the foundation still remains. Remnants of the second temple can be found at London's British Museum.

5 ⊕ The mausoleum at Halicarnassus

Located in southwestern Turkey, this enormous white marble tomb was contructed to house the body of Mausolus, a king of Persian Empire. It was constructed around 350 B.C. by the Greek architects Satuyrus and Pythius and became so well known that the term mausoleum was created to signify any large tomb. An earthquake in the 15th century caused significant damage to the tomb, which was eventually disassembled. Several of its exterior sculptures can be seen in London's British Museum.

6 ⊕ The Colossus at Rhodes

Constructed around 200 B.C. by the Greek sculptor Chares, this 36-meter (120-foot) bronze statue was meant to honor the sun god Helios and celebrate the unity of the city-states of Rhodes. The statue was hollow, supported by stone blocks and iron bars inside its frame. It was destroyed by an earthquake only fifty-six years after its completion.

7 ⊕ The Pharos (lighthouse) of Alexandria or the Walls of Babylon

This lighthouse, completed near 270 B.C., was, at the time, one of the tallest buildings in the known world. Standing over 122 meters (400 feet) high, it guided sailors to the shores of Alexandria, then ruled by King Ptolemy II.

Seven Wonders of the Natural World

1 ⊕ Grand Canyon

Created after millions of years of erosion from the Colorado River and its tributaries, this Arizona landmark is visited by millions of tourists each year.

2 ⊕ Paricutin Volcano

Although it is not one of the largest volcanoes in Mexico, Paricutin has taken a place on the list of natural wonders following its birth in 1943. The eruption spanned ten years and covered about 2.6 square meters (10 square miles). No one was killed from the lava and ash, but it destroyed agricultural land and seriously affected the lives of those living nearby.

3 ⊕ The Harbor at Rio de Janeiro

Located on the east coast of Brazil, the harbor overlooks the Guanabara Bay and the Atlantic Ocean on one side, and mountains on the other. Discovered by Portuguese navigators in 1502, this area houses a huge carnival each year.

4 ⊕ Northern Lights

The northern lights, or aurora borealis, have fascinated people for centuries. Seen as souls, heavenly signs, or even messages from the dead, these shimmering light displays are caused by the interaction of solar winds with Earth's magnetic field. A similar phenomenon occurs in the southern hemisphere as well, but only the northern lights are classified as a natural wonder.

5 ⊕ Mt. Everest

Formed from the collision of Asia and India over 60 million years ago, the Himalayas house Everest, the tallest mountain on Earth. Located in Nepal near the Tibetan border, this snowy peak has fascinated and challenged many climbers and non-climbers alike.

6 ⊕ Victoria Falls

The largest waterfalls in the world, Victoria Falls has a drop of more than 99 meters (325 feet). Flowing from the Zambezi River, the falls were named for Queen Victoria by David Livingstone in 1855, when he became the first European to gaze upon them.

7 ⊕ The Great Barrier Reef

The Great Barrier Reef extends over 1,998 kilometers (1,242 miles) on the northeast coast of Australia. The reef is quite delicate, being comprised of the skeletons of generations of marine life that lived just under the water's surface. The area is home to exotic coral, which is greatly affected by any human or natural interference, and a wide variety of marine life

Selected Sources for Further Study

Books

Arthus-Bertrand, Yann. *Earth from Above for Young Readers*. New York: Harry N. Abrams, 2002.

The Blackbirch Kid's Visual Reference of the World. Woodbridge, CT: Blackbirch Press, 2001.

Brooks, Felicity. *The Usborne First Encyclopedia of Our World*. Tulsa, OK: EDC Publishing, 1999.

Ciovacco, Justine. *The Encyclopedia of Explorers and Adventurers*. New York: Franklin Watts, 2003.

Cunha, Stephen F. *National Geographic Bee Official Study Guide*. Washington, DC: National Geographic, 2002.

Encyclopedia of World Geography. New York: Marshall Cavendish, 2001.

Forina, Rose. *Amazing Hands-on Map Activities*. New York: Scholastic Professional Books, 2001.

Fox, Mary Virginia. *South America*. Chicago, IL: Heinemann Library, 2001.

Furstinger, Nancy. *Get Ready! For Social Studies: Geography*. New York McGraw-Hill, 2002.

Gough, Barry M., editor. *Geography and Exploration: Biographical Portraits*. New York: Scribner, 2001.

Lands and Peoples. Danbury, CT: Grolier Educational, 2003.

Nelson, Robin. *Where Is My Country?* Minneapolis, MN: Lerner Publications, 2002.

O'Brien, Patrick K., editor. *Atlas of World History*. New York: Oxford University Press, 2002.

Oldershaw, Cally. *Atlas of Geology and Landforms*. New York: Franklin Watts, 2001.

Rasmussen, R. Kent, editor. *World Geography*. Pasadena, CA: Salem Press, 2001.

Robson, Pam. *People and Places*. Brookfield, CT: Copper Beech Books, 2001.

Robson, Pam. *Rivers and Seas*. Brookfield, CT: Copper Beech Books, 2001.

Rosenberg, Matthew T. *Geography Bee Complete Preparation Handbook: 1,001 Questions*. Prima Publishing, 2002.

Striveildi, Cheryl. *Continents*. Edina, MN: Abdo Publishing Company, 2003.

Sutcliffe, Andrea. *The New York Public Library Amazing World Geography: A Book of Answers for Kids*. New Jersey: Wiley, 2002.

World Adventure. Chicago, IL: World Book, 2000.

Web Sites

Association of American Geographers. http://www.aag.org/Careers/Intro.html, (accessed May 30, 2003).

"Educational Resources for Cartography, Geography, and Related Disciplines," *U.S. Geological Survey*. http://mapping.usgs.gov/www/html/1educate.html (accessed May 30, 2003).

Geographic.org. http://www.geographic.org/ (accessed May 30, 2003).

"Geography and Map Reading Room," *The Library of Congress*. http://www.loc.gov/rr/geogmap/ (accessed May 30, 2003).

"Marco Polo Xpeditions," *National Geographic*. http://www.nationalgeographic.com/xpeditions/ (accessed May 30, 2003).

National Geographic.com. http://www.nationalgeographic.com/index.html (accessed May 30, 2003).

Postcard Geography. http://pcg.cyberbee.com/ (accessed May 30, 2003).

Queen Elizabeth Islands

Axel
Heiberg I.
Ellesmere I.
Devon I.
Greenland
(DENMARK)
Banks I.
Baffin Bay
Beaufort Sea
Victoria I.
Baffin I.
Brooks Range
Great Bear
Lake
Alaska
(U.S.A.)
Mackenzie
Great Slave
Lake
Alaska Range
Yukon
L.
Athabasca
Hudson
Bay
Labrador
Sea
Bering Sea
Peace
Alaska
Peninsula
C A N A D A
Aleutian Islands
L. Winnipeg
Newfoundland
Vancouver I.
L. Superior
Cape Breton I.
L. Huron
Azores
L. Michigan
R O C K Y
New York
ATLANTIC
OCEAN
Missouri
UNITED
STATES
L. Erie
Sierra Nevada
Appalachian Mts.
Ohio
Ca
Los Angeles
Colorado
Mississippi
M T S.
Rio Grande
SE
Baja California
BAHAMAS
GA
Gulf of Mexico
Coast Mountains
MEXICO
CUBA
GUINEA-
HAITI
SIE
Hawaii (U.S.A.)
DOMINICAN REP.
Mexico
BELIZE
Puerto Rico (U.S.A.)
GUATEMALA
HONDURAS
Caribbean Sea
EL SALVADOR
NICARAGUA
GUYANA
COSTA RICA
VENEZUELA
SURINAME
PANAMA
French Guiana
COLOMBIA
SOLOMON
ISLANDS
PACIFIC
OCEAN
Galapagos Is.
ECUADOR
Amazon
Xingu
VANUATU
PERU
B R A Z I L
FIJI
L.
Titicaca
São Francisco
New Caledonia
(FRANCE)
BOLIVIA
Atacama
Desert
PARAGUAY
Rio de Janeiro
São Paulo
Gran
Chaco
Paraná
North I.
Santiago
URUGUAY
South I.
CHILE
ARGENTINA
NEW ZEALAND
Grande
Isla de Chiloé
Patagonia
Falkland Is.
South Georg
Tierra del Fuego
A N T A R